Collected Essays

Collected Essays

The School of Life

Published in 2023 by The School of Life
930 High Road, London, N12 9RT

Printed in Latvia by Livonia Print

A proportion of this book has appeared online at www.theschooloflife.com/articles

The School of Life publishes a range of books on essential topics in psychological and emotional life, including relationships, parenting, friendship, careers and fulfilment. The aim is always to help us to understand ourselves better – and thereby to grow calmer, less confused and more purposeful. Discover our full range of titles, including books for children, here: www.theschooloflife.com/books

The School of Life also offers a comprehensive therapy service, which complements, and draws upon, our published works: www.theschooloflife.com/therapy

www.theschooloflife.com

ISBN 978-1-915087-10-2

10 9 8 7 6 5 4 3 2 1

MIX
Paper | Supporting responsible forestry
FSC® C002795

Introduction

The School of Life has from its beginning proposed a slightly unusual theory of reading: the point of books is to help us to feel better. That is, to help us to grow into somewhat less agitated, frightened, confused, diffident and panicked versions of ourselves, to edge us towards greater self-awareness, serenity and maturity.

Though aware that many of humanity's ills manifest at the economic and social level, we propose that – far more than is generally appreciated – they almost always have their origins at the psychological one. What we read about in the news lies far downstream from a range of almost humdrum (but in reality hugely consequential) personal dynamics: a mother who couldn't love her child, a father who belittled his son, a family that had no courage for the truth, a mind that didn't understand its own cravings. The improvement of humankind will depend – as much as on grander initiatives – on our collective capacity to master the complexities of our emotional functioning.

This is a collection of our most important essays that takes us through all that The School of Life would most want to teach a friend, and all that we have found – often through great difficulty – possesses the greatest power to calm and illuminate our lives.

Several of the essays touch on the issue of self-knowledge and the ever-present requirement that we become less mysterious to ourselves through a greater understanding of our pasts. We have all, in a variety of ways, entered adult life with what can (with no pejorative intent) be called neuroses; we may be neurotic in love or at work, in our friendships or in our attitudes to creativity or politics. It should be part of every evolved human's mission to seek to understand and unpick the distinctive neurotic elements of their personalities in the name of increased liberation and ease.

These essays are principally interested in healing. Several of them cover the role that relationships can play in returning us to a more balanced and resourceful state of mind. Along the way, The School of Life proposes a distinctly un-Romantic view of what true love should entail. We cannot wait for loving feelings to surge up inside us. We need to work on becoming loving – just as we might otherwise work on becoming rich, fit or popular. And the journey begins when we can take the brave step of admitting that we don't – at this point – probably have too much of a clue how to love, not because we are evil or cold, simply because we've never been nudged to think that this was something we needed to make a concerted effort to learn.

The tone in these essays can be rather melancholic, unapologetically so. We suggest that we should never compound our sorrows by imagining that they are illegitimate or rare. Beneath the smiles, a lot of us are far sadder than we can ever let on. A truly advanced society is one that can give grief all the airtime and imaginative consideration it deserves, one which never forces happiness on unwilling, fragile or privately pained constituents.

A book cannot accomplish very much on its own; it can – at best – be a prompt for the reader to begin their own journey of exploration. We will consider this collection of essays a success if, at frequent intervals, you are tempted to put it down and make a small note in the margin or a journal, or simply stare out of the window and feel renewed energy to explore an old dilemma or a sorrow, a tentative wish or a daydream. This is a book about us, and it is – we hope – very much also a book about you.

Self-Knowledge

I
Self-Ignorance

One of the most striking features of our minds is how little we understand them. Although we inhabit ourselves, we seldom manage to make sense of more than a fraction of who we are. It can be easier to master the dynamics of another planet than to grasp what is at play in the folds of our own brains.

Instances of self-ignorance regularly surprise and perturb us: on certain days, we can be irritable or sad without any idea why. Or we may feel lost in our career, but be unable to say more than that we wish to 'do something creative' or 'help to make the world a better place' – plans so vague that they leave us vulnerable to the more robust plans of others.

It has been the achievement of psychology to instil in us a sense of a basic division between two parts of the mind: the conscious and the unconscious; between what is immediately accessible to us and what lies in shadow, and will surprise us in symptoms, dreams, slips of the tongue and diffuse anxieties, longings and fears. It has also been the work of psychology to insist that maturity must involve a constant drive to turn what is unconscious conscious, to help us master the art of self-knowledge.

We need not blame ourselves for our poor grasp of our own minds. The problem is inherent in the very architecture of the brain, an organ that evolved over millennia for the sake of rapid, instinctive decision-making – not the patient, introspective sifting of ideas and emotions.

However, a degree of emotional squeamishness is also responsible for our failure to look inside. A lot of what is unconscious is tricky material that we shy away from looking at too closely. For example, we may feel troublingly angry towards people we thought we loved. We may be more ruthless

It can be easier to master the dynamics of another planet than to grasp what is at play in the folds of our own brains.

and envious than nice people are ever meant to be. We may have to make enormous changes to our lives, but prefer the ease of the status quo. Across childhood, we may have had instilled in us, so subtly we didn't even notice, strong notions about what are normal and not normal things to experience. Traditionally, boys were not allowed to acknowledge that they felt like crying, and girls weren't allowed to entertain certain kinds of ambitions for fear of being unladylike.

We might not have such obviously naive prohibitions today, but other, equally powerful, ones may have taken their place. We may have picked up covert but forceful indications that no decent person (no-one loved by their parents, at least) could be unable to cope at work, be tempted by an affair, or still be upset over a break-up that took place three years ago. Most of our sexual desires still have no place in our standard understanding of respectability.

When difficult feelings threaten to emerge, the light of consciousness can be counted upon to take fright and shine its beam elsewhere. By failing to investigate the recesses of the mind, we carefully protect our self-image and can continue to think well of ourselves. However, we don't escape from the job of introspection lightly. There is almost always a high price to pay for our reluctance to look within. Feelings and desires that have not been examined tend not to leave us alone; they linger and spread their energy randomly to neighbouring issues. Ambition that doesn't know itself comes out as anxiety. Envy comes out as bitterness; anger turns into rage; sadness evolves into depression. Disavowed material buckles and strains the system. We develop pernicious tics: a facial twitch, impotence, an incapacity to work, alcoholism, a porn compulsion. Most so-called 'addictions' are at heart symptoms of insistent difficult feelings that we haven't found a way to address. Insomnia is revenge for thoughts we have refused to have in the day.

Strangers to ourselves, we end up making bad choices: we exit a relationship that might have been quite workable. We don't explore our own professional talents in time. We alienate friends through erratic, off-putting behaviour. We lack insight into how we come across to others and appal or shock them. We buy the wrong things and go on holiday to places that have little to do with what we really enjoy.

It is no coincidence that Socrates should have boiled down the entire wisdom of philosophy to one simple command: *Know Yourself*. This is a distinctly odd-sounding ambition. Society has no shortage of people and organisations offering to guide us around distant continents, but very few that will help us with the arguably far more important task of travelling around the byways of our own minds. Fortunately, however, there are a number of tools and practices that can help us to reach inside our minds and move us from dangerous vagueness to challenging but redeeming clarity.

II
Philosophical Meditation

Insofar as society encourages us to spend time in our minds, it allots particular prestige to a set of practices collectively referred to by the term 'meditation'. Adherents of meditation typically recommend that we sit in a particular position and strive to empty our consciousness of its normal medley of feelings and ideas. We should still the agitations of what the Buddhists have evocatively termed our 'monkey minds' in a bid for serenity.

There is another approach to consider, not based on Eastern thought, but on ideas that have come down to us from the Western philosophical tradition. We term it Philosophical Meditation, a practice with the premise that a decisive share of the trouble in our minds comes from thoughts and feelings that have not been untangled, examined and confronted with sufficient attention.

Philosophical Meditation needs a time of the day when nothing much will be expected of us. We might be in bed or on the sofa, alone with a notepad and pen. Key to the practice are three well-angled questions:

- *What am I presently anxious about?*
- *What am I presently upset about?*
- *What am I presently excited about?*

Anxiety

We start the Philosophical Meditation by asking: What am I presently anxious about?

Life is generally far more alarming than we allow ourselves to accept. We constantly have to navigate an uncertain world. We are permanent hostages to the whims of fortune. Every minute of the waking day, a skittish radar in one part of our minds is scanning the vast, partly misty, horizon and noting new sources of uncertainty and risk: What will the meeting be like? When do we need to leave? What happened with the letters? Where are we going to be five years from now? Where is the nearest bathroom? We are never more than one piece of bad luck away from a stroke, disgrace or ruin.

During our meditative session, we need to give all our anxieties a chance to understand themselves, for three-quarters of our agitation is not that there are things to worry about, but that we haven't given our worries the time they require to be understood and defused. Only by being listened to can anxieties be drained of some of their intensity. If we were to record our own stream of consciousness in moods of agitation, the result would tumble out in chaotic confusion: '... the biscuits thing all over again, why, why, why, idiot, God the Seoul deal, they can't do it, I have to do it, the bathroom now, I can't do it at 10.30 tomorrow with Luke, why get myself into this, the stupid invoice, why me, my fault, the tree branches, couldn't sleep...'

This fast-moving stream can be gradually tamed, drained, driven into rivulets and evaporated into something far less daunting. Our overall nervousness declines when our anxieties are systematically laid out and examined.

We need to grip our anxieties head-on and force ourselves to imagine what might happen if their vague catastrophic forebodings truly came to pass: What would happen to us if everything we are dimly worried about really came to pass? What are the real dangers? How might we still be OK, even if it all fell apart? Entertaining the most extreme consequences can be the best way to finally neuter an otherwise nagging concern. One by one, we should confront the worst, and see that it is, for the most part, very survivable.

Exercise:
Interpreting Anxiety

Write down what you are anxious about; find at least eight things. Each entry should only be a single word (or just a few words) at this point. Don't worry if some of the anxieties look either incredibly trivial or tragicomically large. If you're having trouble, search for things that may be anxiety-inducing under the following categories:

- *Work*
- *Relationships*
- *Children/Parents*
- *Health*
- *Money*
- *Things I have to do*

Feel the curious release that can come from just making a list of these items.

Huge relief can now come from what we call 'unpacking' an anxiety. There are two kinds of unpacking we might do around any given anxiety.

1. Practical unpacking

Walk yourself through the practical challenge. Ask the following questions:

- *What steps do you need to take?*
- *What do others need to do?*
- *What needs to happen when?*

It is very useful to have a calm and sympathetic part of yourself (or a friend) listening in on the detailed description of what needs to be done to address an issue. It is no longer merely an anxiety; it is a set of steps. They might not all be easy, but at least you are clearer about what they are.

2. Emotional unpacking

Talk yourself through an emotional challenge or set of doubts. Describe the feeling in more detail. What do you feel it points to? Imagine trying to piece it together for a very considerate friend.

The aim here isn't to solve all anxieties; it's to start to get to know them and to experience the relief that comes from this.

Upset

We are ready to turn to the second guiding enquiry behind the Philosophical Meditation: What am I presently upset about?

This could sound odd, because we may have no particular sense of being upset about anything. But the claim here is that we are almost always likely to be upset about something, for the simple reason that we are far more vulnerable than we think and that life constantly places us in the line of fire of little arrows fired by people around us. Without meaning to, our partners and friends daily shoot small darts at us: They didn't ask how the day went, they have forgotten that we have a meeting, they left the towels in a heap... It is from such small humiliations and slights that large blocks of resentment eventually form and render us, for example, unable to love or to bear to be touched. Too much of social existence requires an excessive degree of stoicism from us. There are heavy incentives for us not to feel or notice our pains.

Eventually, this unacknowledged distress may sink our entire characters into depression.

During our introspective sessions, we can throw off our customary and dangerous bravery and let our sadness take its natural, due shape. There may not be an immediate solution to many of our sorrows, but it helps immeasurably to know their contours. As we turn over our sadnesses, large and small, we might imagine we are discussing them with an extremely kind and patient figure who would give us the chance to evoke the hurt in great detail; someone with whom there would be no pressure to rush, be grown-up or brave and who would allow us to admit without fear to the many things that cause us upset. We should, in introspecting, be maximally indulgent with ourselves as a corrective to our normal tendency to be a bit brutal and to insist that we're getting worked up about nothing – when all along, our pain requires a hearing. In the early 19th century, the German poet Heinrich Heine (1797–1856) wrote a poem entitled 'Lorelei' (1823), which opens with a candid admission:

Ich weiß nicht, was soll es bedeuten,
Daß ich so traurig bin;

(I don't know what it means
That I'm so sad at heart.)

The premise here is that there are always some very good reasons why we are sad; it's just that we haven't allowed ourselves to feel them, because we labour under unfair assumptions about what it is right and normal to feel sad about.

Exercise:
Interpreting Upset

As quickly as you can, and without bothering how petty, unreasonable or pretentious it might sound, write a list of current upsets. The more the better. How have others hurt you? What are you sad, nostalgic or wounded about?

Allow yourself in the present safety of this exercise to be, for instance, furious about the way your partner brushes their teeth (too lackadaisical or too smug); the agents of global politics; your boss saying 'yeah, right' in a slightly sarcastic manner; the hotel receptionist who implied you might not be very well off; or your mother commenting on your taste in shoes. These are just starting points and all are valid.

Now ask yourself: If this had happened to a friend, how would you advise them? What might you say?

Again, we're not attempting to resolve these issues as yet. The primary, crucial issue is to be clear about what is actually distressing us. We're allowing our troubles to acknowledge themselves.

Excitement

There is a third question we should consider within a Philosophical Meditation: What am I presently excited about?

Our minds are prone to become clogged up by unexamined sources of excitement that can, once they are decoded, point the way to important changes we might want to make in our lives. An excitement is a curious kind of signpost to new directions we might take, usually in our working or personal lives. We might experience it when we read an article in the newspaper about a new kind of business or hear of a colleague's plans to relocate to another city, but often we don't pause to analyse the excitement any further and thereby miss out on opportunities for development.

All of us have impulses towards growth and development and, when we are alert, can perceive slightly better versions of ourselves thanks to the messages we are receiving in garbled forms via our pulses of interest. The job of introspection is to help us ask ourselves: If this attractive experience (it might be a view, a book, a place, a biography) could talk, what might it want to tell me? Who is it inviting me to be? If other parts of my life were more like this, how might things go? Anything that arouses our curiosity or yields a certain pleasure is providing data – in a slightly illegible form – about something important missing or in short supply in our lives. We should pause to acknowledge the direction we are being inarticulately but perhaps wisely pointed towards.

Philosophical Meditation does not magically solve problems, but it may help hugely in creating an occasion when we can identify our thoughts and get them in some kind of order. Fears, resentments and hopes become easier to name. We become less scared of the contents of our own minds; we grow calmer, less resentful and clearer about our direction in life. We start, at last, to know ourselves a little better.

Exercise:
Interpreting Excitement

Rapidly list several things that have caught your attention and excited your interest since the last Philosophical Meditation. A word or a brief phrase is sufficient for now.

Your list might include:
- *Moments of envy*
- *Daydreams: ideas about how life might ideally be*
- *How nice someone or something was*

Pass these through a sieve of further questions:
- *Describe your excitement as if to a sympathetic, interested friend.*
- *If you could realistically change your life in certain ways, what would it be to change in light of this?*
- *This exciting thing holds a clue to what is missing in your life; what might that be?*
- *If this thing could talk, what might it tell you?*
- *If this thing could try to change your life, what changes might it advise?*

III
Emotional Identity

Our personalities can usefully be divided up into a range of different identities, each of which sheds light on a specific side of who we are: a political identity, a sartorial identity, a financial identity, a culinary identity, and so on.

Perhaps the most important and telling of these identities is our Emotional Identity: the characteristic way in which our desires and fears manifest themselves and our personalities respond to the behaviour – negative and positive – of others. There are four main themes around which our Emotional Identities are structured:

- Self-Love
- Candour
- Communication
- Trust

It is their particular dosage and arrangement within us that decisively shapes who we are.

To get to know ourselves is in large part a question of coming to understand the distinctive configuration of our Emotional Identity.

Self-Love

Self-love is at the core of answering the riddle of who we are emotionally. It is this quality that determines the extent to which a person feels warmly towards themselves, can forgive and accept who they are, and is able to remain steadfast in the face of opposition and reversals.

Evidence of our degree of self-love emerges particularly clearly around the threats posed to us by other people. When we meet a stranger who has things that we don't (a better job, a nicer partner, etc.), when self-love is low, we may quickly feel ourselves worthless and pitiful. Or, if our levels of self-love are more substantial, we may remain assured by the decency of what we already have and who we are. When another person frustrates or humiliates us, we may be able to let the insult go and even shrug it off, confident in our right to exist, or we may we need to enforce respect from others, remaining brooding and devastated, cut to the core of our being by a few unkind words. When we are faced with a need to risk making a fool of ourselves, we may feel the danger to be far too great, or we might be able to withstand the disapproval of others due to a sufficient degree of internal ballast.

The strength and nature of our self-love can be tracked with particular clarity within relationships. When a love affair isn't working for us (perhaps because we're getting hurt or ignored), do we have enough self-love to leave it quickly? Or are we so down on ourselves that we carry an implicit belief that harm is all we deserve from close relationships? In a different vein, when in love, how good are we at apologising for things that may be our fault? If we have sizeable reserves of self-love, we might feel we can afford to admit mistakes and still believe in our basic decency. Yet if our self-love is very fragile, no admission of guilt or error is ever possible; it would sap the last of our limited self-regard. We become very brittle to be around.

In the bedroom, how clean and natural or alternatively disgusting and sinful do our desires feel? If there is a sufficient quantity of self-love in our personalities, it will be possible to recognise that one's desires are – admittedly – sometimes a bit odd, but not feel that they are bad or dark. They can't really be, since we have them and are inwardly sure that we are not inherently sinful. We don't have to be ashamed of ourselves.

Self-love is a factor in our working lives too, determining how much, at the office, we can assert our needs. Do we have a reasonable, well-grounded sense of our worth and so feel able to ask for (and properly expect to get) the conditions that enable us to work most effectively? The issue of self-love decides how independent we can be, how well we can hold onto a thought-through idea that we believe is right when others don't get it. With high enough levels of self-love, we can say no; we are not committed to manic people-pleasing. We may also be able to ask for a raise when we feel we deserve it. We are aware of our genuine contribution. Honourable self-love is not selfishness: it's the feeling of correctly respecting ourselves.

Candour

Candour is another key constituent of our Emotional Identity. The degree to which someone possesses this quality determines the extent to which difficult ideas and troubling facts can be consciously admitted into the mind, soberly explored and taken seriously. How much can we admit to ourselves about who we are – even if, or especially when, it's not very nice? How much do we need to insist on our own normality and sanity? Can we explore our own minds and look into their darker and more troubled corners without flinching too much? Can we admit mistakes? Can we admit to envy, sadness and confusion?

Around others, how ready are we to learn? Do we need always to be defensive, taking a criticism of one part of us as an attack on everything about us? How quickly do we put up a barrier when there is feedback? How ready are we to learn, given that valuable lessons usually come in painful guises?

Honourable self-love is not selfishness: it's the feeling of correctly respecting ourselves.

Communication

Our Emotional Identity is further brought into focus by looking at our communicative styles. Can we put our disappointments into words that, more or less, enable others to see our point? Or do we internalise pain, act it out symbolically or discharge it onto innocents with counterproductive rage?

When other people upset us, do we feel it is OK to communicate our internal state? Do we feel we have the right to let others understand us? Are we sulkers? In other words, when the desired response isn't forthcoming, do we quickly give up and go in for aggressive silence? Or can we have a plausible second go: Can we take seriously the thought that the other person isn't necessarily evil or stupid? Can we be calm enough to teach? To what degree can we admit that it is legitimate for others not to understand us, and additionally feel that there is a plausible, convincing journey we can take them on towards a proper appreciation of our point of view?

Trust

When it comes to Emotional Identity, trust concerns our instinctive feelings about how safe or dangerous we, other people and the wider world are likely to be. We can have greater or lesser degrees of trust in our capacity to survive challenges. Theoretically we know that a speech, a performance review, a romantic rejection or a bout of financial trouble won't necessarily be life-threatening, but internally they may feel like an enormous danger.

A degree of stress is often called for, but its overall level is very individual. How close are we, at any time, to catastrophe? Around others, how much do we suspect that people are, at heart, out to get us? Are strangers generally nice or likely to be quite nasty? Do we generally imagine new acquaintances will like us or wound us? How fragile are others? If we are a touch assertive, will others collapse and break, or remain more or less fine?

Around love, degrees of trust determine our anxiety about the future with our partner. How tightly do we need to cling to them? If they go off us for a bit, will they return? How much do we imagine we would suffer if they don't come back? How 'controlling' do we need to be? Does such controlling behaviour stem from a basic lack of trust in the other person? How much of a risk can we take? Can we approach an interesting-looking stranger? Can we make the first move around a kiss or sex?

At work, how resilient are we? Failure isn't appealing, but does one see the world as a forgiving place in which it is normal to get second and third chances? Do we feel the world is big enough, and reasonable enough, for us to have a legitimate shot at doing our own thing, or must we be subservient, meek serfs?

Testing Emotional Identity

It is symptomatic of the way our minds work that we cannot directly ask ourselves who we are in terms of Emotional Identity. We need to ask ourselves smaller questions and answer them without pausing too long, thereby attempting to bypass our rationalising filters. Then we need to wheel back and sift through our answers to assemble a plausible picture of who we might be emotionally.

We need to sit an Emotional Identity Questionnaire:

Emotional Identity Questionnaire

Give a score to each of the statements below, on a scale from 1 to 5:

1 = That's not true.

2 = That's not very true, but there's a glimmer of recognition.

3 = I don't know – maybe, maybe not.

4 = A bit true, but I have a few reservations.

5 = Yes, that's true.

Self-Love

1. If people knew who I really was deep down, they would be shocked.
2. It can be embarrassing to ask where the bathroom is.
3. In relationships, it can feel pretty disturbing when someone you like starts to like you back.
4. I sometimes feel a bit disgusting.
5. When people approve of you, a lot of it comes down to what you've managed to achieve.

Candour

1. People tend to think too much.
2. I'm not a jealous person
3. I'm basically very sane.
4. I don't mind feedback in theory, but most of what I've received has been really off the mark.
5. There's far too much 'psychobabble' around these days.

Communication

1. People you're close to should be naturally good at understanding how you feel in a lot of areas.
2. When I feel misunderstood, I need to be alone.
3. I'm not a good teacher.
4. I sulk every now and then.
5. People rarely 'get it' when you're trying to explain.

Trust

1. It's not going to be OK in the end.
2. I worry about my health.
3. Civilisation is pretty fragile.
4. When someone is late, I sometimes wonder if they might have died.
5. If you don't watch them closely, people will try to swindle you.

Count up your scores in each category. The lower the score, the more you have of each quality. The higher the score, the less you have of Self-Love, Candour, Communicative Skills and Trust.

Emotional Inheritance

What creates Emotional Identity? Why do we have the Emotional Identity we do and not a different one?

A big modern response looks to genetics for answers: it tells us that we have a specific genetic inheritance and (via many complex processes) that this inheritance shapes our adult personality. We're not saying that genetics are irrelevant, but we want to focus attention on another kind of inheritance: Emotional Inheritance.

One of the characteristic possessions of all European nobles for many centuries was an elaborate depiction of their family tree, showing their lineage down the generations. The idea was that the person sitting at the bottom of the tree would see themselves as the product of – and the heir to – all who had come before them. The tree gave a quick visual guide to who they were and what others should know about them. If two aristocrats were contemplating marriage, the first thing they would do was to carefully examine each other's trees.

It can seem like a quaint preoccupation, wholly tied to another age and solely of interest to members of a few grand and ancient families. But the idea of such a tree sits upon a universal and still highly relevant concern: irrespective of the financial and status details of our families, we all have another significant legacy to grapple with, in that each of us is the recipient of an Emotional Inheritance, largely unknown to us, yet enormously influential in determining our day-to-day behaviour, and normally in rather negative or complex directions. We need to understand the details of our Emotional Inheritance a little before we are able to ruin our own and others' lives by acting upon its often antiquated and troublesome dynamics.

Some of what we inherit psychologically from our families can, of course, be positive. Marcus Aurelius (121–180 CE), the philosopher and emperor of Rome, began his *Meditations* with a touching list of the many positive things he had learned from his relatives:

> *From my grandfather Verus I learned good morals and the government of my temper.*
> *From my father, modesty and a manly character.*
> *From my mother, piety and beneficence, and abstinence, not only from evil deeds, but even from evil thoughts; and further, simplicity in my way of living, far removed from the habits of the rich.*
> – Marcus Aurelius, *The Meditations* (161-180 CE)

Few of us are as lucky as this. Alongside positives, we tend to inherit many predispositions that make it harder than necessary for us to cope with adult life, especially in the area of relationships and of work. Were we to repeat Marcus Aurelius's exercise, it might run in a far darker direction:

> *From my mother, I learnt to lose my temper quickly and give up on being heard properly by people close to me.*
> *From my father, I learnt to judge myself by my external achievements only and therefore to feel intense jealousy and panic in the face of professional setbacks.*

A lot in our inheritance works against our chances of fulfilment and well-being because its logic does not derive from the present; it involves a repetition of behaviour and expectations that were formed and learnt in childhood, typically as the best defence we could cobble together in our immaturity in the face of a situation bigger and more complex than we were. Unfortunately, it is as if part of our minds hasn't realised the change in our external circumstances, but insists on re-enacting the original defensive manoeuvre even in front of people or at moments that don't warrant or reward it. For example, it might once have made sense to try to see the good side and attract the loyalty of a parent even though they were neglectful and sometimes violent: there were few other options when one was three. But to continue to associate affection with violence and neglect is to impose intolerably narrow restrictions on one's adult love choices.

Our Emotional Inheritance clings to us because it was bequeathed in conditions of total helplessness. The early years were periods of acute vulnerability. We were utterly at the mercy of the prevailing environment. We could not properly move, speak, control or contain ourselves; we could not calm ourselves down or recover our equilibrium. We had no choice about whom to direct our feelings towards and no way to defend ourselves adequately against what injured us. We could not even string thoughts together, needing the language eventually lent to us by others in order to begin to interpret our requirements. Even in the most benign of circumstances, with only the best intentions at play, the possibilities for warps and distortions are enormous. Few of us ever come through entirely unscathed.

Psychotherapists have developed a special term to capture what we inherit emotionally from the past: they call it our 'transference'. In their view, each of us is constantly at risk of 'transferring' patterns of behaviour and feeling from the past to a present that doesn't realistically call for it. We feel a need to punish people who aren't to blame; we worry about a humiliation that isn't on the cards; we are compelled to betray as we were once betrayed, three decades before.

Ideally, we would build up a storehouse of knowledge of what exactly we had inherited (and from whom), a kind of emotional family tree that would show us, and others, the issues that had been transferred across generations and were liable to disrupt our lives today.

Learning to Deal with Emotional Inheritance

Maturity involves accepting with good grace that we are involved in multiple transferences, along with a commitment to try to disentangle them rationally. The job of growing up means realising with due humility the exaggerated dynamics we may constantly bring to situations and monitoring ourselves more accurately and more critically so as to improve our capacity to judge and act in the here and now with greater fairness and neutrality. The idea is to grow a little wiser as to where our troubles come from and around what areas of our lives we need to be especially careful.

Traditionally, family trees didn't just exist to tell people about themselves; they were public objects intended to convey to strangers what they needed to know about us. Before grand people got married, they would carefully scan each other's trees to know what was at stake. An emotional family tree would have a similar value in letting others know more about us in contexts when they might still be sympathetic, before we've had a chance to damage or enrage them with our inheritance. Knowing the risks of transference prioritises sympathy and understanding over irritation and judgement. We can come to see that sudden bursts of anxiety or hostility in others may not always be directly caused by us, and so should not always be met with fury or wounded pride. Bristling and condemnation can give way to compassion for the difficulties all of us have with our pasts.

In a perfect world, two people on an early dinner date would swap beautifully drawn family trees called, perhaps, 'My Emotional Inheritance'. Such a tree would also be something to give at a wedding and would be required at work, as a supplement to a CV. Having a complex Emotional Inheritance would not be a source of shame; the pride would be that one understood its constituent parts. We don't need people to be perfect; we simply need them to be able to explain the greater part of their inherited imperfections calmly and in good time, before we are enmeshed in the sufferings they can otherwise cause us.

Fully getting to grips with your Emotional Inheritance is a long-term task. It takes a lot of time and involves asking ourselves questions again and again. So, it is worth wondering what the point is of realising the ways your Emotional Inheritance has shaped your current identity. There seem to be three major benefits of this therapeutic exercise:

1. We become aware of ways in which we are a bit crazy (that is: puzzling to others and inappropriate in our responses). We can catch ourselves before we do too much damage. But we also grasp why we are like this. We don't have to hate ourselves; we can become more sympathetic to our awkward legacies and realise that we have learnt a few somewhat counterproductive ways of coping.

2. We can more calmly explain ourselves to others. Even if we can't entirely change, we can flag up what might be challenging about living around us. If we understand ourselves better, we can help others understand us more sympathetically too.

3. We begin to see that we have a degree of freedom and opportunity to change (to a limited but useful degree) the difficult parts of who we are. We don't have to keep on repeating exactly what we've been doing. There are other options.

Emotional Inheritance Questionnaire

Our Emotional Identities have a history; they are an Emotional Inheritance from our families. Knowing more about our Emotional Inheritance enables us to watch out for peculiar behaviour, feel sympathy for ourselves, explain ourselves to others and, in small ways, change.

Consider the inherited, familial aspects of the central pillars of your Emotional Identity:

Self-Love

- Did you feel loved?
- How much of who you really are were you allowed to be?
- Were you allowed to fail?
- Were you made to feel guilty and ashamed? How?
- How was the 'bad' side of you received?

Candour

- Did you have to be very normal?
- Did people around you admit to being afraid and sad?
- Did it matter what people thought?

Communication

- Did people communicate patiently and clearly with you?
- Were you allowed to tell others how you really felt?

Trust

- Were the people around you confident about the world?
- Did they panic acutely?
- Did they lose their temper regularly?
- How worried were they about your health?

Probe gently. Be sympathetic. If you get stuck, be patient. Each answer might be a novel, or at least a short story.

IV
Honesty and Denial

A major obstacle to self-knowledge, and in turn, to a flourishing life, is the tendency of one part of the mind to lie to the other. We lie to ourselves for what might seem like a very understandable reason: we want to avoid pain. We become experts at pushing disturbing thoughts far into the unconscious because we are squeamish.

The things we lie to ourselves about

There are four things we particularly tend to lie to ourselves about:

1. *Things we need to change about our lives*
We lie about all the problematic aspects it would take considerable effort to alter: our jobs, our relationships, our friendships, our relations with our families, our health, our habits and our ideas.

2. *Things that might disturb our self-image*
We lie because we need to think well of ourselves and are devoted to imagining that we are essentially normal, without peculiar loves, hates and deviant thoughts.

3. *Things we really want and can't have*
We lie because we don't want to feel so inadequate, and yet because we lack so many good things.

4. *Things we are angry with others about*
We lie because we are furious with certain people who we are supposed to love. And we lie because what we are furious about feels so minor and petty for a grown-up to care about.

How we lie to ourselves

Given how risky the truth about us can feel, we have had to learn to be masters of deception. Our techniques are wide-ranging, devilish and often hugely imaginative. Here are some of the leading manoeuvres we employ to pull the wool over our own eyes:

Distraction or addiction
We identify something that can very effectively keep our thoughts away from troubling inner confrontations. Online pornography is a favourite, the news another, alcohol a third, work a fourth. We don't so much like these elements in and of themselves; we like them for their ability to keep us away from what we fear.

Manic cheeriness
A sadness that we haven't been able to admit to is often covered up with exaggerated doses of manic cheeriness. We aren't happy so much as incapable of allowing ourselves to feel even the slightest sadness, in case we were to be overwhelmed by our buried grief. We develop a brittle, insistent tendency to say that all is very well. 'This is lovely, isn't it?' we might press, leaving no room for any ideas to the contrary.

Irritability

Denied anger with a particular person or situation often seeps out into a generalised irritability. So successful is the lie, we don't really know what's up: we just keep losing our tempers. Someone has moved the TV remote, there aren't any eggs in the fridge, the electricity bill is slightly higher than expected... anything can set us off. Our brains are so filled with how frustrating and annoying things are that we have cleverly left no space for focusing on the true, very sad issue.

Denigration

We tell ourselves that we simply don't care about something – love or politics, career success or intellectual life, that beautiful student or the house we can't afford. And we are very emphatic about our lack of interest and disdain. We go to great lengths to make it clear to others and ourselves how absolutely unconcerned we are. There must be no mistake. We simply and absolutely don't care. They're all stupid. It's a waste of money. What idiots. We might go in for long, erudite and argumentative explanations about why something doesn't impress us. We get very rational and factual. We're being more eloquent and clever in fending off any idea that we might be interested in something than in defending anything we actually love.

Censoriousness

We grow censorious and deeply disapproving of certain kinds of behaviour and people. What we don't admit is that we are so full of condemnation only because we need to ward off awareness that a part of us in fact really likes the condemned element. We attack certain sexual tastes as deviant and beyond the pale, precisely because we half-know that we share them somewhere inside ourselves. We are delighted when particular people are arrested or shamed in the press; what they did was utterly awful, we insist, our outrage shielding us from any risk of spotting the connection between them and us.

When our feelings become very tricky, we just pass them on to someone else. Rather than accepting them as our own, we convince ourselves that they exist only in other people, whom we duly attack and censor. Perhaps your partner has started speaking about a party being thrown by a moderately famous person. You're thrilled about it, but frightened to be thrilled. You are meant to be egalitarian and serious, so you can't want this. So, conveniently, it seems it must be just your partner who wants this, and you then accuse them of being a 'serious social climber'. You have found the perfect person on whom to land your unacceptable desires.

Defensiveness

When there is unwelcome news, we may resort to a highly successful diversionary tactic: taking offence. A colleague tries to give us a bit of feedback. Instantly we accuse them of rudeness, arrogance and a sense of entitlement. A partner points something out and we become furious that they are piling pressures on us at a difficult point. Feeling offended takes up all our attention. It muddies the waters. We no longer have to pay attention to information that is correct but challenging.

Cynicism or despair

We are sad about particular things, but confronting them would be so arduous that we generalise and universalise the sadness. We don't say that X or Y has made us sad; we say that everything is terrible and everyone is awful. We spread the pain in order that its particular, specific causes can no longer be the focus of attention. To put it metaphorically, our sadness becomes lost in the crowd.

The idea of being dishonest with ourselves may not sound especially decent, but why shouldn't we just lie if it is more pleasant to do so? What is the issue with keeping things from ourselves if we suffer so much from the truth? Why is the truth necessarily good?

The drawbacks of lying to ourselves

The defence of honesty must ultimately be a cautionary, egoistic one. We need to tell ourselves the truth when we can for the simple reason that we often pay a high price for the short-term calm of our lies.

We miss key opportunities for growth and learning
The things we are in denial about are painful, but they simultaneously contain material that is potentially vital to our overall growth and development.

If we could stop, for a time, looking at naked people, or drinking, or checking the news, and face up to what we need to do, we might – gradually – end up in a much better place.

If we could accept that we wanted certain things, even if we didn't end up with all of them, we could still secure some sort of substitute or a portion of them.

If we could face up to our stranger desires, we'd learn to navigate more freely in our minds and be alive to a wider range of our own thoughts, which could render us more creative and interesting.

We're not nice to be around
Our defences might be hidden from ourselves, but their consequences are often evident to others. They are the ones who suffer our irritability, gloom, manufactured cheerfulness or our defensive rationalisations. We act unfairly, so they back off and keep a distance. We grow isolated and friendless.

We develop harmful symptoms

The truth will out. And when we don't let it emerge, it has a tendency to reveal itself through involuntary (often physical) symptoms. We become insomniac or impotent, an eyelid starts twitching, we acquire a stutter, we scream in our sleep, we lose energy, we fall into depression...

The way to greater honesty follows some of the techniques evident from the rehabilitation of crimes. We must reduce the shame and danger of confession. And we must improve the chances of rehabilitation.

To bolster the courage to look more frankly into ourselves, we need a broader, more reassuring sense of what is normal. Of course, it is normal to be envious, crude, sexual, weak, in need, child-like, grandiose, terrified and furious. It is normal to be excited by people who are younger and older than us and to desire random adventures even within loving and committed unions. It is normal to be hurt by signs of rejection, and to be made insecure by any evidence of neglect by a partner. It is normal to be weird; sometimes we want to jump on the railway tracks or lick the toilet seat. It is normal to harbour hopes for ourselves professionally far beyond what we have been able to achieve. It is normal to envy other people, many times a day, to be upset by any kind of criticism of our work or performance, and to be so sad that we think a lot of suicide or flight.

We don't think in this free and honest way because we're scared that we could never come back from such confessions. But recognising a feeling doesn't mean you follow it to a conclusion. Admitting to a fantasy or desire doesn't have to mean acting it out – in fact, it is usually an alternative to doing so.

Understanding how self-deceit works can help us with ourselves, but also with others. We start to see them as beset by the same problems as us. Quite often they say things that are not in line with their true feelings or desires – mean things when they are feeling vulnerable, perhaps, or arrogant things when they are feeling small – and we will identify that it is charitable to forgive them for not always managing to be reliable correspondents of their inner lives. It is not sinister to think this way of others; it is a kindly move that gives us the energy to lend a second, more compassionate, look at behaviour that might initially appear horrifying.

Exercise:
An Experiment in Honesty

Consider our list of defensive, self-deceiving moves:

- Distraction or addiction
- Manic cheeriness
- Irritability
- Denigration
- Censoriousness
- Defensiveness
- Cynicism or despair

We all practise them all the time.

Can you remember specific incidents in your life when you employed them as strategies? What were you trying to hide from yourself?

It can help if this exercise happens in a group, because the enemy of such an effort is often the sense that we're all alone. The solution is always the normalisation of the disavowed parts of ourselves.

V
Self-Judgement

The Inner Voice

Somewhere in our minds, removed from the day-to-day, there sits a judge. They watch what we do, study how we perform, examine the effect we have on others, track our successes and failures, and then, eventually, they pass a verdict. So consequential is this judgement, it colours our entire sense of ourselves. It determines our levels of confidence and self-compassion; it lends us a sense of whether we are worthwhile beings, or conversely, should not really exist. The judge is in charge of what we call our self-esteem.

The verdict of the judge is more or less loving, more or less enthusiastic, but not according to any objective rulebook or statute. Two individuals can end up with wildly different levels of self-esteem even though they may have done much the same things. Certain judges simply seem more predisposed than others to lend us an essentially buoyant, warm, appreciative and generous view of ourselves. Others encourage us to be hugely critical, often disappointed and sometimes close to disgust.

The origin of the voice of the inner judge is simple to trace: it is an internalisation of the voice of people who were once outside us. We have absorbed the tone of a kind and gentle caregiver, who liked to laugh indulgently at our foibles and had endearing names for us, or else the voice of a harassed or angry parent, the menacing threats of an elder sibling keen to put us down, the words of a schoolyard bully, or a teacher who seemed impossible to please. We take in these voices because at certain key moments in the past they sounded so compelling and irresistible. The authority figures repeated their messages over and over until they became lodged in our own way of thinking – for better and for worse.

Why the Inner Voice Matters

Our level of self-love is very consequential across our lives. It can be tempting to suppose that being hard on ourselves, although painful, is ultimately useful. Self-flagellation can feel like a survival strategy that steers us clear of the many dangers of indulgence and complacency. But there are equal, if not greater, dangers in an ongoing lack of sympathy for our own plight. Despair, depression and suicide are not minor risks.

Afflicted by a lack of self-love, romantic relationships become almost impossible, for one of the central requirements of a capacity to accept the love of another turns out to be a confident degree of affection for ourselves, built up over the years, largely in childhood. We need a legacy of feeling that we in some basic way deserve love in order not to respond obtusely to affections granted to us by prospective adult partners. Without a decent amount of self-love, the kindness of another will always strike us as misguided or fake, even as strangely insulting, for it suggests that they haven't even begun to understand us, so different are our relative assessments of what we happen to deserve. We end up self-destructively – although unconsciously – disappointing the intolerable, unfamiliar love that has been offered to us by someone who clearly has no clue who we are.

Changing the Inner Voice

It may feel tempting to say that we shouldn't judge ourselves at all. We should simply approve and love. But a good internal voice is rather like (and just as important as) a genuinely decent judge: someone who needs to separate good from bad but who can be merciful, fair, accurate in understanding what's

Exercise:
An Audit of Our Inner Voice

We can catch the sound of what our inner voice is like when we prompt ourselves to finish certain sentences:

- When I do something stupid, I usually tell myself...
- When I succeed, I usually tell myself...
- When I'm feeling lazy, my inner voice says...
- When I think of what I want sexually, my inner voice says...
- When I get angry with someone, my inner voice says...

Does the inner judge strike you as kindly or punitive?

Whose outer voice became your inner voice in the context of each question?

going on and interested in helping us deal with our problems. It's not that we should stop judging ourselves; rather, it's that we should learn to be better judges of ourselves.

Part of improving how we judge ourselves involves learning – in a conscious, deliberate way – to speak to ourselves in a new and different manner, and this means exposing ourselves to better voices. We need to hear constructive, kindly voices often enough and around tricky enough issues that they come to feel like normal and natural responses – so that, eventually, they become our own thoughts.

One approach is to identify a nice voice we knew in the past and give it more scope. Perhaps there was a kindly grandmother or aunt who was quick to see our side of things and who would offer us deft words of encouragement. When things don't go as we want, we can ask ourselves what this person would say – and then actively rehearse to ourselves the words of consolation they would most likely have offered (we'll tend to know immediately).

The other major strategy for changing the voices in our heads is to try to become an imaginary friend to ourselves. In friendship, we know instinctively how to deploy strategies of wisdom and consolation that we stubbornly refuse to apply to ourselves.

There are three key moves a good friend would typically make that can provide a model for what we should, with a new commitment to self-love, be doing with ourselves in our own heads. Firstly, a good friend likes you pretty much as you are already. Any suggestion they make, or ambition they have about how you could change, builds on a background of acceptance. When they propose that you might try a different tack, it's not an ultimatum or a threat. They are emphatically not saying that you have to change or be abandoned. The friend insists that we are good enough already. But they want to join forces with us to solve a challenge they feel we would properly benefit from overcoming.

Without being flattering, good friends also constantly keep in mind certain things we're getting right. They don't think anything wrong with the odd compliment and emphasis on our strengths. It's quite galling how easily we can lose sight of all of our good points when troubles strike. The friend doesn't fall into this trap; they can acknowledge the difficulties while still holding on to a memory of our virtues. The good friend is compassionate. When we fail, as we will, they are understanding and generous around our mishaps. Our folly doesn't exclude us from the circle of their love. The good friend deftly conveys that to err, fail and screw up is what we humans do. We all emerged from childhood with various biases in our character that evolved to help us cope with our necessarily imperfect parents. These acquired habits of mind will reliably let us down in adult life. But we're not to be blamed, because we didn't deliberately set out to be like this. We didn't realistically have a lot of better options. The good friend knows that failures are not, in fact, rare. They bring, as a starting point, their own and humanity's vivid experience of messing up into play as key points of reference. They are continually telling us that our specific case might be unique but that the general structure is common. People don't just sometimes fail. Everyone fails; we just don't know about it.

It is ironic, yet essentially hopeful, that we usually know quite well how to be a better friend to near strangers than we know how to be to ourselves. The hopefulness lies in the fact that we already possess the relevant skills of friendship. It's just that we haven't yet directed them to the person who probably needs them most – namely, of course, ourselves.

A successful search for self-knowledge should end up with an admission of how little we do – and perhaps ever can – properly know of ourselves.

VI
Emotional Scepticism

The outcome of any concerted attempt at self-knowledge could be presumed to be a deep understanding of ourselves. But strangely, the real outcome is rather different. It appears that the more closely we explore our minds, the more we start to see how many tricks these organs can play on us – and therefore the more we will appreciate how often we are likely to misjudge situations and our own emotions. A successful search for self-knowledge should end up with an admission of how little we do – and perhaps ever can – properly know of ourselves. It is an apparent paradox summed up by Socrates (c. 470–399 BCE): *I am wise not because I know, but because I know I don't know.*

This critical attitude towards our own minds can be given a special name: Emotional Scepticism. Emotional Scepticism involves remaining highly cautious around our instincts, impulses, convictions and strong passions. Our brains are brilliant instruments, able to reason, synthesise, remember and imagine at an extraordinary pitch and rate. But these brains – let's call them walnuts in honour of their appearance – are also very subtly and dangerously flawed machines. They are flawed in ways that typically don't announce themselves to us and therefore give us few clues as to how on guard we should be about our mental processes. Most of the walnut's flaws can be attributed to the way the instrument evolved over millions of years. It emerged to deal with threats, some of which are no longer with us; at the same time, it had no chance to develop adequate responses to a myriad of challenges generated by our own complex societies.

The flaws of the faulty walnut

We should feel pity for the walnut's situation and compassion for ourselves. But we should also remain very vigilant. Here are just some of the many things we need to watch out for with our faulty walnuts:

The walnut is influenced by the body to an extent it doesn't recognise

The walnut is extremely bad at understanding why it is having certain thoughts and ideas. It tends to attribute them to objective conditions out in the world, rather than seeing that they might be stemming from the impact of the body upon the mind. It doesn't typically notice the role that levels of sleep, sugar, hormones and other physiological factors play upon the formation of ideas. The walnut adheres to an intellectual interpretation of plans and positions that are, at base, frequently merely physiological. Therefore, it can feel certain that the right answer is to divorce or leave the job rather than go back to bed or eat something to raise blood sugar levels.

The walnut is influenced by its past, but can't see its distortions

The walnut believes it is judging each new situation on its own merits, but it is inevitably drawing upon patterns of action and feeling shaped in previous years. It might, for example, assume that any older man who speaks in a confident way is out to humiliate them, when actually it was just one man – their father – who did this.

The walnut is bad at self-control and gets passionate about, and scared of, the wrong things

The walnut constantly gets excited about things that aren't good for it: sugar, salt and sex with strangers, for a start. Advertising knows how to exploit this cognitive frailty to perfection. Our confusions can generally be traced back to targets that would once have been crucial and fitting for us to focus on in simpler environments, but cause chaos in the complicated conditions of modernity.

The walnut is egocentric

The walnut is primed to look at things from its own point of view – or the way of looking that is long established as normal in its tribe. It often simply can't believe that there are other ways of considering an issue. Other people can therefore seem perverse, or horrible to it – sparking outrage or self-pity. It's only in the last second, from an evolutionary point of view, that the walnut has started to try to imagine what it might be like to be someone else (a symptom of this is that it's learnt to take pleasure in novels). But this is still a fragile empathetic capacity, which tends to collapse, especially when the walnut is tired, and someone is trying to persuade it of a strange-sounding idea.

The Characteristics of the Emotional Sceptic

There are three key things that characterise the outlook of an emotionally sceptical person.

They distinguish between feeling and action

They don't automatically act on their feelings. The sceptic opens up the equivalent of a demilitarised zone between emotions and actions. Having surveyed the fragilities of our minds, the Ancient Greek Sceptics recommended that we learn to develop an attitude of what they called *epoche*, translated as 'reserve' or 'suspension of judgement'. Aware of our proclivities towards error, we should never rush into decisions; we should let our ideas settle so they can be re-evaluated at different points in time. We are to be especially vigilant about the impact of sexual excitement, tiredness and public opinion on the formation of our plans.

They are modest about rationality

They are deeply conscious of the ways in which what seems like pure cold reason is in fact the slave of passion. The emotional sceptic acknowledges that they can't be sure that what they feel is right actually is right. They become more modest, more ready to admit that there might be something to be said on the other's side, more open to ideas that strike them as initially implausible. Their scepticism leads them to be more generous to others and more modest in their own claims.

They are open to revising their beliefs and attitudes

They may feel pretty sure and committed just now but they are aware that their conclusions are provisional. The emotional sceptic knows there is more in their minds than they can access at any given point, and so remain tentative about their initial positions.

Our vulnerability to emotional distortion is not our fault: it is the result of a mismatch between the system of reasoning we have been bequeathed by our evolutionary history and the complex nature of the life tasks we are challenged by. We can't wholly refashion who we are: we will inevitably be swept about by egotism, jealousy, wounded pride, projection and bursts of tired panic and anger. In other words, we are condemned by nature to address the world and shape our lives via the mechanisms of an at times catastrophically faulty brain.

However, we will go a long way to counteract the problems of our machinery if we prepare ourselves for it: if we accept that we stare out at reality through a highly unreliable and distorted pane of glass and must, therefore, frequently suspend judgement, moderate our impulses, watch over our diet and strive to get to bed early.

We will finally have learnt how to know ourselves when we have a complete picture at once of what we can know – and of what we have to remain very modest about ever knowing.

On Confidence

I

Introduction

It can be humbling to realise just how many great achievements have not been the result of superior talent or technical know-how, but merely that strange buoyancy of the soul we call confidence.

We spend vast amounts of time acquiring confidence in narrow technical fields: quadratic equations or bioengineering, economics or pole vaulting. But we overlook the primordial need to acquire a more free-ranging variety of confidence – one that can serve us across a range of tasks: speaking to strangers at parties, asking someone to marry us, suggesting a fellow passenger turn down their music, changing the world.

We so often lack confidence because we implicitly regard its possession as a matter of slightly freakish and irreplicable good luck. Some people simply are very confident, for reasons that neuroscientists may one day uncover. But, we tell ourselves, there isn't much we can do about our particular situation. We are stuck with the confidence levels we were born with.

In fact, the opposite is true. Confidence is a skill, not a gift from the gods. And it is a skill founded on a set of ideas about the world and our natural place within it. These ideas can be systematically studied and gradually learnt, so that the roots of excessive hesitancy and compliance can be overcome. We can school ourselves in the art of confidence.

Confidence
is a skill,
not a gift from
the gods.

II
Idiocy and Confidence

In well-meaning attempts to boost our confidence ahead of challenging moments, people often try to draw our attention to our strengths: our intelligence, our competence, our experience. However, this can have awkward consequences. There is a type of underconfidence that arises specifically when we grow too attached to our own dignity and become anxious around any situation that might seem to threaten it. We hold back from challenges in which there is any risk of ending up looking ridiculous – which comprises, of course, almost all the most interesting situations.

In a foreign city, we grow reluctant to ask anyone to guide us to the nice bars, because they might think us an ignorant, pitiable lost tourist. We might long to kiss someone, but never let on, in case they dismiss us as a predatory loser. At work, we don't apply for a promotion, in case the senior management deems us delusionally arrogant. In a concerted bid never to look foolish, we don't venture very far from our cocoon. Consequently – from time to time, at least – we miss out on the best opportunities of our lives.

At the heart of our underconfidence is a skewed picture of how dignified a normal person can be. We imagine that it might be possible, after a certain age, to place ourselves beyond mockery. We trust that it is an option to lead a good life without regularly making a complete idiot of ourselves.

One of the most charming books written in early modern Europe was *In Praise of Folly* (1509), by the Dutch scholar and philosopher Erasmus (c. 1469–1536). In its pages, Erasmus advances a hugely liberating argument. In a warm tone, he reminds us that everyone, however important and learned they might seem, is a fool. No one is spared, not even the author. However well-schooled he himself was, Erasmus remained – he insists – as much of a nitwit as anyone else: his judgement is faulty; his passions get the better of him; he is prey to superstition and irrational fear; he is shy whenever he has to meet new people; he drops things at elegant dinners. This is deeply cheering, for it means that our own repeated idiocies do not have to exclude us from the best company. Looking like a prick, making blunders, and doing bizarre things in the night does not render us unfit for society; it makes us a little more like the greatest scholar of the northern European Renaissance.

There is a similarly uplifting message to be drawn from the work of Pieter Bruegel the Elder (c. 1525–1569). His painting *Netherlandish Proverbs* (1559) presents a comically disenchanted view of human nature. Everyone, he suggests, is pretty much deranged: here's a man throwing his money into the river; there's a soldier squatting on the fire and burning his trousers; someone is intently bashing his head against a brick wall; someone else is biting a pillar. Importantly, the painting is not an attack on just a few unusually awful people: it is a picture of parts of all of us.

Bruegel's and Erasmus's works propose that the way to greater confidence is not to reassure ourselves of our own dignity; it's to come to peace with our inevitable ridiculousness. We are idiots now, we have been idiots in the past, and we will be idiots again in the future – and that's OK. There aren't any other available options for human beings.

We grow timid when we allow ourselves to be overexposed to the respectable sides of others. Such are the pains people take to appear normal, we collectively create a phantasm that suggests that normality might be possible, and this is problematic for everyone.

Once we learn to see ourselves as already, and by nature, foolish, it won't matter so much if we do one more thing that might look stupid. The person we try to kiss could indeed think us ridiculous. The individual from whom we asked directions in a foreign city might regard us with contempt. But if

Pieter Bruegel the Elder,
Nederlandse Spreekwoorden
(Netherlandish Proverbs), 1559

these people did so, it wouldn't be news to us. They would only be confirming what we had already gracefully accepted long ago: that we, like them – and every other person on the earth – are a nitwit. The risk of trying and failing would have its sting substantially removed. The fear of humiliation would no longer stalk us in the shadows of our minds. We would grow free to try things by accepting that failure was the norm. And every so often, amid the many rebuffs we would have factored in from the outset, it would work: we'd get a kiss, we'd make a friend, we'd get a raise.

The road to greater confidence begins with a ritual of telling oneself solemnly every morning, before heading out for the day, that one is a muttonhead, a cretin, a dumbbell and an imbecile. A few more acts of folly should, thereafter, not matter very much.

III
Impostor Syndrome

Faced with challenges, we often leave the possibility of success to others, because we don't seem to ourselves to be the sort of people who win. When we approach the idea of acquiring responsibility or prestige, we quickly become convinced that we are 'impostors', like an actor in the role of a pilot, wearing the uniform and making sunny cabin announcements while incapable of even starting the engines.

The root cause of impostor syndrome is a hugely unhelpful picture of what people at the top of society are really like. We feel like impostors not because we are uniquely flawed, but because we can't imagine how deeply flawed the elite must also be beneath a more or less polished surface.

The impostor syndrome has its roots far back in childhood – specifically in the powerful sense children have that their parents are very different from them. To a 4-year-old, it is incomprehensible that their mother was once their age and unable to drive a car, tell the plumber what to do, decide other people's bedtimes and go on trips with colleagues. The gulf in status appears absolute and unbridgeable. The child's passionate loves – bouncing on the sofa, Pingu, Toblerone – have nothing to do with those of adults, who like to sit at a table talking for hours and drinking beer that tastes like rusty metal. We start out in life with a very strong impression that competent and admirable people are not like us at all.

This childhood experience dovetails with a basic feature of the human condition. We know ourselves from the inside, but others only from the outside. We are aware of all our anxieties and doubts from within, yet all we know of others is what they happen to do and tell us – a far narrower and more edited source of information.

We are often left to conclude that we must be at the more freakish and revolting end of human nature. Really, however, we're just failing to imagine that others are every bit as fragile as we are. Without knowing what it is that troubles or wracks outwardly impressive people, we can be sure that it will be something. We might not know exactly what they regret, but there will be agonising feelings of some kind. We won't be able to say exactly what kind of sexual kink obsesses them, but there will be one. And we can know this because vulnerabilities and compulsions cannot be curses that have descended upon us uniquely; they are universal features of the human mental equipment.

The solution to the impostor syndrome lies in making a crucial leap of faith: that others' minds work in much the same way as ours do. Other people must be as anxious, uncertain and wayward as we are.

Traditionally, being a member of the aristocracy provided a fast track to confidence-giving knowledge about the true characters of the elite. In 18th-century England, an admiral of the fleet would have looked deeply impressive to outsiders (more or less everyone), with his splendid uniform (cockaded hat, loads of gold) and thousands of subordinates to do his bidding. But to a young earl or marquis, who had moved in the same social circles all his life, the admiral would appear in a very different light. He would have seen him losing money at cards in the club the night before; he would know that his pet name in the nursery had been 'Sticky' because of his inept way of eating jam tarts; his aunt would still tell the story of the ridiculous way the admiral had tried to proposition her sister in the Yew Walk; he would know the admiral was in debt to his grandfather, who regarded him as pretty dim. Through acquaintance, the aristocrat would have reached a wise awareness that being an admiral was not an unattainable position reserved for gods; it was the sort of thing Sticky could do.

The solution to the impostor syndrome lies in making a crucial leap of faith.

The other traditional release from underconfidence of this type came from the opposite end of the social spectrum: being a servant. 'No man is a hero to his valet,' remarked the 16th-century French essayist Michel de Montaigne (1533–1592) – a lack of respect that may at points prove deeply encouraging, given how much our awe can sap our will to rival or match our heroes. Great public figures aren't ever so impressive to those who look after them, who see them drunk in the early hours, examine the stains on their underpants, hear their secret misgivings about matters on which they publicly hold firm views and witness them weeping with shame over the strategic blunders they officially deny.

The valet and the aristocrat reasonably and automatically grasp the limitations of the authority of the elite. Fortunately, we don't have to be either one to liberate ourselves from inhibiting degrees of respect for the powerful; imagination will serve just as well. One of the tasks that works of art should ideally accomplish is to take us more reliably into the minds of people we are intimidated by and show us the more average, muddled and fretful experiences unfolding inside.

At another point in his *Essays* of 1580, Montaigne playfully informed his readers in plain French that 'Kings and philosophers shit and so do ladies'. Montaigne's thesis is that, for all the evidence that exists about this shitting, we might not guess that grand people ever had to squat on a toilet. We never see distinguished types doing this – while we, of course, are immensely well informed of our own digestive activities. Therefore, we build up a sense that because we have crude and sometimes rather desperate bodies, we can't be philosophers, kings or ladies, and that if we set ourselves up in these roles, we'd just be impostors.

With Montaigne's guidance, we are invited to take on a saner view of what powerful people are actually like. But the real target isn't just an underconfidence about bodily functions; it is psychological timidity.

Montaigne might have said that kings, philosophers and ladies are wracked by self-doubt and feelings of inadequacy, sometimes bump into doors and have weird lustful thoughts about members of their own families. Furthermore, instead of considering only the big figures of 16th-century France, we could update the example and refer to CEOs, corporate lawyers, news presenters and successful startup entrepreneurs. They too can't cope, feel they might buckle under pressure and look back on certain decisions with shame and regret. No less than shitting, such feelings belong to us all. Our inner frailties don't cut us off from doing what they do. If we were in their roles, we'd not be impostors, we would simply be normal.

Making a leap of faith around what other people are like helps to humanise the world. Whenever we encounter a stranger, we are not really encountering such a person; we are encountering someone who is in basic ways very much like us, despite surface evidence to the contrary. Therefore, nothing fundamental stands between us and the possibility of responsibility, success and fulfilment.

IV
Trust in the System

When we take our ideas out into the world, there is no more common response than to hear a 'no' in return.

We develop a proposal at work that seems pretty good to us. We do some research, put together strategic options and hand it to a senior colleague who agrees to give it some thought. Then, after six weeks, a message comes back: the firm is grateful for the suggestion, but won't be taking the plan further. There is no precise explanation, just a general view: the timing is wrong; it doesn't fit with general policy; it's not the kind of thing that's right for the team. We may be disappointed, but we take the comments on the chin. Our suggestion couldn't really have been a good one. Perhaps we should be more careful in the future.

Or maybe we've hit upon an idea for a new kind of product. It looks to us as if there might be a significant gap in the market. We call in a business advisor and talk it through. But they tell us, with a striking degree of sarcasm, that it's not going to work. They wear very elegant spectacles and once worked with BMW and Google. Later, we delete the whole presentation from our laptop.

Or, perhaps for years, we've been happily using our old phone. It's not terribly sophisticated but it does just the things we want. Unfortunately, we leave it on a train. At the shop, they're not at all helpful. They tell us our model is absurdly outdated, equipped with a stone-age processor and a 960 x 540-pixel resolution display that doesn't respond well to any of the new swipe commands. There's nothing to be done. We accept the suggestion of a phone we don't like so much. Then, a few weeks later, at a conference, we see someone happily using exactly the phone we wanted.

In big and small instances, we cave in to the judgements of the system, beside whose might and invincibility our own hopes seem feeble and disposable. The root of our underconfidence is a touching, but ultimately hugely dangerous, degree of trust – a legacy of times in our lives when those in charge had our best interests in mind and took the time to assess every one of our needs. When a parent told us we couldn't use the computer in our bedroom or that it wasn't advisable for us to go on the school trip to Spain, we could trust that they weren't being merely mean or unimaginative; they were the bearers of bad news out of mature benevolence.

From such experiences, we may develop a more generalised belief in the open-heartedness of those who frustrate us. The senior manager, business advisor or sales assistant are, we feel, in their own ways as careful about their judgements as our own families. But this, of course, can't be true.

At the end of the Classical period, on the cusp of the 4th and 5th centuries of the modern era, as the Roman Empire in the West was collapsing, the Christian philosopher St Augustin (354–430 CE) e tried to describe the essential, un-avoidable flaws of all human systems. He drew a fundamental contrast between two realms. One he called the City of God, an imagined ideal in which institutions could be exactly the way we'd like them to be: wise, altruistic and benign. On the other hand, there was what he called the City of Man, a realm that described institutions as they actually were: occasionally well-meaning, but frequently lazy, casual, corrupt or indifferent.

The dark brilliancy of Augustine's diagnosis was his conviction that it would by nature be impossible for human institutions ever to meet our hopes. They could never be the wise and kindly organisations that they presented themselves as being. Such aspirations belonged to what he thought of as the afterlife – or, as we might now more reasonably put it, to nowhere.

Children have great trouble imagining the inner lives of those in authority. A young school child can be deeply puzzled to see their teacher on a Sunday morning at the shops or jogging round the park. In their minds, this mighty person is simply and exclusively 'the teacher'. Their whole life (the child thinks) revolves around the classroom and the large desk they stand behind. They have no history; they couldn't have been a child themselves; they have no problems or frustrated dreams or wakeful nights. Our childish selves struggle to flesh out the reality of adult existence.

However, maturity means, ideally, going from the myth of a person, however high their status in a system, to a full recognition of their humanity. We finally pay others a strange but valid compliment when we accept them as versions of the same complex and imperfect creatures we know ourselves to be. This may feel like disenchantment, but it is also a crucial vehicle for a future in which the word 'no' seems just a little less impartial and beyond question.

V
History is Now

One of the things that separates confident from diffident people is their approach to history. Broadly speaking, the unconfident believe that history is over; conversely, the confident trust that history is still in the process of being made – and possibly by themselves one day.

The way we enter the world carries with it an inherent bias towards an impression that history has been settled. Everything around us conspires to convey a sense that the status quo is entrenched. We are surrounded by people far taller than us, who follow traditions that have been in place for decades – centuries, even. Our understanding of time hugely overprivileges the immediate moment. To a 5-year-old, last year feels like a century ago. The house we live in appears as immutable as an ancient temple; the school we go to looks as though it has been performing the same rituals since the earth began. We are constantly told why things are the way they are and encouraged to accept that reality is not made according to our wishes. We come to trust that human beings have fully mapped the range of the possible. If something hasn't happened, it's either because it can't happen, or it shouldn't.

The result is a deep wariness around imagining alternatives. There is no point starting a new business (the market must be full already), pioneering a new approach to the arts (everything is already set in a fixed pattern), or giving loyalty to a new idea (it either exists or is mad).

When we study history, however, the picture changes sharply. Once time is speeded up and we climb up a mountain of minutes to survey the centuries, change appears constant. New continents are discovered; alternative ways of governing nations are pioneered; ideas of how to dress and whom to worship are transformed. Once people wore strange cloaks and tilled the land with clumsy instruments. A long time ago, they chopped off a king's head. Way back, people got around in fragile ships, ate the eyeballs of sheep, used chamber pots and didn't know how to fix teeth.

We come away from all this knowing, in theory at least, that things do change. However, in practice, and almost without noticing, we tend to distance ourselves and our own societies from a day-to-day belief that we belong to the same ongoing turbulent narrative and are, at present, its central actors. History, we feel, is what used to happen; it can't really be what is happening around us in the here and now. In our vicinity at least, things have settled down.

To attenuate this insensitivity to the omnipresence of change, and by extension the passivity it breeds, we might turn to some striking lines in T.S. Eliot's cycle of poems *The Four Quartets* (1943):

> So, while the light fails
> On a winter's afternoon, in a secluded chapel
> History is now and England.

Winter afternoons, around 4 p.m., have a habit of feeling particularly resolved and established, especially in quiet English country chapels, many of which date back to the Middle Ages. The air in such chapels is still and musty. The heavy stone floors have been slowly worn away by the feet of the faithful. There might be a leaflet advertising an upcoming concert and a charity box hoping to catch our eye. Over the altar, a stained-glass window of the saints (Peter and John, holding a lamb each) glows from the last of the light. These are not places and times to think about changing the world; everything hints that we would be wiser to accept the way things are, walk back home across the fields, light a fire and settle down for the evening. Hence the surprise of Eliot's third line, his resonant: 'History is now and England.'

In other words, everything that we associate with history – the impetuous daring of great people, the dramatic alterations in values, the revolutionary questioning of long-held beliefs, the upturning of the old order – is still going on, even at this very moment, in outwardly peaceful, apparently unchanging places like the countryside near Shamley Green, in Surrey, where Eliot (1888–1965) wrote the poem. We don't see it only because we are standing too close to it. The world is being made and remade in every instant. Therefore, any one of us has a theoretical chance of being an agent in history, on a big or a small scale. It is open to our own times to build a new city as beautiful as Venice, to change ideas as radically as the Renaissance, to start an intellectual movement as resounding as Buddhism.

The present has all the contingency of the past, and is every bit as malleable. It should not intimidate us. How we love, travel, approach the arts, govern, educate ourselves, run businesses, age and die are all up for further development. Current views may appear firm, but only because we exaggerate their fixity. The majority of what exists is arbitrary, neither inevitable nor right, simply the result of muddle and happenstance. We should be confident, even at sunset on winter afternoons, of our power to join the stream of history and, however modestly, change its course.

VI
Experience

One of the greatest sources of despair is the belief that things should have been easier than they have turned out to be. We give up not simply because events are difficult, but because we hadn't expected them to be so. The struggle is interpreted as humiliating proof that we do not have the talent required to carry out our wishes. We grow subdued and timid and eventually surrender, because a struggle this great seems impossibly rare.

The capacity to remain confident is, therefore, to a significant extent a matter of having internalised a correct narrative about what difficulties we are likely to encounter. Unfortunately, the narratives we have to hand are deeply misleading, for a range of reasons. We are surrounded by stories that conspire to make success seem easier than it is, and therefore that unwittingly destroy the confidence we can muster in the face of our obstacles.

Some of the explanations for the preponderance of optimistic narratives are benign. If we told a small child what lay in store for them – the loneliness, the fractious relationships, the unfulfilling jobs – they might cave in and give up. We prefer to read them the adventures of Miffy, the adorable bunny.

At other points, the reasons for the silence around difficulty are slightly more self-serving: we are trying to impress people. The successful artist or skilled entrepreneur go to great lengths to disguise their labours and make their work appear simple, natural and obvious. 'Art lies in concealing art,' opined the Roman poet Horace (65–8 BCE).

The great stand-up comic does not reveal the time spent agonising over every detail of their performance. They will not tell us of the anxieties around whether it was best to deliver the last line sitting, to convey an impression of stunned passivity, or standing, to imply a stifled energy about to be released; or whether it was preferable to use the word 'tiny' or simply go with 'very, very small' as the punchline to the opening joke. Appearing to say the first thing that comes into one's head is the result of decades of rehearsal.

As customers, we pay to have news of struggle kept from us. We don't wish to read the novelist's early drafts; we don't want to hear about the company's difficulties in setting up the hotel or the engineer's complaints about the hydraulic system. We want to admire the polished surface of the gadget without a reminder of the cramped circuits beneath.

But there comes a point, when we move from consumers to producers, that we start to pay in heightened currency for our ignorance: the currency of confidence and self-respect. We see our early failures as proof of conclusive ineptness rather than as the inevitable stages on every path to mastery. Without an accurate developmental map, we can't position ourselves properly with regards to our defeats. We have not seen enough of the rough drafts of those we admire, and therefore cannot forgive ourselves the horror of our own early attempts.

Certain societies have been wiser than our own in communicating the challenges of all noble endeavours. For instance, the ancient temple dedicated to the Goddess Aphaia, on the Greek island of Aegina, was decorated with prominent pieces of sculpture that set out to portray a very precise idea of what your life would be like as a warrior. Someone would try to stab you with a spear; the person standing next to you in the phalanx would collapse; you'd be pushed over backwards, bash your head with your own sword and a determined adversary would probably fire an arrow in your back as you turned to flee.

Those who commissioned the temple were deliberately preparing their people for the hardships of battle, so they would be ready when they entered the field. At the same time, they were dignifying the lives of those

TOP Sculpture of a warrior from the east pediment of the Temple of Aphaia II, c. 505–500 BCE

BOTTOM Pedimental figures from the Temple of Aphaia on Aegina, c. 500/490–490/480 BCE

The statues in Aegina's Temple of Aphaia showed the gritty realities of warfare to prepare soldiers for the battlefield.

who dared undergo these titanic struggles. The warriors deserved prestige, the temple builders were saying, because war was never a route to easy glory. It was imperative that such statuary not be hidden away but displayed right in the centre of town, so that one would encounter it on serious and important occasions from youth onwards. Despite their limited resources, ancient Greek communities went to astonishing lengths to remind themselves of what the most prestigious job available actually involved: namely, a lot of hardship.

We are, by contrast, recklessly short on detailed, honest and compelling accounts of what to expect around key aspects of our professional lives. To shore up our confidence, we would need regularly to encounter the modern equivalents of the works of the classical sculptors: films, poems, songs and novels that would represent for us the agonies that unfold in the unglamorous but hugely representative hubs of modern capitalism: the world's distribution centres, tax offices, airport lounges, HR conferences and management retreats.

The confidence-boosting artists would show us, without reserve or coyness, what a successful life truly involves. They would take us through the tears we will shed in office cubicles; the meetings in which our ideas will be rejected and our projections thwarted; the mocking articles we will read about ourselves in newspapers; the hours we'll spend in lonely foreign hotel rooms while we miss out on our children's school plays; the sense that our best insights have arrived far too late; the inability to sleep from worry and confusion.

Thereby, we'd be better placed to meet our own eventual experiences against a realistic set of expectations. Our setbacks would take on a different meaning. Instead of looking like confidence-destroying evidence of our incapacities, they would much more readily strike us as proof that we were on the standard path to what we admire. We'd interpret our worries, reversals and troubles as unavoidable landmarks, not aberrations or fateful warnings.

Confidence isn't the belief that we won't meet obstacles: it is the recognition that difficulties are an inescapable part of all worthwhile contributions. We need to ensure we have plenty of narratives to hand that normalise the role of pain, anxiety and disappointment in even the best and most successful lives.

VII
Death

There is so much that we put off every day: the relationship that, for the sake of both participants, it would be better to end; the new person it would be thrilling to get close to; the alternative career that promises to utilise our deepest talents; the house with the beautiful views over water. And yet we do nothing. There may be distressed moments of recognition at three in the morning, but in the light of day we bury our longings and muddle on. We find ourselves musing on the interesting things we'll do when we retire. We let life leak away.

Our hesitation is grounded in a sense of risk. Every move presents us with appalling dangers. The new house might not be right; the change of career might lead to ruin; the beloved might reject us; we could regret leaving the old relationship. But our inaction is not in itself cost-free, for in the wings, out of regular conscious awareness, there is something arguably even more frightening than failure: the tragedy of wasting our lives.

We too easily ignore the most stupid yet deepest fact about our existence: that it will end. The brutal fact of our mortality seems so implausible that we live in practical terms like immortals, as if we will always have the opportunity to address our stifled longings one day. There will be time next year, or the year after. But by hyping up the dangers of failure in action, we underrate the seriousness of the dangers lurking within passivity. In comparison with the horror of our final exit, the pains and troubles of our bolder moves and riskier ventures do not, in the end, seem so terrifying. We should learn to frighten ourselves a bit more in one area to be less scared in others.

Frans Hals, *Young Man Holding a Skull (Vanitas)*, 1626–1628
This painting typifies the genre of the Vanitas – a reminder of the fleetingness of life, usually featuring a skull.

It is hardly surprising that we struggle with the notion of how long we will be here. At first, life seems quite endless. At 7, it feels like an eternity till Christmas. At 11, it is almost impossible to imagine what it might be like to be 22. At 22, 30 feels absurdly remote. Time does us a disservice in seeming so long, and yet turning out to be so resolutely short. Typically, people only become gripped by the idea of mortality at a few select points in their lives. Turning 40 or 50 can bring a sudden reversal of perspective. We panic or become morose. We buy a new car or take up a musical instrument. However, what this really indicates is a dramatic failure of anticipation. The extraordinary aspect is not that we're dying, but that the reality of the nature of existence did not get fixed firmly enough in our brains at an earlier, more appropriate, moment. A midlife crisis is not a legitimate awakening; it's a sign of being shamefully ill prepared.

We should never need to be awoken. In an ideal culture, our mortality would be systematically impressed upon us from the earliest age. There would be a specific day each month when everyone attended a stranger's funeral. Every news bulletin would be followed by a live feed from a hospice. Career guidance would start with a brief meditation on the preponderance of heart attacks and pancreatic cancers. We'd have impressively grim monuments across our cities (in supermarket car parks and around football stadia): 'To Those Who Wasted Their Lives'. Worrying about where life was going would be treated as an admirable and important characteristic. You'd often overhear people saying: 'I really like X; they're so concerned about wasting their life.'

Even without this ideal society-wide support there are moves we can make ourselves to usefully intensify our awareness of our own limited spans: we should assemble our own repertoire of reminders, perhaps a skull, a set of cancer statistics or a close-up of the sort of capillary that can unleash a stroke.

We need regular, forceful encounters with reminders that there is something else we should be far more frightened of than embarrassment around holding someone's hand or a bit of trouble as we change the subject of our university degree.

VIII
Enemies

Learning that someone hates us deeply, even though we have done nothing ostensibly to provoke them, can be one of the most alarming situations we face. At a bar after work, we might be told, via a malevolent third party, that two people in the office deem us arrogant and disrespectful and that, for the last few months, they haven't lost a chance to put us down behind our backs. Or we learn that a friend of a friend, a senior professor, has forceful objections to a paper of ours; they called it 'naive' and 'stuck in the 1970s' and made sarcastic jokes at our expense at a conference. Furthermore, because of technology, we're now aware of a vast new range of potential enemies scattered around the digital universe. We are only ever a few seconds of online searching away from pitiless, personally targeted assessments of all that we are.

For the underconfident among us, enemies are a catastrophe. In our psychological make-up, the approval of the world effectively supports our approval of ourselves. Consequently, when enemies agitate against us, we lose faith not in them (they continue to exert a mesmeric authority over us), but, more alarmingly, in ourselves. We may, when with our friends, casually profess to hate the haters (and curse their names with bravado), but in private, over the ensuing months, we simply cannot dismiss their judgements, because we have accorded them a status logically prior to our own in our deep minds. Their objections may feel unbearable, like a physical discomfort we cannot correct, but we can't reject them as unwarranted either. In despair, it feels as if we do not know how to carry on, not only because we've been called idiots or egotists, but because, as a result, we must simply be idiots and egotists.

The judgements of others have been given a free pass to enter all the rooms of our minds. There is no one manning the border between them and us: the enemies are freely in us, wandering wildly and destructively through the caverns of our inner selves, ripping items off the shelves and mocking everything we are. In our distress, we may keep harping back to the idea (it brings tears to our eyes) that the situation is profoundly 'unfair': we did nothing especially wrong, our intentions are benevolent and our work is acceptable. Why, therefore, has our name been trampled upon and our reputation trashed? Either because we truly are fools (which is an unendurable truth) or because we're not fools (in which case the hatred is an unendurable error). Whatever is right, we can't just walk away and get on with our lives. We feel compelled to take some kind of corrective action to scrub away the stain our enemies have applied. In the middle of the night, we contemplate a range of responses: angry, passive-aggressive, self-harming, charming, begging... Our partner might implore us to drop it and return to bed. We cannot: the enemy refuses to leave our heads.

Where does such underconfidence around enemies come from? We should, as ever, begin with parents and sketch an imaginary portrait of types who could unwittingly create such tortured mindsets. However ostensibly loving these parents might have been, they are also likely to have felt a high degree of trust in the system. If the police were investigating one of their friends, their guess would be that the authorities were correct in their suspicions. When reading a newspaper, if they were to read a destructive review of a novel, even one by an author whose work they'd much enjoyed in the past, it would seem evident that the author had lost their talent and was now kidding the public. If the parents were friends with an architect who was up for a major prize that was then awarded to somebody else, they'd feel the friend – whose buildings they admired – must have lacked talent in comparison with the winner, whose dark asymmetrical structures they would vow at once to take a second, more respectful, look at.

When it came to their own children, these underconfidence-generating parents would have applied a similar method of judgement: the issue of how much and where to love would have been to a large extent determined externally. If the world felt the baby was adorable, they probably were (and if not, then not so much). Later, if the child won a maths prize, it was a sign not just of competence at algebra but of being, far more broadly, a love-worthy person. Conversely, if the school report described the child as an easily distracted dreamer who looked as if he would flunk his exams, that might mean the offspring didn't quite deserve to exist. The lovability of the child in the eyes of the parents rose and fell in accordance with the respect, interest and approval of the world.

To be on the receiving end of such parenting is a heavy burden. We, the recipients of conditional love, have no option but to work manically to fulfil the conditions set up by parental and worldly expectations. Success isn't simply a pleasant prize to stumble upon when we enjoy a subject or a task interests us; it is a psychological necessity, something we must secure in order to feel we have the right to be alive. We don't have any memories of success-independent affection and therefore constantly need to recharge our batteries from the external power source of the world's flickering and wilful interest. Unsurprisingly, when enemies come on the horizon, we are quickly in deep trouble, for we have no ability to hold in our minds the concept that they might be wrong and we right, that our achievements are not our being and that the failure of our actions does not presuppose failure of our entire selves. Rendered defenceless by our upbringing, we have no border post between inside and out. We are at the mercy of pretty much anyone who might decide to hate us.

Contrast this with the blessed childhood of the confident. Their parents would have maintained a vigorously sceptical relationship to the system. The world might sometimes be right, but then again, on key occasions, it could be gravely and outrageously wrong. Everyone was, in their eyes, endowed with their own capacity to judge. It is not because the crowd is jeering that the accused is guilty, or vice versa. The chief of police, the lead reviewer of *The Times*, or the head of the Pritzker Architecture Prize might well be idiotic; these things happen. In their role as parents, the messages of the confidence-inducing were no less generous in their scepticism: 'You are loved in and of yourself because of what you are, not what you do. You aren't always admirable or even likeable, but you are always deserving of affection and charity of interpretation. It doesn't matter to me if you end up the president or the street cleaner. You will always be something more important: my child. If they don't have the wisdom to be kind, fuck them!' Without necessarily intending this, the parents set up a soothing voice that still plays on a loop in the recesses of the mind, especially at moments of greatest challenge. It is the voice of love.

We cannot go back and change the past that made us. However, by understanding the structure of what we are missing, we may at least strive to integrate emotionally healthier voices into our agitated interiors. The verdict of the system is never totally wrong, but nor is it ever more than occasionally right: police forces get muddled; reviewers redirect their disappointments onto innocent targets; prize committees fall under the sway of fashion. The world doesn't reliably 'know'. We cannot change the presence of an enemy, but we can change what an enemy means to us. These figures can shift from being devoted, impartial agents of truth about one's right to exist to being – more sanely – people who have an opinion, probably only ever a bit right, about something we once did, and never about who we are (that is something we decide).

Panicking about having acquired a few enemies can be a symptom of a dangerous trust in human beings as a whole. Underconfident types work with the assumption that almost everyone they encounter will be sane, measured, intelligent, judicious, and in command of themselves. If, despite these attributes, certain people still write nasty things online or describe us as a nuisance, the attacks simply have to be true. Yet the more psychologically robust are saved from such dispiriting assumptions by a highly useful skill: fierce pessimism. They assume from the start that most people, even grand and supposedly intelligent ones, are riddled with prejudice, beset by low motives, and capable of deliberate cattiness and meanness better suited to a playground of the under-fives. They lie, they slander, they project, they say things to make themselves feel better, they are envious and inadequate, cruel and close to evil. Why should we be surprised and disturbed if a few people happen to be nasty to us, given that nastiness is more or less the fundamental truth of human nature? The benefit of thinking a lot less of everyone can be a calmer attitude towards the specific meanness of a few.

Armed with darker thoughts, the confident know that every decent and interesting person is going to accumulate a string of enemies as they make their way through life. It would be impossible for it to be otherwise, given human nature. The specific reasons will be varied and somewhat random: some of these enemies will flare up because they have vested interests in a status quo we are challenging; some may be uncomfortably reminded of their own renounced ambitions when they encounter our skills; some may find our achievements humiliating to their sense of self-worth; some are people who might have wanted to be our friends or even our lovers, and then turned sour when this proved impossible. We will constantly be the target of anger, but we don't have to believe ourselves to be its true cause.

In the 17th century, the Dutch developed a tradition of painting ships in violent storms. These works, which hung in private homes and in municipal

Ludolf Bakhuysen, *Warships in a Heavy Storm*, c. 1695

buildings around the Dutch republic, were not mere decoration. They had an explicitly therapeutic purpose: they delivered a moral to their viewers, who lived in a nation critically dependent on maritime trade, about confidence in seafaring and life more broadly. The sight of a tall sailing ship being tossed to a twenty-degree angle in a rough sea looks like a catastrophe to an inexperienced person. But there are many situations that look and feel much more dangerous than they really are, especially when the crew is prepared and the ship internally sound. Consider Ludolf Bakhuysen's work *Warships in a Heavy Storm* (c. 1695). The scene looks chaotic in the extreme: How could they possibly survive? But the ships were well designed for just such situations. Their hulls had been minutely adapted through long experience to withstand the tempests of the northern oceans. The crews practised again and again the manoeuvres that could keep their vessels safe: they knew how to take down sails at speed and ensure that the wind would not shred the mast. They understood about shifting cargo in the hull, tacking to the left and then abruptly to the right, and pumping out water from the inner chambers. They knew how to remain coolly scientific in responding to the storm's wilful, frantic motions. The picture pays homage to decades of planning and experience. One can imagine the older sailors on the ship saying to a terrified novice, with a laugh, that just last year off the coast of Jutland there was an even bigger storm – and slapping him on the back with paternal playfulness as the youth was sick overboard. Bakhuysen wanted us to feel proud of humanity's resilience in the face of apparently dreadful challenges. His painting enthuses us with the message that we can all cope far better than we think, that what appears immensely threatening may be highly survivable.

What is true of storms in the North Sea may be no less true of enemies at the office. Their aggression can be terrifying, like the giant waves off Den Helder, yet in reality – with deft emotional skill and internal reorganisation – can prove eminently manageable. The storms are not really about us, and we can survive them by refusing to let the verdicts of others become our verdicts on ourselves. We should keep in mind a confident distinction between the hater and the critic, aim to correct our genuine flaws and otherwise forgive the injured, roaring winds that seek to punish us for pressures that have nothing to do with us. The storms will die down, we will be battered, a few things will be ripped, but eventually we will return to safer shores – as the sun rises over the spires of Alkmaar.

IX
Self-Sabotage

It is normal to expect that we will always – almost by nature – actively seek our own happiness, especially in two big areas of potential satisfaction: relationships and careers.

It is therefore odd and a little unnerving to find how often many of us act as if we were deliberately out to ruin our chances of getting what we want. When going on dates with candidates we are keen on, we may lapse into unnecessarily opinionated and antagonistic behaviour. When we are in a relationship with someone we love, we may drive them to distraction through repeated unwarranted accusations and angry explosions, as if we were somehow willing to bring on the sad day when, exhausted and frustrated, the beloved would be forced to walk away, still sympathetic but unable to take our elevated degree of suspicion and drama.

Similarly, we might be led to destroy our chances of a major promotion at work when, just after giving a particularly convincing presentation to the board, we grow bizarrely strident with the CEO or become drunk and insulting at a crucial client dinner.

Such behaviour can't be put down to mere bad luck. It deserves a stronger, more intentional term: self-sabotage. We are familiar enough with the fear of failure, but it appears that success can sometimes bring about as many anxieties, which may ultimately culminate in a desire to scupper our chances in a bid to restore our peace of mind.

What could possibly explain this suspicion of success? In certain cases, an unconscious desire to protect those who love us, particularly those who cared for us in childhood, from a sense of envy and inadequacy that might be triggered by our gains. The beautiful new partner or the promotion to a senior role may prove silently devastating to those around us, prompting them to wonder about how little they have achieved by comparison and to fear that they will be deemed no longer good enough to merit our company.

It can feel odd to accept that those who loved us as children could harbour envious feelings towards us, especially when they might be devoted to us in most other ways. Yet these caregivers may nevertheless be carrying a private layer of regret within them about the course of their own lives and attendant fears of being neglected and thought unimportant by others, even their own children. As we were growing up, there might have been telling reminders about not getting too big for one's boots and not forgetting where one came from, disguised pleas not to be forgotten and overlooked. We can end up in a bind: the success we long for threatens to hurt the feelings of those we love.

The solution, once we discover the impasse, is not to sabotage ourselves; it is to grow deeply generous and proactive around the real reasons why our caregivers could have ended up feeling so apprehensive about our achievements. We should recognise that these caregivers are not, ultimately, afraid of our success so much as they are afraid of being abandoned and reminded of their own inadequacies. The task, therefore, isn't to ruin our chances; it is to try to reassure our nervous companions of our essential loyalty and of their primordial value.

A second common type of self-saboteur is one who finds the price of hope too high to pay. When we were younger, we may have been exposed to exceptionally brutal disappointments at a time when we were too fragile to withstand them. Perhaps we hoped our parents would stay together and they didn't. Or we hoped our father would eventually come back from another country and stay. Perhaps we dared to love someone and, after a few weeks of happiness, they swiftly and oddly changed their attitude and mocked us in front of our peers. Somewhere in our characters, a deep association has been forged between hope and danger, along with a corresponding preference to live quietly with disappointment rather than more freely with hope.

The solution is to remind ourselves that we can, despite our fears, survive the loss of hope. We are no longer those who suffered the disappointments responsible for our present timidity. The conditions that forged our caution are no longer those of adult reality. The unconscious mind may, as is its wont, be reading the present through the lenses of decades ago, but what we fear will happen has, in truth, already happened; we are projecting into the future a catastrophe that belongs to a past we have not had the chance to fathom and mourn adequately.

Furthermore, what fundamentally distinguishes adulthood from childhood is that the adult has access to a great many more sources of hope than the child. We can survive a letdown here or there, because we no longer inhabit a closed province, bounded by the family, the neighbourhood and the school. We can use the whole world as an orchard in which to nurture a diversity of hopes that will always outstrip the inevitable, yet only ever occasional and survivable, crushing disappointment.

Lastly, we may destroy success from touching modesty: from the sense that we cannot really deserve the bounty we have received. We may turn to consider our new job or lover in the light of all the sides of ourselves that we know to be less than perfect – our laziness, cowardice, stupidity and immaturity – and conclude that there must have been a mistake and that we must therefore return our gifts to the more deserving. But this is kindly, though balefully, to misunderstand the way success and pain are allotted. The universe does not distribute its gifts and its horrors with divinely accurate knowledge of the good and bad within each of us. Most of what we win is not quite deserved and most of what we suffer isn't either. Cancer wards are not filled with the exceptionally wicked.

When we feel oppressed by a sense of not meriting our favours, we need only remind ourselves that we will soon enough not deserve our maledictions either. Our diseases, public falls from grace and romantic abandonments will in time be as undeserved as our beauty, elevations and loving partners might now be. We should not worry so much about the latter, nor complain quite so bitterly about the former. We should accept from the start, with good grace and dark premonition, the sheer randomness and amorality of fate.

It can be useful to keep the concept of self-sabotage in mind when interpreting our and others' odder antics. We should start to get suspicious when we catch ourselves pulling off erratic performances around people we deep down really like or need to impress.

Furthermore, faced with certain kinds of viciousness and unreliability in others, we should dare to imagine that things are not quite as they seem; we might have on our hands not a malevolent opponent, but an almost touchingly wounded self-saboteur, who chiefly deserves a little patience and should gently be coaxed out of doing themselves further harm.

We should come to terms with, and help others to see, just how hard and unnerving it can sometimes be to get close to the things we truly want.

X
Confidence in Confidence

Although we assume that we, like everyone else, must want to be confident, we may harbour private suspicions that confidence is in fact an unappealing state of mind. We might, without fully realising it, find the idea of being truly confident strangely offensive, and secretly remain attached to hesitancy and modesty.

We may take quiet pride in the fact that we aren't the types to complain in restaurants. We don't kick up a fuss about our salary. We don't ask all our friends to rearrange their holidays for our sakes. We don't play our music loudly. Our meekness protects us from some deeply off-putting associations around self-assertion. These might have been forged early on in our lives in the presence of people who were both hugely unpleasant and highly certain of their right to exist. They may have been terrifyingly demanding, impatient, dismissive and brash. They might have shouted in service situations and slammed the phone down on people they believed didn't respect them enough. We may have started to think that this is how people needed to behave in order to succeed and that if this were the case, then conspicuous success wouldn't be for us.

We shouldn't forget that suspicion of confidence has traditionally enjoyed immense cultural endorsement. Christianity, for centuries the greatest influence on the mindset of the West, was highly sceptical about those who might think too well of themselves. While the meek basked in divine favour, the arrogant would be the last to enter the kingdom of heaven. The political theory of Karl Marx (1818–1883) added to this argument a set of theories apparently proving that economic success was always founded upon the exploitation of others. No wonder it may feel as if, to be moral citizens, we should steer clear of all overly robust assertions of our own interests.

Yet this attitude too can carry dangers. We may lack the confidence not to be cruel and promote idiocy, but to fight for kindness and wisdom. Our lack of confidence in confidence may allow degraded versions of self-assertion to thrive.

Our attitude may also be unfair. Our negative view of confidence may be overly dependent on the quirks of our own histories, on the sort of people we first encountered confidence in who were not its best or most reliable representatives. Our real problem may not be confidence so much as a lack of other virtues such as manners, charm, wit and generosity. We may be wrongly diagnosing the root of our objections. There may be a few people at risk of growing into braggarts, self-seekers and blowhards. But confidence is in its essence entirely compatible with remaining sensitive, kind, witty and soft-spoken. It might be brutishness, not confidence, that we hate.

Furthermore, our attraction to meekness may mask some cowardly resentment against self-assertion. We might not so much admire timidity as fear trying confidence. It was this species of self-protective deception that particularly fascinated the German philosopher Nietzsche (1844–1900). He thought it a typical error of many Christians, who might pride themselves on their 'forgiveness' while in reality simply trying to excuse their 'inability to take revenge'. We should take care not to dress up our base deficiencies as godly virtues.

Unfortunately it isn't enough to be kind, interesting, intelligent and wise *inside*: we need to develop the skill that allows us to make our talents active in the world at large. Confidence is what translates theory into practice. It should never be thought of as the enemy of good things; it is their crucial and legitimate catalyst. We should allow ourselves to develop confidence in confidence.

What is Psychotherapy?

I

Introduction

Psychotherapy is one of the most valuable inventions of the last one hundred years, with an exceptional power to raise our levels of emotional well-being, improve our relationships, redeem the atmosphere in our families and assist us in mining our professional potential.

However, psychotherapy is also profoundly misunderstood and the subject of a host of unhelpful fantasies, hopes and suspicions. Its logic is rarely explained and its voice seldom heard with sufficient directness.

This book attempts to explain psychotherapy: what the needs are in all of us to which it caters; the methods by which it addresses these needs; and what the outcome of a therapeutic intervention could ideally be.

The book reflects a fundamental belief of The School of Life that psychotherapy is the single greatest step any of us can take towards self-understanding and fulfilment. A course of therapy stands to render us slightly less angry, self-defeating, unconfident, lost and sad.

This is a guide to the purpose and meaning of psychotherapy.

II
Why We Need Therapy

A primal wound

The origins of our need for psychotherapy lie deep in our pasts. No one intends for this to happen, but somewhere in childhood, our trajectory towards emotional maturity will almost certainly have been impeded. Even if we were sensitively cared for and lovingly handled, we can be counted upon not to have passed through our young years without sustaining some kind of deep psychological injury – what we can term a 'primal wound'.

Childhood opens us up to emotional damage in part because, unlike all other living things, *Homo sapiens* have an inordinately long and structurally claustrophobic pupillage. A foal can stand up thirty minutes after it is born. By the age of 18, a human will have spent around 25,000 hours in the company of its parents. A female grouper mother will unsentimentally dump up to 100 million eggs a year in the sandy banks off the north Atlantic seaboard, then swim away without seeing a single one of her offspring again. Even the blue whale, the largest animal on the planet, is sexually mature and independent by the age of 5.

But for our part, we dither and linger. It can be a year until we take our first steps and two before we can speak in whole sentences. It is close to two decades before we are categorised as adults. In the meantime, we are at the mercy of that highly peculiar and distorting institution we call home, and its even more distinctive overseers, our parents.

Across the long summers and winters of childhood, we are intimately shaped by the ways of the big people around us: we come to know their favourite expressions, their habits, how they respond to a delay, the way they address us when they're cross. We know the atmosphere of home on a bright July morning and in the afternoon downpours of mid-April. We memorise the textures of the carpets and the smells of the clothes cupboards. As adults, we can still recall the taste of a particular biscuit we liked to eat after school and know intimately the tiny sounds a mother or father will make as they concentrate on an article in the newspaper. We can return to our original home for a holiday when we are parents ourselves and find – despite our car, responsibilities and lined faces – that we are 8 again.

During our elongated gestation, we are at first, in a physical sense, completely at the mercy of our caregivers. We are so frail, we could be tripped up by a twig; the family cat is a tiger. We need help crossing the road, putting on our coat, writing our name.

Our vulnerability is also emotional. We can't begin to understand our strange circumstances: who we are; where our feelings come from; why we are sad or furious; how our parents fit into the wider scheme; why they behave as they do. We necessarily take what the big people around us say as an inviolable truth; we can't help but exaggerate our parents' role on the planet. We are condemned to be enmeshed in their attitudes, ambitions, fears and inclinations. Our upbringing is always particular and peculiar.

As children, we can brush off very little of this. We are without a skin. If a parent shouts at us, the foundations of the earth tremble. We cannot tell that some of the harsh words were not really meant, had their origins in a difficult day at work, or are the reverberations of the adult's own childhood; it feels as if an all-powerful, all-knowing giant has decided, for good (if unknown) reasons, that we are to be annihilated.

Nor can we understand when a parent goes away that they didn't leave us because we did something wrong or because we are unworthy of love, but because even adults aren't always in control of their own destinies.

If parents are in the kitchen raising their voices, it can seem as though these two people must hate one another inordinately. To children, an overheard altercation (with a slammed door and swear words) may feel catastrophic, as though everything safe will disintegrate. There is no evidence in the child's grasp that arguments are a normal part of relationships; that a couple may be committed to a life-long union and at the same time forcefully express a wish that the other go to hell.

Children are equally helpless before their parents' idiosyncratic ideologies. They can't understand that an insistence that they not mix with another family from school, or that they follow particular dress codes, or hate a given political party, or worry about dirt or being less than two hours early for a flight, represents a partial understanding of priorities and reality.

Children don't have a job. They can't go elsewhere. They have no extended social network. Even when things are going well, childhood is an open prison.

As a result of the peculiarities of the early years, we become distorted and unbalanced. Aspects within us start to develop in odd directions. We find that we can't easily trust, or become unusually scared around people who raise their voices, or can't tolerate being touched. No one needs to do anything particularly shocking, illegal, sinister or wicked to us for serious distortions to unfold. The causes of our primal wound are rarely outwardly dramatic, but their impact can often be momentous and long-lasting. Such is the fragility of childhood that nothing outwardly appalling need have happened to us for us to wind up profoundly scrambled.

We know this point from tragedy. In the tales of the Ancient Greeks, it is not enormous errors and slips that unleash drama; it is the tiniest, most innocent, errors. Terrible consequences unfurl from seemingly minor starting points. Our emotional lives are similarly tragic in structure. Everyone around us may have been trying to do their best with us as children, yet we have ended

We are reluctant historians of our emotional pasts.

up now, as adults, nursing major hurts that ensure we are much less than we might have been.

Imbalances

As a result of our childhoods, we are unbalanced; over most issues, we tend to list excessively, like a sailing yacht in high wind, in one direction or another. We are too timid or too assertive; too rigid or too accommodating; too focused on material success or maddeningly lackadaisical. We are obsessively eager around sex or painfully wary and nervous in the face of our own erotic impulses. We are dreamily naive or sourly down to earth; we recoil from risk or embrace it recklessly; we are determined never to rely on anyone or are desperate for another to complete us; we are overly intellectual or unduly resistant to ideas.

The encyclopedia of emotional imbalances is a volume without end. What is certain is that these imbalances come at vast cost, rendering us less able to exploit our talents and opportunities, less able to lead satisfying lives and a great deal less fun to be around.

Yet because we are reluctant historians of our emotional pasts, we easily assume that our imbalances are things we could never change; that they are innate. It is just how we are made. We simply are people who micromanage, or can't get much pleasure out of sex, or scream when someone contradicts us, or run away from lovers who are too kind to us. It may not be easy, but nor is it alterable or up for enquiry.

The truth is likely to be more hopeful, although more challenging in the short term. Our imbalances are invariably responses to something that happened in the past. We are a certain way because a primal wound knocked us off a more fulfilling trajectory years ago. In the face of a viciously competitive parent, we took refuge in underachievement. Having lived around a parent disgusted by the body, we became frightened by sex. Surrounded by material unreliability, we had to overachieve around money and social prestige. Hurt by a dismissive parent, we fell into patterns of emotional avoidance. A volatile parent pushed us towards our present meekness and inability to make a fuss. Early overprotectiveness inspired timidity and, around any complex situation, panic. A continually busy, inattentive parent was the catalyst for a personality marked by exhausting attention-seeking behaviour.

There is always a logic and always a history.

We can tell that our imbalances date from the past because they reflect the way of thinking and instincts of the children we once were. Without anything pejorative being meant by this, our way of being unbalanced tends towards a fundamental immaturity, bearing the marks of what was once a young person's attempt to grapple with something beyond their capacities.

When they suffer at the hands of an adult, children almost invariably take what happens to them as a reflection of something that must be wrong with them. If someone humiliates, ignores or hurts them, it must be because they are imbecilic, repugnant and worth neglecting. It can take many years, and a lot of patient inner exploration, to reach an initially less plausible conclusion: that the hurt was undeserved and that there were many other things going on, off-stage, in the raging adult's interior life for which the child was blameless.

Similarly, because children cannot easily leave a difficult situation, they are prey to powerful, limitless longings to fix the broken person they depend on. In the infantile imagination, it becomes the child's responsibility to mend all the anger, addiction or sadness of the grown-up they adore. It may be the work of decades to develop a wiser power to feel sad about, rather than eternally responsible for, those we cannot change, and perhaps to move on.

Communication patterns are beset by comparable childhood legacies. When something is wrong, children have no innate capacity to explain their cause. They lack the confidence, poise and verbal dexterity to get their points across with the calm and authority required. They tend to dramatic over-reactions instead: insisting, nagging, exploding, screaming. Or, conversely, to excessive underreactions: sulking, sullenness, silence, avoidance. We may be well into middle age before we can shed our first impulses to explode at or flee from those who misunderstand our needs and more carefully and serenely try to explain them instead.

It is another feature of the emotional wounds of childhood that they tend to provoke what are in effect large-scale generalisations. Our wounds may have occurred in highly individual contexts: with one particular adult who hit their particular partner late at night in one particular terraced house in one particular town in the north. Or the wound may have been caused by one specific parent who responded with intense contempt after one specific job loss from one specific factory. But these events give rise to expectations of other people and of life more broadly. We grow to expect that everyone will become violent, that every partner will turn on us, and that every money problem will unleash depression and then abandonment. The character traits and mentalities that were formed in response to one or two central actors of childhood become our templates for interpreting pretty much anyone. For example, the always jokey and slightly manic way of being that we evolved to keep a listless mother engaged becomes our second nature. Even when she is long gone, we remain people who need to shine at every meeting, who require a partner to be continually focused on us, and who cannot listen to negative or dispiriting information of any kind. We are living the wide-open present through the narrow drama of the past.

Similarly, a childhood craving to pacify and never bother two squabbling, unhappy parents can far outlast our actual presence in their company.

Decades later, we may still harbour a powerful desire to evade all confrontation, even though the original source of our hesitancy has long disappeared and such avoidance bears a heavy price.

It is a complicating factor that our imbalances don't cleanly reveal their origins – either to our own minds or to the world at large. We aren't really sure why we run away, get angry, have a proud and haughty air, miss every deadline, or cling excessively to people we love. Because the sources of our imbalances escape us, we miss out on garnering important sources of possible sympathy. The world judges us on the behaviours that our wounds inspire, rather than on the wounds themselves. The damage may have begun with a feeling of invisibility – a poignant enough phenomenon – but to a world that doesn't care to know more, we now come across as somewhat sickening show-offs. Maybe the damage began with being let down, but now we simply appear crazily controlling. Perhaps it started with a bullying, competitive father; now it seems as if we are just spineless.

We make our lives tougher than they should be because we insist on thinking of people as inept and mean rather than (as is usually the case) victims of what we have all travelled through: a tricky early history.

Amnesia and denial

What happened to us in childhood is the single greatest cause of how we function emotionally as adults. Therefore, what is surprising and unfortunate is how little of the past we can properly remember. We can recall the basic facts and a few incidents, but in terms of grasping in detail, with visceral emotion, how our present is influenced by the personalities and circumstances of our early years, we are often novices or simply sceptical as to the point of a close look backwards. In many cases, it would not be too strong to speak of willed amnesia.

The tendency to forget the primal wound of childhood is not hard to understand. It is implausible, but also humiliating, to imagine that events from so long ago might influence the bulk of our feelings and actions in the present. Blunt and clichéd-sounding psychological determinism negates our hopes for a life of dignified adult liberty. It seems crushing and, from certain perspectives, plain daft to suppose that our personalities might remain forged by incidents that unfolded before our fifth birthday. We would like to make sense of our moods in terms of what is happening in the present. If we feel angry with someone, we would like the cause to lie with them, rather than something three decades ago that has made us especially prone to taking offence.

We tend to adopt a sentimental attitude towards the past that is far more attentive to the occasional endearing exception than the more challenging norm. Family photos, almost always snapped at the happier moments, guide the process. There is much more likely to be an image of one's mother by the pool smiling with the expression of a giddy young girl than of her slamming the back door in rage at the misery of her marriage; there will be a shot of one's father genially performing a card trick, but no visual record of his long, brutal mealtime silences. A lot of editing goes on, encouraged by all sides.

With age, we naturally look at the world through the eyes of an adult rather than try to recover the distinctive and peculiar perspective of a child. To any grown-up, it is obvious that a 3-year-old having a tantrum in a restaurant is to be condemned as irritating, theatrical and bad-mannered. But that is chiefly because we lack the encouragement or empathy to try to recreate the strange inner world of a small person (an inner world that was once our own) in which she might feel tired and bewildered, fearful that an unfamiliar dish is going to be forced on her, or lonely and humiliated by being the smallest person in a large and lugubrious dining room, far from her toy rabbit, left by mistake in the room upstairs.

When an adult locks a kitchen door to ensure silence during an hour-long business call, it is far from normal to picture the scene from the viewpoint of the very young child on the other side of the door, for whom this endless exclusion may seem proof that everything good and kind has mysteriously and suddenly died. It becomes difficult for us to keep in mind how much in all our characters was marked by what are (from a grown-up perspective) almost laughably minor yet hugely potent incidents.

It is not simply that we have forgotten the past. We could in principle re-enter the emotional spaces we once inhabited. It is for deeper reasons that we push aside the memories and actively restrict reflection on our histories.

We keep away from ourselves because so much of what we could discover threatens to be painful. We might discover that we were furious with, and resentful about, certain people we were only meant to love. We might discover how much ground there was to feel inadequate and guilty on account of the many errors and misjudgements we have made. We might find that, although we wanted to be decent, law-abiding people, we harboured fantasies that went in deviant and aberrant directions. We might recognise how much was nauseatingly compromised and needed to be changed about our relationships and careers.

We not only have a lot to hide, we are liars of genius. It is part of the human tragedy that we are such natural self-deceivers. Our techniques are multiple and close to invisible.

We become addicted. Not to heroin or whisky, but to innocuous, everyday activities that attract no alarm or suspicion. We become addicted to checking the news or tidying the house, exercising or taking on fresh projects at work. To the world, it can look as if we are just being productive, but the clue to our compulsiveness lies in our motives. We are checking the news to keep the news from ourselves at bay; we are working for the company as an alternative to working on our soul. What properly indicates addiction is not what someone is doing, but their way of doing it to avoid encounters with themselves. We are addicts whenever we develop a manic reliance on something – anything – to keep our darker and more unsettling feelings at bay.

We lie by being very cheerful. It seems almost imperceptible from happiness. But with its remorseless and insistent upbeat quality, aggressive jolliness has very little to do with true satisfaction. The jolly person doesn't just want the mood to be happy; they can't tolerate that it might in any way be sad, so unexplored and potentially overwhelming are their own background feelings of disappointment and grief.

We lie by attacking and denigrating what we love, but haven't managed to get. We dismiss the people we once wanted as friends, the careers we hoped one day to have, the lives we tried to emulate. We reconfigure what a desired but painfully elusive goal meant to us in the hope of not needing to register its loss properly.

We lie through a generalised cynicism, which we direct at everything and everyone so as to ward off misery about one or two things in particular. We say that all humans are terrible and every activity is compromised so that the specific cause of our pain does not attract scrutiny and feelings of shame.

We lie by filling our minds with impressive ideas, which blatantly announce our intelligence to the world but subtly ensure we won't have much room left to rediscover the long-distant feelings of ignorance or confusion upon which the development of our personalities may rest.

We write dense books on the role of government bonds in the Napoleonic wars or publish extensively on Chaucer's influence on the mid-19th-century Japanese novel. We secure degrees from Institutes of Advanced Study or positions on editorial boards of scientific journals. Our minds are crammed with arcane data. We can wittily inform a dining table of guests who wrote the Enchiridion (Epictetus) or the life and times of Dōgen (the founder of Zen Buddhism). But we don't remember much about how life was long ago,

We not only have a lot to hide, we are liars of genius.

back in the old house, when father left, mother stopped smiling and our trust broke in pieces.

We deploy knowledge and ideas that carry prestige to stand guard against the emergence of more humble but essential knowledge from our emotional past. We bury our personal stories beneath an avalanche of expertise. The possibility of a deeply consequential intimate enquiry is deliberately left to seem feeble and superfluous next to the supposedly grander task of addressing a conference on the political strategies of Dona Maria the First or the lifecycle of the Indonesian octopus.

We lean on the glamour of being learned to make sure we won't need to learn too much that hurts.

We lie by pretending that we are simpler than we really are and that too much psychology might be fuss and nonsense. We lean on a version of robust common sense to ward off intimations of our own awkward complexity. We imply that not thinking very much is evidence of a superior kind of intelligence.

In company, we deploy bluff strategies of ridicule against more complex accounts of human nature. We sideline avenues of personal investigation as unduly fancy or weird, implying that to lift the lid on inner life could never be fruitful or respectable. We use the practical mood of 9 a.m. Monday morning to ward off the complex insights of 3 a.m. the previous night, when the entire fabric of our existence came into question against the backdrop of a million stars, spread like diamonds on a mantle of black velvet. Deploying an attitude of vigorous common sense, we strive to make our moments of radical disquiet seem like aberrations rather than the central occasions of insight they might actually be.

We appeal to the understandable longing that our personalities are non-tragic, simple and easily comprehended so as to reject the stranger, but more useful, facts of our true, intricate selves.

A defence of emotional honesty has nothing to do with high-minded morality. It is ultimately cautionary and egoistic. We need to tell ourselves a little more of the truth because we pay too high a price for our lies. Through our deceptions, we cut ourselves off from possibilities of growth. We shut off large portions of our minds and end up uncreative, tetchy and defensive, while others around us have to suffer our irritability, gloom, manufactured cheerfulness or defensive rationalisations. Our neglect of the awkward sides of ourselves buckles our very being, emerging as insomnia or impotence, stuttering or depression; revenge for all the thoughts we have been so careful not to have. Self-knowledge is not a luxury so much as a precondition for a measure of sanity and inner comfort.

The emotionally healthy childhood

We can sometimes be so modest about our power to know what might be good for others or ourselves, we forget it might be possible to hazard generalisations about what constitutes an emotionally healthy childhood. It can't be idiosyncrasy or good luck; there are distinct themes and goals to identify. With a map of optimal development in mind, we could more clearly appreciate where dislocation begins, what we have to be grateful for, and what there is to regret. At a collective level, we could have more of a sense of what there is to achieve to generate a more emotionally privileged and therefore slightly saner world.

In the course of an emotionally healthy childhood, we could expect some of the following to occur.

Someone will put themselves profoundly at our service. If as adults we have even a measure of mental health, it is almost certainly because, when we were tiny, helpless infants, there was a person (to whom we essentially owe our lives) who pushed their needs aside for a time to focus wholly on our own. They interpreted what we could not say; they guessed what might be ailing us; they settled and consoled us. They kept the chaos and noise at bay and cut up the world into manageable pieces for us. They did not ask that we thank them, understand them or show them sympathy. They did not demand that we enquire how their day went or how they were sleeping at night. They treated us like royalty, so that we would later on be able to submit to the rigours and humiliations of an ordinary life. This temporarily one-sided relationship guaranteed our eventual ability to form a two-sided kind.

We may think of egoists as people who have grown sick from too much love. But the opposite is the case: an egoist is someone who has not yet had their fill. Self-centredness has to have a clean run in the early years if it isn't to haunt and ruin the later ones. The so-called narcissist is simply a benighted soul who has not had a chance to be inordinately and unreasonably admired at the start.

In an emotionally healthy childhood, someone is on hand to put the most positive spin on our behaviour. We are given the benefit of the doubt. We are assessed by what we might be one day, not by what we are right now. Someone is kind.

A harsh judge, for example, might say that we were 'attention-seeking'. Our caregiver imagines that what we most need is a hug and some encouraging words. We might have acted meanly. Our caregiver adds that we must have been feeling threatened. It looked as if we were negligent; the caregiver remembers that tiredness could have explained it.

Our carer constantly searches beneath the surface for more sympathetic explanations. They help us to be on our own side, to like ourselves, and therefore not to be too defensive about our flaws, the existence of which we grow strong enough to accept.

In a good childhood, the relationship with our caregiver is steady, consistent and long-term. We trust that they will be there tomorrow and the day after. They aren't volatile or fragile. They are almost boringly predictable and happy to be taken for granted. As a result, we develop a trust in relationships that spreads throughout our life. We are able to believe that what has gone well once can go well again and let such an expectation govern our choice of adult partners. We aren't mesmerised by people who are off-hand and unreliable; we don't relish being punished. We can pick out candidates who are kind and nurturing, and don't judge them as weak or deficient for being so.

If trouble strikes with our kindly partners, we don't panic anxiously or avoidantly turn away. We can confidently set about trying to repair a love we know we deserve.

In an emotionally healthy upbringing, we aren't always required to be wholly good boys or girls. We are allowed to get furious and sometimes revolting, at points to say 'absolutely not' and 'because I feel like it'. The adults know their own flaws and do not expect a child to be fundamentally better than they are. We do not have to comply at every turn to be tolerated. We can let others see our shadow sides.

This period of freedom prepares us one day to submit to the demands of society without having to rebel in self-defeating ways (rebels being, at heart, people who have had to obey too much too early). We can knuckle down and toe the line when it's in our long-term interest to do so. At the same time, we're not overly cowed or indiscriminately obedient either. We find a sound middle point between slavish compliance and self-destructive defiance.

In an emotionally healthy home, our carer isn't jealous of or competitive with us. They can allow themselves to be overtaken and superseded. They have had their moment in the limelight, or else are having it elsewhere beyond the family. They can be proud rather than rivalrous of the achievements of the (usually same-sex) child. It doesn't need to be all about them.

The good carer isn't overly ambitious on the child's behalf. They want them to do well, but for their own sake, and in their own way. There is no particular script that the offspring has to follow to be loved; the child isn't required to support the carer's frayed self-belief or burnish their image in the eyes of the world.

In an emotionally healthy upbringing, the child learns that things that break can be fixed. Plans can go awry, but new ones can be made. The carer models for the child how to calm down, plough on and remain hopeful. A voice of resilience, originally external, becomes the way the child learns to speak to themselves. There are alternatives to panic.

Importantly, plenty goes wrong in the emotionally healthy childhood. No one has staked their reputation on rendering the whole thing perfect. The carer does not see it as their role to remove every frustration. They intuit that a lot of good comes from having the right, manageable kind of friction, through which the child develops their own resources and individuality. In contact with bearable disappointment, the child is prompted to create their own internal world, in which they can dream, hatch fresh plans, self-soothe and build up their own resources.

The child can see that the good carer is neither entirely good nor wholly bad, and therefore is worthy of neither idealisation nor denigration. The child accepts the faults and virtues of the carer with melancholy maturity and gratitude and thereby, by extension, becomes ready to accept that everyone they like will be a mixture of positive and negative. As adults, they won't fall deeply in love and then become furious at the first moment of letdown. They have a realistic sense of what can be expected of life alongside another good enough human.

Soberingly, despite all our advances in technology and material resources, we are not much more advanced in the art of delivering emotionally healthy childhoods than previous generations. The number of breakdowns, inauthentic lives and broken souls shows no marked signs of decline. We are failing to offer one another tolerable childhoods not because we are evil or

Plenty goes wrong in the emotionally healthy childhood.

indifferent but because we still have so far to go before we know how to do that most apparently simple yet infinitely complicated of things: love.

The tool that might just get us there is psychotherapy.

The markers of emotional health

One way to start assessing how badly we have been knocked by our early years – and where we might therefore need to direct most of our repair work and attention – is to identify a range of markers of emotional health and imagine how we fare in relation to them. At least four markers suggest themselves.

1. Self-love

Self-love is the quality that determines how much we can be friends with ourselves and remain on our own side.

When we meet a stranger who has things we don't, how quickly do we feel ourselves pitiful, and how long can we remain assured by the decency of what we have and are? When another person frustrates or humiliates us, can we let the insult go, able to perceive the senseless malice beneath the attack, or are we left brooding and devastated, implicitly identifying with the verdict of our enemies? How much can the disapproval or neglect of public opinion be offset by the memory of the steady attention of a few significant people in the past?

In relationships, do we have enough self-love to leave an abusive union? Or are we so down on ourselves that we carry an implicit belief that harm is all we deserve? In a different vein, how good are we at apologising to a lover for things that might be our fault? How rigidly self-righteous do we need to be? Can we dare to admit mistakes, or does an admission of guilt or error bring us too close to a background sense of nullity?

In the bedroom, how clean and natural or alternatively disgusting and sinful do our desires feel? Might they be a little odd, but not bad or dark, since they emanate from within us and we are not wretches?

At work, do we have a reasonable, well-grounded sense of our worth, and so feel able to ask for (and expect to get) the rewards we are due? Can we resist the need to please others indiscriminately? Are we sufficiently aware of our genuine contribution to say no?

2. Candour

Candour determines the extent to which difficult ideas and troubling facts can be consciously admitted into the mind, soberly explored and accepted without denial. How much can we admit to ourselves about who we are – even if, or especially when, the matter is unpleasant? How much do we need to insist on our own normality and wholehearted sanity? Can we explore our own minds and look into their darker and more troubled corners without flinching too much? Can we admit to folly, envy, sadness and confusion?

Around others, how ready are we to learn? Do we need always to take a criticism of one part of us as an attack on everything about us? How ready are we to listen when valuable lessons come in painful guises?

3. Communication

Can we patiently and reasonably put our disappointments into words that, more or less, enable others to see our point? Or do we internalise pain, act it out symbolically or discharge it with counterproductive rage?

When other people upset us, do we feel we have the right to communicate or must we slam doors and retreat into sulks? When the desired response isn't forthcoming, do we ask others to guess what we have been too angrily panicked to spell out? Or can we have a plausible second go and take seriously the thought that others are not merely being nasty in misunderstanding us? Do we have the inner resources to teach rather than insist?

4. Trust

How risky is the world? How readily might we survive a challenge in the form of a speech, a romantic rejection, a bout of financial trouble, a journey to another country or a common cold? How close are we, at any time, to catastrophe? What material are we made of?

Will new acquaintances like us or wound us? If we are a touch assertive, will they take it or collapse? Will unfamiliar situations end in a debacle? Around love, how tightly do we need to cling? If our lover is distant for a while, will they return? How controlling do we need to be? Can we approach an interesting-looking stranger? Or move on from an unsatisfying relationship?

Overall, do we feel the world to be wide, safe and reasonable enough for us to have a legitimate shot at contentment, or must we settle, resentfully, for inauthenticity and misunderstanding?

It isn't our fault (or, in a sense, anyone else's) that many of these questions are so hard to answer in the affirmative. But, by entertaining them, we are at least starting to know what kind of shape our wounds have and, therefore, what kind of bandages might be necessary.

III
How Therapy Works

Psychotherapy is a tool; like all tools, it has been designed to help us overcome an inborn weakness and to extend our capacities beyond those with which nature originally endowed us. In this sense, it is not metaphysically different from a bucket, which remedies our problems of holding water in our palms, or a knife, which makes up for the bluntness of our teeth.

What is distinctive about therapy is what it is a tool for: it is an invention to help improve the way our emotions operate. It has been devised to correct the otherwise substantial difficulties we face in understanding ourselves, trusting others, communicating successfully, honouring our potential and feeling adequately serene, confident, authentic, direct and unashamed.

For such an important invention, psychotherapy is low on overt signs of innovation. Technically speaking, it requires only a comfortable room free of any interruptions, fifty minutes, possibly twice a week for a year or so, two chairs and some chat. But at the level of training, the psychotherapist needs to undertake a period of extensive education in the workings of the mind, which – in the more responsible jurisdictions – has some of the rigour, intellectual ambition and periods of hands-on experience demanded by the acquisition of a pilot's licence.

To deliver on its promises, psychotherapy relies on at least eight distinct moves.

1
Witnessing

Most of what we are remains a secret to the world, because we appreciate how much of it flouts the laws of decency and sobriety by which we would like to live. We know that we would not last long in society if a stream of raw data ever leaked out of our minds.

A lot of what is inside us can seem daft: how we felt a strange impulse to burst into tears when reading a children's book about an elephant befriending a baby sparrow; how often we imagine acquiring a power to go back in time and correct the missed opportunities of our adolescence. From a harsh angle, some of what is inside is distinctly pathetic: how worried we are about asking where the bathroom is; how envious we are of a close acquaintance; how much we worry about our hair. A significant part is alarming and quasi-illegal: our fantasies about a work colleague and a family member; our plans for what we would ideally do to an enemy.

In response to our isolation, we are often told about the importance of friends. But we know that the tacit contract of any friendship is that we will not bother the incumbent with more than a fraction of our madness. A lover is another solution, but it is not in the remit of any partner to delve into, and accept, more than a modest share of what we are.

In every social interaction, we sensibly ensure that there remains a large and secure divide between what we say to people and what is truly going on inside our minds.

The exception lies with psychotherapy. Here, remarkably, we can say pretty much anything we want – and, indeed, should strive to do so. We don't have to impress the therapist or reassure them of our sanity. We need to tell them what is going on. There is no need to stop them thinking we are perverted, odd or terrified. We can gingerly hint at some very dark things about us and will find that our interlocutor is not horrified or offended but only calmly interested. We will learn that we are not monsters or freaks. We arrive at the opposite of loneliness.

2
Worldliness

Therapists know a lot about the unvarnished truths of human nature. They have close-up experience of the greatest traumas – incest and rape, suicide and depression – as well as the smaller pains and paradoxes: a longing provoked by a glance at a person in a library that took up the better part of twenty years; an otherwise gentle soul who broke a door; a handsome, athletic man who can no longer perform.

They know that inside every adult there remains a child who is confused, angry, hurt and longing to have their say and their reality recognised. They appreciate that this child has to get to know itself again and will want to be heard, perhaps through tears or near-incomprehensible mutterings, which might be at odds with the surface maturity and self-command normally associated with grown-ups.

Therapists have sufficiently acclimatised themselves to the reality of what people are like not to need to censor or deliver moralistic judgements. They have done this not primarily through books, but by being courageous about knowing their own nature. They may not share our fantasies exactly, but they accept that their own are as colourful and as complex. They don't have our precise anxieties, but they know well enough the powerful and peculiar fears that hold us all hostage.

They can start to help us because they have an accurately broad grasp of what it means to be normal – which is, of course, so far from what we insist on pretending is normal. They don't require us to be conventionally good or typical to shore up their fragile sense of self or of reality. Their only requirement is that we admit, without too much defensiveness, to some of what is going on inside us.

3
Kindness

Therapists are, very gratifyingly, on our side. Without ill intention, most people are not particularly; they are intermittently jealous, bored, vindictive, keen to prove a point or distracted by their own lives. But the therapist brings a focused, generous attention to our case. Their room is safe and set aside from day-to-day pressures. They are sorry that we have suffered. They understand that it must have been worrying, enraging or exciting. They know we didn't do it on purpose or that we had our reasons if we did. Without flattering us in a rote way, merely because it is their job to do so, they strive to enter into our experience and to side with it. They look at reality through our eyes so as to start correcting a legacy of shame and isolation.

At the same time, their kindness makes ours a little less necessary. Normal life requires that we constantly weigh the impact of our words on other people. We have to consider their priorities, ask how their children are, and hold their concerns in mind.

Here there is no such call. Like a parent who doesn't need a small child to reciprocate, the therapist voluntarily foregoes equality in the relationship; they won't talk of their regrets or insist on their anecdotes. They simply want to help us find what is best for us, understood on our terms. They won't have a preconceived view of how we are meant to live, just sympathy for the complexities and suffering we have endured and a desire to help us with the future.

That said, kindness is not merely pleasant. Knowing that we have someone on our side is designed to lend us the courage to face up to experiences we normally evade. In a sufficiently calm, reassuring and interested environment, we can look at areas of vulnerability we otherwise lack the courage to tackle. We can dare to think that perhaps we were wrong or that we have been angry for long enough, that it might be best to outgrow our justifications or cease trying to seduce every audience.

The kindness of another person gives us the security needed to probe constructively at our clever, puzzling, evasive minds.

4
Listening

One of the structural flaws of these minds is that it is immensely hard for us to think deeply and coherently for any length of time. We keep losing the thread. Competing, irrelevant ideas have a habit of flitting across the mental horizon and scrambling our tentative insights. Every now and then, consciousness inexplicably goes blank for a moment. Left to our own devices, we quickly start to doubt the value of what we are trying to make sense of, and can experience overpowering urges to check the news or search out a biscuit. As a result, some of the topics we most need to examine – where our relationship is going; what we might do next at work; how we should best answer a letter; what bothers us so much about the way our partner returns our hand after an attempt at a caress – founder into the mental sands, to our grave psychological cost.

What helps enormously in our attempts to know our own minds is, surprisingly, the presence of another mind. For all the glamour of the solitary seer, thinking usually happens best in tandem. The curiosity of someone else gives us the confidence to remain curious about the thickets of our own minds. It is the application of a light pressure from outside us that firms up the jumbled impressions that lie within. The requirement to verbalise our intimations mobilises our flabby reserves of concentration.

Occasionally a friend might be unusually attentive and ready to hear us out. But it isn't enough for them merely to be quiet. The highest possibilities of listening extend far beyond the polite fact of not being interrupted. To really be heard means being the recipient of a strategy of 'active listening'.

From the start, the therapist will use a succession of very quiet but significant prompts to help us develop and stick to the points we are circling. These suggest that there is no hurry but that someone is there, following every utterance. At strategic points, the therapist will drop in a mission-critical and hugely benign 'do say more' or an equally powerful 'go on'. Therapists are experts of the low-key positive sound: the benevolent, nuanced 'ahh' and the potent 'mmm', two of the most significant noises in the aural repertoire of psychotherapy that together invite us to remain faithful to what we were starting to say, however peculiar.

As beneficiaries of active listening, our ideas, memories and concerns don't have to fall into neat, well-formed sentences. We are allowed to stumble and get confused. But the active listener contains and gardens the emerging confusion. They gently take us back over ground we covered too quickly and prompt us to address a salient point that we might have sidestepped; they will help us chip away at an agitating issue while continually reassuring us that what we are saying is valuable. All the while, they will note minor changes in our facial expressions and tone of voice. They will be interested in the way we choose our words, and attentive not only to what we actually express but to how we might otherwise have put it.

They do not treat us like unusually unsophisticated beings or strangely ineffective communicators; they are simply immensely alive to how difficult it is for anyone to piece together and express what they really have on their minds.

5
Time

Therapy is built on the understanding that we will not be able to transmit our key experiences in one or two self-contained blocks of time. We live in time and have to decode ourselves in time. We can't be in all the moods we need to access on every occasion. Some weeks will find us readier than others to investigate particular memories or consider certain viewpoints. The therapist allows us to start the conversation anywhere we want, permits us to wander through our internal corridors, confident that so long as we keep showing up and sharing, we will eventually drop enough clues to assemble a psychological portrait of the self, like an ancient vase slowly being pieced together from fragments sifted from mounds of debris.

6
Interpretation

The therapist's active listening is not meandering: what underpins it is an attempt to understand – for our sake – what the subterranean operations of the past are doing to the present.

We arrive in therapy with questions. We have a presenting problem that hints at, but does not fully capture, the origins of our suffering. Why, for instance, do we repeatedly fall for people who attempt to control and humiliate us? How can we be so convinced we need to leave a job and yet have remained resolutely unable to locate a more satisfying replacement? Why are we paralysed by anxiety in public ? Why do we sabotage sexual possibility?

By their questions and their attention, their careful probing and investigative stealth, the therapist tries – harder than anyone has probably yet done – to discover how our presenting problem might be related to the rest of our existence and, in particular, the turmoils of childhood. Over many sessions, a succession of small discoveries contributes to an emerging picture of the sources of our emotional wounds, and of the way in which our character slowly evolved in response to them in a way that hampers our possibilities today.

We may, for example, start to sense how a feeling of rivalry with a parent led us to retire early from workplace challenges in order to hold on to their love, as well as seeing, perhaps for the first time, that the logic of our self-sabotage no longer holds. Or we might perceive the way an attitude of aggressive cynicism, which restricts our personalities and our friendships, might have had its origins in a parent who let us down at a time when we could not contain our vulnerability, and thereby turned us into people who try at every juncture to disappoint themselves early and definitively rather than allowing the world to mock our emerging hopes at a time of its own choosing.

It is unhelpful to state any of this too starkly or harshly. An interpretation delivered in its bare bones will be anticlimactic and bathetic and most likely prompt resistance or aggression. For the interpretation to work its effect, we as clients need to move from merely assenting to it intellectually to having an internal experience of the emotions it refers to. We need to feel for ourselves (rather than take on trust) the continued presence, within our adult selves, of the poignantly susceptible person we once were.

For the process to work, the therapist must tactfully let it seem as if the discovery of the structure of our troubles is almost entirely our own unhurried work.

7
A relationship

The ongoing contact between ourselves and the therapist, the weekly sessions that may continue over months or years, contribute to the creation of something that sounds, in a professional context, distinctly odd: a relationship.

We are almost certain to have come to see a therapist in the first place because, in some way, having relationships has become beset with difficulties that we sense, but don't quite understand: maybe we try to please people at once, secure their admiration, but then feel inauthentic and inwardly numb and pull back. Perhaps we fall in love very powerfully, but then always discover a major flaw in a partner that puts us off and makes us end the story and restart the cycle.

The relationship with our therapist may have little in common with the sort of unions we have in ordinary life. We won't ever be shopping together or watching TV side by side in bed. But, unavoidably and conveniently, we bring to our encounters with the therapist the very tendencies that emerge in our relations with other people in our lives. Here too we may be seductive but then cold, or prone to idealisation then seized by an impulse to flee. Except that now, in the presence of the therapist, our tendencies will have a chance to be witnessed, slowed down, discussed, sympathetically explored and – in their more damaging manifestations – overcome. The relationship with the therapist becomes a litmus test of one's behaviour with people more generally and thereby allows us, on the basis of greater self-awareness, to modify and improve how we relate to others.

In the therapy room, our proclivities and habits are noticed and can be commented on, not as reproaches but as important information about our character that we deserve to become aware of. The therapist will (with kindness) point out that we're reacting as if we had been attacked, when they only asked a question; they might draw our attention to how readily we seem to want to tell them impressive things about our finances (yet they like us anyway), or how we seem to rush to agree with them when they're only trying out an idea of which they themselves are not very sure. They will signal where we are prone to pin to them attitudes or outlooks that they don't actually have. They may note how invested we seem to be in the idea that they are disappointed in us, or find us boring or are revolted by our sexuality. They will point out our habit of casting people in the present in roles that must derive from the past and will search with us for the origins of these attributions, which are liable to mimic what we felt towards influential caregivers and now shape what we expect from everyone.

The therapeutic relationship acts as a microcosm of our relationships in general and so can be used as a unique vehicle for learning about our more imperceptible emotional tendencies. By re-experiencing relational problems with an empathetic other who will not respond as ordinary people will, who will not shout at us, complain, say nothing or run away, we can be helped to understand what we are up to and given a chance to let new patterns of relating emerge.

The relationship with the therapist becomes a template for how we might form relationships with others going forward, freed from the manoeuvres and background assumptions that we carried within us from childhood, and that can impede us so grievously in the present.

The therapeutic relationship may be for us the first properly healthy relationship we have had, one in which we learn to hold off from imposing our assumptions on the other and trust them enough to let them see the larger, more complex reality of who we are, without too much intervening shame or embarrassment. It becomes a model – earned in a highly unusual situation – that we start to apply in the more humdrum but consequential setting of daily life, with our friends and our partners.

8
Inner voices

Somewhere in our minds, removed from the day-to-day, there sits a judge. They watch what we do, study how we perform, examine the effect we have on others, track our successes and failures – and then, eventually, they pass a verdict. The origin of the voice of the inner judge is simple to trace: it is an internalisation of the voice of people who were once outside us. We absorb the tones of contempt and indifference or of charity and warmth that we will have heard across our formative years. Sometimes, a voice is positive and benign, encouraging us to run those final few yards. More often, the inner voice is not nice at all. It is defeatist and punitive, panic-ridden and humiliating. It does not represent anything like our best insights or most mature capacities.

Part of what therapy offers us is a chance to improve how we judge ourselves and the voices we hear in our heads. It can involve learning – in a conscious, deliberate way – to speak to ourselves in the way the therapist spoke to us over many months. In the face of challenges, we can enquire of ourselves, 'And what would they say now?' After we have heard their constructive, kindly voice often enough and around tricky enough issues, it will come to feel like a natural response; eventually, it will become our own thoughts.

IV

Case Studies

One of the best ways to understand what psychotherapy involves is to read accounts of what happened to people when they went: the problems they came in with, the discussions that were had, and how things changed as a result. What follow are four representative case studies of the therapeutic process.

Underachievement

It ought to be a source of immense satisfaction for a parent to see their child secure success and esteem in their chosen career. In reality, this is only possible if the parent has learnt to be comfortable with being superseded by their child, if they have the inner resources not to mind surrendering leadership, if their own sense of self is robust. It is not enough to know how to feel tender around the helplessness of an infant; an equally crucial, though less recognised, challenge is to cope with their eventual strength as an adult.

Twenty-seven-year-old Nathan [not his real name] arrives in therapy complaining of a sense of listlessness and despair.

He had always seemed marked out for a special destiny. His father is one of the city's most powerful bankers, a self-made man who overcame a deprived childhood to achieve extraordinary wealth and renown. His mother, a former beauty queen, is on the board of the opera, the museum and several children's charities.

Nathan is their only son. There has long been a feeling that he would achieve something commensurate with the status of his parents. At a young age, his mother called him 'little genius'. Family friends would joke to his father that his son looked exactly like him (the resemblance is striking, even though the son retains a handsome head of hair) and would soon be one to watch in the trading world.

But none of the early promise has borne fruit. Nathan did not feel his grades in maths were good enough to follow his father into business. He was more naturally drawn to the arts and, after graduating, tried to write a novel. He kept at it for three years, but after yet another rejection letter he put the manuscript aside. He also started and abandoned three film scripts.

He complains about his love life. He is often in the role of pursuing women who want to be his friend but not his lover. Sex can be awkward.

Nathan is currently working in a basic administrative role in an art gallery in a run-down part of the city. His salary doesn't start to cover his rent, which is taken care of by his father. Payment involves a complex administrative rigmarole, in which Nathan is required to show up at his father's office every month with a receipt from the landlord and is asked by the PA to wait outside for up to an hour while his father finishes apparently urgent business inside.

Nathan calls himself, in a dry sardonic voice, with shoulders stooped, the ultimate loser.

On the surface, parents invariably speak of wanting the best for their child. But if they are nursing, somewhere within, a wound of neglect and humiliation, it may be intolerably envy-inducing to see a child succeed against odds smaller than those they had to endure.

The adult will feel compelled to keep winning, even against the child they ostensibly love: it might be at table tennis or Monopoly, in exam grades or political arguments. Or at life more generally. There is a basic sense that there cannot be two winners in the same household and that it is the senior party who has to triumph.

Nathan has always admired but been intimidated by his father. He mentions in an early therapy session that when he was no more than 7 he tried to identify something to buy his father for his birthday but realised he would never be in a position to afford anything this potentate of finance actually needed.

He also remembers a time – the first and only time – he beat his father at tennis. They were at their house in the Bahamas. Nathan was 15. The father was proud of his game. But this time, Nathan won. Clearly and unambiguously. Yet the father accused Nathan of being a 'cheat' and stormed off the court in fury. They didn't speak all day, and never played again.

In the unconscious mind, a child facing parental competitiveness understands that they are being offered a deal: a choice between love and early retirement or success and possible expulsion. Unfortunately, it mostly doesn't feel like a choice. The capacity to stand up for oneself requires enough of an experience of unconditional love at the outset for the threat of its loss to seem endurable down the line. But without inner ballast, the child has no realistic way forward other than to put aside their ambitions and submit to (imperceptible and never quite stated) parental edicts.

For Nathan, the work of therapy involves seeing that his father's seeming support is really an expression of rivalry. His father is generous with money, but the way it is distributed serves to reinforce the idea of Nathan's dependent, inferior position.

At the same time as bringing the father's competitiveness to consciousness, therapy helps Nathan to appreciate its origins. The father is not so much vindictive as fragile. His power in the world is almost inversely proportionate to his feeling of inner security.

The more he dwells on his father's past, the more Nathan starts to feel sorry for, and almost protective of, him. It cannot be much fun to be an adult threatened by an adolescent's growing skill at backhand.

One way to meddle with the ambitions of a child is to imply that the child cannot be a success; the other, equally harmful way, is to insist that he or she must be one.

Nathan's mother's greatest wish had once been to study literature and become a university professor. It didn't happen.

She has always been extremely encouraging to Nathan – in a way. When he was little, he started reading early, which began her habit of referring to him as a genius. When he turned 13, she gave him the complete works of Nabokov. Now she sends him links to literary articles and talks about new novels that he must read. She took the rejection of her son's novel very badly – perhaps worse than Nathan himself did. She urges him to try again and to meet up with a creative writing teacher she met who has offered to help with plot structure. Nathan can't bear to tell her that he's thrown away his book and all its accompanying notes. He dreads that one day he will have to inform his mother of a greater truth: that he is not the genius she needed him to be.

It is as harmful to require a child to succeed as it is to require them to fail. In both cases, the child's true developmental needs are sacrificed to the parent's psychological requirements. Sincere love is neutral in this area; it doesn't mean needing someone either to succeed or to fail, but rather to grow on their own terms, which might be compatible with being either quite ordinary or, perhaps, exceptional.

In the course of a year of therapy, Nathan recognises that the world is broader and more robust than he had first imagined. A client of the gallery where he works offers him a new job in his architecture firm. Nathan accepts that he won't ever write a novel, and perhaps never even wanted to. This causes an uncomfortable lunch with his mother, but it's only one lunch.

Although it means dramatically tightening his expenditures, Nathan decides that he doesn't need his father's money for his rent. He tells him politely but firmly that he won't come uptown for another cheque. This creates an unexpected response. His father immediately offers to give him a large lump sum upfront, no questions asked. Nathan is grateful but hasn't touched the money yet.

At around the same time, he develops a new confidence around women, and meets a young German architect in the office. The sex is pretty good.

Step by step, Nathan is starting to discover something even more satisfying than knowing how to please his parents: leading his own life.

The good child

We tend to assume that all is well with good children. They don't pose immediate problems; they keep their bedroom tidy, do their homework on time and are willing to help with the washing up. But the secret sorrows – and future difficulties – of the good child are tied to the fact that they behave this way not out of choice but because they feel under irresistible pressure to do so. They are trying to cope with a legacy of caregivers who had no capacity to deal with their more complicated, and inevitably darker, reality.

Eva works in a top law firm. She is hugely coveted and has been made a partner at the age of only 30 – an almost unparalleled achievement.

Eva comes to therapy because she recently collapsed on stage at a conference where she was delivering the keynote speech. This was hugely embarrassing but also deeply mysterious. The doctors could find nothing wrong. Eva interprets it as an almost deliberate act of self-sabotage. She registers an impulse in herself to let her firm down, to fail and mess up – like she has never done before.

Eva does not know where the impulse comes from but, after too long of being very good, she has an occasional and powerful longing to try to be bad. 'I wonder what it would be like to blow everything sky high,' she tells her therapist, with a burst of almost childlike glee, which she then quickly checks, feeling a need to reassure the therapist of her fundamentally law-abiding nature.

On one occasion, Eva rather enjoyed taking a day off work, pretending that she was ill in bed, and then spending many hours with a girlfriend at an upscale shopping mall instead. But she became terrified that wind of her 'bad behaviour' might reach her colleagues.

We imagine good children to be fine because they do everything that is expected of them. But the good child isn't good because, by a quirk of nature, they simply have no inclination to be anything else. They are good because they lack other options. Some good children are good out of love of a depressed, harassed parent who makes it clear they just can't cope with any more complications or difficulties. Others are good at soothing a violently angry parent who threatens to become catastrophically frightening at any sign of less than perfect conduct.

Eva's parents were immigrants. From the first, they instilled in her a ferocious work ethic. When Eva's father left the family, her mother had to support three children on her own. Eva was the oldest. She remembers hearing her mother wake up at 4 a.m. to start her first shift.

There was little room for laughter. Eva took school very seriously, was desperate to get good grades, and pulled herself through university, working in the evenings and at weekends in a care home. There has been a lot of disappointment in Eva's mother's life. Eva always struggled hard to ensure she would not be another.

Now her mother, who lives very near her, expects to hear every detail of her daughter's life and invariably has a lot of very firm advice about what Eva should do.

The repression of the good child's share of challenging emotions, although it produces short-term pleasant obedience, stores up enormous difficulty. The good child becomes a keeper of too many secrets and a poor communicator of unpopular but important things.

In one session, Eva arrives having cut her hair short, and shows the therapist a small new tattoo she has had done on her wrist. She is excited by these steps but nervous about the reaction her mother might have when she sees her at the weekend. The session focuses on how to understand her mother's worries. Eva's mother will think that it is impossible for Eva to be a partner in a law firm and have short hair or a discreet tattoo. These fears are exaggerated, of course, but her mother is trying to express as best she can her intense hopes for, and love of, her child. Her mother will be angry, but that's because she's frightened, she cares and she is sure that any indication of unorthodox behaviour will be catastrophically punished by the world. But with the therapist, Eva can consider the evidence: the law firm is quite conservative, but there's no reason to think that her new hairstyle will damage her career.

The trouble of the good child is that they have no experience of other people being able to tolerate, or remain calm in front of, their badness. They have missed out a vital privilege accorded to the healthy child: that of being able to display confident, envious, greedy or aggressive sides and yet be met with toleration and love nevertheless. Perhaps a rebellion isn't always easy for a resilient family, but, like a storm, everyone takes it in their stride.

The excessively good person typically has particular problems around sex. As a child, they may have been praised for being pure and innocent. As they become an adult, however, like all of us, they discover the ecstasies of sex, which can be beautifully perverse and excitingly disgusting – and radically at odds with what they believe is right. In response, they may disavow their desires, grow cold and detached from their bodies, or perhaps give in to their longings only in a disproportionate way that is destructive to other parts of their lives and leaves them disgusted and frightened.

Eva has not been in a sustained relationship. There have been people, both men and women, who she has really liked, but it's always been difficult when things become sexual. She becomes very wary and unresponsive. At work she has overheard people talking about 'the ice queen' and she is sure they were referring to her.

She has had some intense sexual encounters – once in the restroom of a restaurant – that she is deeply embarrassed to mention and that she describes as 'sordid'. They were with people she hardly knew, who she would 'never normally have anything to do with'.

It has been difficult for Eva to discuss her sexual fantasies in sessions; she was sure the therapist would be appalled by some of her 'perverted' imaginings. It took many months to reassure her that there was no surprise or horror at her revelations, and that someone could entirely respect her and also properly understand her sexual character. It had seemed to her impossible that anyone competent and decent could do both. This wasn't something she realised in one go; it took many re-encounters with the same anxiety for a degree of trust gradually to evolve.

Now Eva has become interested in finding someone 'for love and sex'. She is still looking, but she has recently had dates with a couple of people she loves talking to and with whom she can imagine having the kind of sex she really wants. It is still early days, but it no longer feels impossible.

Maturity involves a frank, unfrightened relationship with our own darkness, complexity and ambition. It involves accepting that not everything that makes us happy will please others or be honoured as especially 'nice' by society, but that it can be important to explore and hold on to it nevertheless. The desire to be good is one of the loveliest things in the world, but in order to have a genuinely good life, we may sometimes need to be (by the standards of the good child) fruitfully and bravely bad.

After a year in therapy, Eva has started to see less of her mother. She is genuinely grateful and considerate, but can politely yet firmly push back on her excessive demands to be informed about everything. The phrases 'I love you, but I can't see you on Sunday' and 'I love you, but I'm going to keep that one to myself' have been important to her: they put into words the idea that she can let her mother down in certain ways and still appreciate her mother's past efforts.

At work, Eva has had a fruitful, though tricky, confrontation with a senior partner: when a number of impossibly tight deadlines were imposed on her team, she was able to explain that they couldn't all be met; she couldn't be a good colleague simply by pretending that everything could be done; she could only do her job well by making a bit of a fuss and getting extra resources assigned to the project, even though that wasn't the answer her superiors wanted to hear.

Splitting

The pioneering mid-20th-century Viennese psychoanalyst Melanie Klein (1882–1960) drew attention to something dramatic that happens in the minds of babies during feeding sessions with their mothers. When feeding goes well, the baby is blissfully happy and sees their mother as 'good'. But if, for whatever reason, the feeding process is difficult, the baby can't grasp that it is dealing with the same person it liked a lot only a few hours ago.

Therefore, it splits off from the actual mother a second 'bad' version, whom it deems to be a separate, hateful individual, responsible for deliberately frustrating its wishes and, in the process, protecting the image of the good mother in its mind. In the baby's world, there is a 'good' mother who is ideally lovely and perfect and another 'bad' mother who is entirely horrible. When there is any difficulty, the baby feels that the 'bad' mother has turned up, and that if she could just be made to go away, by being annihilated or banished, the 'good' mother would come back and everything would be fine. This process is known in therapy as 'splitting'. It can cause us immense difficulties, and it doesn't just happen in babies.

Miriam is strikingly beautiful; she has a very engaging personality: open, direct and friendly. She has worked in various impressive roles around the media. She has an assured, cosmopolitan air. What has brought her to therapy is that for years she has been in a painful romantic cycle with men: she falls madly in love with someone wonderful, then, after around three months, and normally after a relatively small incident, she falls dramatically out of love with them again.

Miriam is savagely funny when she describes what turned out to be wrong with each of the men she's been out with. There was the fantastically 'anal' graphic designer who was obsessed with ironing his socks and underpants and who would 'practically froth at the mouth' if he discovered a fork in the knife section of the cutlery drawer. There was a Finnish filmmaker with a habit of going into extended monologues about (here she copies his accent) 'how he wanted to get back to the ways of the forest'. There was a banker who (she says) was in love with his own sister.

But behind the wit, there is a grim pattern: the people Miriam loves all turn out to be 'buffoons, narcissists, lost boys, scumbags, weirdos or maniacs – or some combination of them all'.

Ideally, over time, the child manages to put together the two images of their carer. Painfully, and with much constructive disappointment, they see that there aren't really two versions: there is just one person who is a bearable combination of nice and frustrating; who is delightful in some ways and a bit disappointing in others. If things go well, the child comes, sadly but realistically, to grasp that there is no ideal, 'perfect' mother, just one person who is usually lovely but can also be cross, busy, tired, who can make mistakes, and be very interested in other people. By extension, they see that this is how other people generally are. What look like failings are often tied to what is attractive about them: they are a bit fussy because they are so caring; they are a touch boring because they are serious about one or two things. In the best possible scenario, the child comes to be reconciled to reality, and able to love people as they are.

Miriam lost her father when she was young. She cherishes memories of him. He was great fun, clever and kind. She loved it when he took her swimming. He often read to her at night and put on different voices for all the characters. But she never discovered the full reality of who he was. She didn't get to know the more complex sides of his character; she has never really heard anything about his sexuality or what he was like in relationships. She has an idealised picture of her father. This means that her frustration around the men in her life is built on a background accusation that they are not as good as someone whose true nature she never knew.

A central theme of therapy for Miriam has been realising that she could imagine ways in which her father was far from perfect, without feeling that this is being unfair to him or damaging to her loyalty to the good things she remembers. He could have been (and certainly was) both a very good father and a very ordinarily flawed and muddled man. Had he lived, she would inevitably have clashed with him in lots of ways, found him annoying, embarrassing and disappointing – because these are standard parts of growing up. Miriam realises the cost of not having had an adolescence around her father.

Although childhood may be long over, the tendency to 'split' those close to us is always there. We can find it hard to accept that the same person might be very nice and good in some ways and very disappointing in others. The bad version can appear to destroy the good one, although these are just different and connected aspects of one complex human being.

In therapy, Miriam has been reconsidering her past relationships. The men she is so good at mocking were indeed annoying in certain ways, but they were also (to varying degrees) kind, intelligent, generous, tender and hard-working. And they were all fascinated by her. She was disturbed by flaws that need not have been fatal. She realises that there will be something wrong with whoever she is with, not because she has 'crazy taste in men' but because everyone is odd and frustrating when we get to know them well.

Recently Miriam has become closer to her grandmother – her father's mother. Her grandmother has fleshed out the picture of her son in loving, but not always flattering, ways. Miriam has been able to accept that her father could be moody, sly, underhand and at times irresponsible about money. He was far from perfect – and yet he was lovely.

Now Miriam has started going out with a man who, she admits, she wasn't mad about at first. His taste in clothes leaves something to be desired; he talks too much about his work; she doesn't like all his friends. But they have had some very interesting weekends together and she likes the way he warmly makes fun of her more eccentric sides. He's also hit it off with her grandmother.

Anxious and avoidant attachment

Depending on what happened when we were growing up, many of us tend as adults to have a bias towards either an anxious or an avoidant way of behaving in relationships. With an anxious pattern of being around our lovers, when there is difficulty we may grow officious, procedural and controlling over small matters of domestic routine. We feel our partners are escaping us emotionally, but rather than admitting to our sense of loss and our fear, we respond by trying to pin them down administratively. We get unduly cross when they are eight minutes late; we chastise them for not having done certain chores; we ask them strictly if they have completed a task they had vaguely agreed to undertake. All this rather than admit the underlying, poignant emotional truth: 'I'm worried that I don't matter to you...'

Jayathri (a GP) and Arun (who works in IT) have been together for four years. Eighteen months ago, they bought a house together with the idea that they might start a family one day. But increasingly they've been arguing a lot. The rancour can last for days. There are sulks, bitterness and a bad atmosphere that refuses to budge. They both regret it, but are at a loss as to what to do. They have come for couples therapy.

In the first session, Jayathri complains that Arun is appallingly unreliable: he says he'll pick up the dry cleaning, and then not actually do so; or when they've arranged to go out to dinner, he'll tell her at the last minute that he'll be fifteen minutes late. At home she finds it maddening when Arun checks his phone just when she's trying to tell him something important about a food delivery or his mother.

When she complains, to make matters worse, he doesn't say anything. He just looks into the middle distance, then sneaks off to do some computer thing in the room upstairs. It seriously annoys her that he can't even speak. Almost in tears, she describes how he 'tunes out' and how she ends up having to take charge of everything herself.

Avoidant attachment is a pattern of relating to lovers whereby, when there is difficulty, we grow unusually cold and distant, and deny our need for anyone. We may desperately want to communicate, to be reassured and to get our point across, but feel so unconfident that we may be unheard or unwanted that we disguise our need behind a façade of indifference. Rather than stay present and struggle towards closeness, we say that we're busy, we pretend our thoughts are elsewhere, we become sarcastic and dry; we imply that a need for reassurance would be the last thing on our minds.

Visibly agitated, Arun says he often feels he would rather be on his own than have his girlfriend nagging him. Why can't she just be kind? He resents the way she's so bossy and tries to direct what he does with his phone. The worst thing is when Jayathri stands on the landing and shouts at him through the door of his study. She can go on for half an hour or more. Arun is normally quite reserved during this tirade, but it eventually makes him furious. Sometimes he'll scream at her to 'fucking leave me alone', and then return apparently calmly to his computer.

Patterns of attachment are not easy to budge, but it is hugely beneficial to understand which one we might have so as better to warn those we love, and apologise after the storm.

Arun grew up in a lively, busy family; his parents (originally from India) were – and still are – academics, often at conferences and preoccupied by work. When he was a child, they entertained a lot at home; no one minded if he left the grown-ups having long, loud conversations around the dining table and went to watch television in his bedroom.

On one occasion he wasn't feeling very well and went down to the kitchen to tell his mother. She gave him a hug, but didn't stop talking to her friends. He felt his parents weren't very bothered about what was happening at school. They were so taken up with teaching students it was as if they didn't think anything really mattered 'until you went to university'. When he was 14, he tentatively tried to tell his father there was a girl he was interested in and his father (Arun rolls his eyes as he says this) went off into a kind of lecture about 'the Western Myth of Romantic Love'. In that kind of setting, it was pretty pointless trying to explain very much.

The crucible of avoidant attachment is the child's sense that a parental figure lacks concern. To seek closeness is to guarantee humiliation. The child gives up on hoping for warmth and closeness; they withdraw and bury their longing for affection so as to avoid any rebuff. They learn not to care whether anyone says anything sweet or tender; they close down any interest in gentle signs of reassurance or playful gestures of affection. They feel cautious and uneasy around the expression of emotion, whether in themselves or by others. They may find this an advantage in a professional environment, but in relationships they can instinctively push away a partner who seeks a deeper connection. At their core, they are not without emotional needs, but they have, over the years, committed a lot of resources to coming across this way.

For her part, Jayathri spent her childhood in Sri Lanka, where her family were involved in a number of businesses, mainly around textiles and construction. It was a volatile and chaotic upbringing; her parents could be bountiful and warm one day and cold and frightening the next; there was a huge falling out across their extended family over an inheritance. Twice, when she was 7 and then 9, she had to abruptly change schools for reasons that were never made clear to her. When she was 15, she was sent to a school in England. She was very lonely at first but later did well, winning prizes in biology and chemistry: 'I had to pull myself together and just get on with it.'

Across sessions, without ever being direct, the couples therapist gets Arun and Jayathri to focus on the underlying concepts of 'anxious' and 'avoidant' relationship styles. As a child, Arun had developed an avoidant strategy to cope with his parents' lack of attention. When he goes off to his room now, it's not because he doesn't care but because he feels he'll never be listened to and that he can't explain anything to another person. Technology appeals to him because it's automatically responsive; it won't ask him to account for himself or shout when there's a distracted look in his eyes.

Jayathri's anxious pattern of behaviour stems from her childhood way of coping with family relationships that she felt were unstable and untrustworthy. She resorted to imposing external order as a way of coping with a sense of emotional flux. When she feels lonely or sad, her instinct is to try to micromanage. It is not that she's essentially domineering: when she says 'turn off your phone' or 'take the rubbish out now, how many times do I have to ask you?', it is her garbled way of trying to say 'I need you and I want to be close to you.'

When we are anxious in relationships, we can't (we believe) force the partner to be generous and warm. We can't force them to want us (even if we haven't asked them to). The goal isn't really to be in charge all the time; it's just that we can't admit to our terror at how much we need the other. A tragic cycle then unfolds. We become shrill and unpleasant. To the other person, it feels as if we can't possibly love them anymore. Yet the truth is we do: we just fear too much that they don't love us. As a final recourse, we may ward off our vulnerability by denigrating the person who eludes us. We pick up on their weaknesses and complain about their extensive shortcomings. Anything rather than ask the question that so much disturbs us: Does this person love me? Yet, if this harsh, graceless, anxious behaviour could be understood for what it is, it would be revealed not as a rejection, but as a strangely distorted – yet very real and touching – plea for tenderness.

Initially, these interpretations of their own and each other's behaviour felt very alien to Arun and Jayathri. But after several months of weekly sessions together, the true meaning of their behaviour to one another is starting to come into view.

Arun is learning to say 'I feel you're not listening and that makes me feel like running away from the terror of not being heard' rather than retreat to his 'cave'. Jayathri can sometimes say 'I'm feeling overwhelmed and I'm worried you don't love me' rather than 'we're meeting Karen and David at 7.30 so you'll need to be back by 6.50 at the latest; the taxi is at 7.15 and you should wear the dark blue shirt'.

They still squabble quite often and things are far from perfect, but the tensions tend to get resolved much more quickly; they can sometimes calm down after a few minutes. They are more accepting of their needs. Jayathri can admit that Arun is more solitary than she is, and it's not a rejection of her. Arun can see that Jayathri likes to plan and organise and that this doesn't have to be seen as an attack on him. It is not a perfect match – there are still tensions – but on the whole they are much more comfortable with their life together.

V
Conclusion

Our suspicions of therapy

It is easy, and even important for a while, to be suspicious of therapy. Our doubts tend to cluster in five main areas.

1. Therapy is only for the crazy

A widespread belief implies that therapy is a resource reserved for the mad. Only on the basis of having drastically failed as a human being would we ever consider going to 'see someone'.

But therapy is merely a sophisticated response to the very normal distresses of the human condition. Everyone is a touch crazy, if we define craziness as the inevitable result of having been confronted at too young an age with problems too large and too threatening to be dealt with optimally and thereby acquiring coping strategies – of which we're largely ignorant – that hurt us and others and limit our capacities for fulfilment. In this specific sense, we are all mad and therefore prime candidates for assistance of some kind. What qualifies us for therapy is not a unique stain on our identity; it is membership of the human race.

Therapy can usefully be compared with certain traditional religious practices, such as atonement or confession, that were also interpreted as universally relevant rather than set aside for a few exceptionally persistent sinners. Every moderately self-aware and modest person was presumed to understand that they had done things they regretted and knew of ways they might improve. Participating in religious rituals was hence no marker of extreme depravity; it was, as therapy continues to be, an appropriate response to one's allotted share of frailty and confusion.

2. Therapy is self-indulgent

It is tempting to declare an activity one is suspicious of a 'luxury'. Depending on the perspective, it can be deemed a 'luxury' to read all the time, exercise every day, bake one's own bread or buy an Italian car. The term 'luxury' is simply an insult for what one has no interest in rather than a category defined by cost.

Psychotherapy is routinely accused of being a self-indulgence by people who see nothing especially luxurious about going on a skiing holiday or hiring a personal trainer. The underlying worry seems to be that, by talking closely about ourselves once a week or more, our personalities are at risk of growing dangerously egoistic. The interest of the therapist within the consulting room may, the assumption goes, breed a belief that everyone can and should find moments of our psychological history as compelling as they proved in therapy. But this is to misunderstand the origins of egoism, which lie not in excessive intelligent attention but in neglect. Therapy is unlikely to make us less interested in the lives of others; the greater probability is that it will free us from certain inner torments that have to date prevented us from participating fully in the experiences of those around us.

Another worry is that therapy is a costly replacement for friendship, and indicates a failure to develop the empathy and kindness involved in making true friends. But this apparent defence of friendship fails to acknowledge the rules and codes of conduct that govern the institution. We cannot expect an ordinary friend to listen with huge intelligence, care and persistence on a weekly basis to our secret troubles, put their own needs to one side and formulate subtle interpretations of our histories dating back to early childhood. This would be as ambitious, and as unattuned to the legitimacy of professional skill, as wishing that a friend could fly us to another country or perform open heart surgery on us simply on the basis that they like us. It is appropriately respectful of friendship to know all that it cannot be and do.

3. Therapy robs us of dignity

Therapy works with ideas that challenge notions of adult dignity. Through its processes, we are led to contemplate some distinctly awkward possibilities: that a lot of what we are today is motivated by processes we have in common with a bewildered 3-year-old; that in a sense we haven't matured very much in many decades.

The solution to the apparently dispiriting aspect of this thesis is to reconfigure what it might mean to be, in certain areas, 'younger' than our biological age. To remain a bewildering mixture of an adult and a wounded child is no rare or insulting proposition. We shouldn't fear it as a dark possibility to be contemplated in the shadows, but rather embraced in the daylight with good humour and wry self-deprecation. We are never quite done with the business of growing up.

4. Therapy lacks confidence

Some of our suspicions of therapy can be traced back to the way it looks and feels. We may understandably associate it with some slightly odd-sounding unkempt figures who practise it from attics or pokey basement rooms. They might turn up to a cocktail party wearing sandals; they can seem devoid of any aura of prestige or confidence. This is legitimately disconcerting. It is natural to hope to see outward signs of success before we entrust our inner lives, especially their more broken and failed parts, to another person. But this is an accident of history rather than a structural problem of therapy. The shabby externals indicate that the practice has not yet reached its full stature, and that doing so might involve smartening up a bit.

5. Therapy will change everything

The last but most acute charge is that therapy over-promises. It can, unwisely, be presented as the key to transforming us into rich, invincible achievers who will triumph in love and work. Such inflated promises rightly invite doubt. But ultimately they are not a true reflection of what therapy hopes to do for us. Its authentic aim is more limited: to assist us in the task of becoming slightly more mature, slightly less compulsive and occasionally more self-aware participants in the human drama. Therapy cannot annul the essential pains of existence, but it can equip us to cope with them with a touch more courage and dignity.

How therapy might change us

What sort of person might we be after therapy, if the process were to go as well as could be hoped?

We will still quite often be unhappy. People will continue to misunderstand us; we'll meet with opposition; there will still be things that will be out of reach; success will come to people who don't appear to deserve it, and much that is good about us won't be fully appreciated by others. We will still have to compete with and submit to the judgement of others; we will still be lonely sometimes; and therapy won't stop us falling ill, dying and watching the people we love pass away. Therapy can't make life better than it truly is. However, with these caveats in place, there are still substantial benefits that therapy can bring us.

1. We will have slightly more freedom

A key feature of the defences we build up against our primal wound is that they are rigid and limit our room for manoeuvre. For example, we may have a distinctive but unfortunate type that we go for in love; or we can't be touched in certain places; or we have to be constantly cynical or else insistently jolly. Our sense of who we are allowed to be and what we can do is held prisoner by the shocks of the past.

The more we understand the original challenges and the logic of our responses to them, the more we can take a risk of deviating from whom we once felt we had to be to survive. Perhaps we can, after all, afford to hope; or to go on top, or to spend some time alone, or to try a new job.

We realise that what we had believed to be our inherent personality was just a position we had crouched into to deal with the prevailing atmosphere. Having taken a measure of the true present situation, we may accept that there could be other, sufficiently safe, ways for us to be.

2. We can be readier to explain ourselves

We had learnt to be ashamed and silent. But the therapist's kindness and attention encourages us to be less disgusted by ourselves and furtive around our needs. Having once voiced our deeper fears and wishes, they can become slightly easier to bring up again with someone else. There may be an alternative to silence.

With a greater sense of our right to exist, we may become better at articulating how it feels to be us. Instead of just resenting another person's criticism, we might explain why we believe they have been unjust to us. If we are upset by our partner, we don't need to accuse them of evil and flee the house. Rather than escape, we will know to explain how (perhaps strangely) sensitive we are and how much reassurance we need to feel secure in their affection. Instead of trying to pretend that nothing is ever our fault, we can offer a candid explanation of our limitations and commit to trying to do better going forward.

3. We can be more compassionate

In the course of therapy, we will realise how much we were let down by certain people in the past. A natural response might be blame. But the eventual, mature reaction (building on an understanding of how our own flaws arose) will be to interpret their harmful behaviour as a consequence of their own disturbance. The people who caused our primal wound almost invariably didn't mean to do so; they were themselves hurt and struggling to endure.

We can develop a sad but more compassionate picture of a world in which sorrows and anxieties are blindly passed down the generations. The insight isn't only true to experience; holding it in mind will mean there is less to fear. Those who wounded us were not superior, impressive beings who knew our special weaknesses and justly targeted them. They were themselves highly frantic, damaged creatures trying their best to cope with the litany of private sorrows to which every life condemns us.

In these ways, therapy will have done some of its most important work.

How to Find Love

I
Introduction: From Reason to Instinct

We should feel sympathy for ourselves. The challenges of finding love are highly complex, seldom systematically explored, and relatively new. We have been looking for love the way we do now for, at best, only 260 years. We are still at the dawn of determining how to get into good relationships. Signs of our missteps are all around us.

For most of history, relationships were very different in two main ways. Firstly, people didn't marry for love. They did so for reasons of status, money, household skills and beauty. We didn't expect to *love* our partners; we hoped – at best – to tolerate them. We made Marriages of Reason. Secondly, we didn't have to find our partners ourselves. The task of locating a spouse was left to our families or society more broadly. We would wait to be presented with options vetted for us according to 'objective' criteria.

Then, in the middle of the 18th century in Europe, a revolution of ideas began that has now spread around the world; a movement known to us today as Romanticism. Romanticism declared that the only real foundation for a relationship was an intense bond of love. All practical considerations (heirs, status, property) were deemed either negligible or irrelevant. The Marriage of Reason gave way to the Marriage of Feeling. We were now left to choose our own partners, without reference to the wishes of anyone else, be it family or society. The ideal lover was to be found by Instinct, not by Reason.

The idea of following an 'Instinct' took on an enormous role in the story of love. Far from being a passing folly, the feeling of being 'in love' was now interpreted as a supremely reliable guide to half a century or more of conjugal happiness. The arrival of this feeling was understood to be a little mysterious: one couldn't predict it, justify it, or wish it to occur at will. It would simply descend upon us in the presence of certain people for reasons that lay outside conscious understanding. It had elements in common with a religious visitation. One would become aware of a variety of symptoms, amply described in literature and art: a quickened heartbeat, a sense of having alighted on 'The One', difficulty sleeping, an urge to speak (to almost everyone) about the beloved and a desire to listen to music and go into nature, together with The One.

Romanticism's faith in the power of instinctive attraction has been touching and at points exhilarating, but it has also proved enormously problematic. In comparison with the hopes we harbour of love, the way most of our lives turn out can appear extremely disappointing. When we take into account the statistics on marital unhappiness and divorce, we must conclude that raw instinct alone cannot be judged an especially reliable method of locating the right partner. Our belief in instinct has been no friend of our chances of happiness. We can't go back to the Marriage of Reason, but we may need to look for a future beyond the Relationship of Instinct. At The School of Life, we anticipate – and are trying to create tools for – what we call a Psychological Relationship: a union where the best insights of psychology are brought to bear on the complex business of finding and maintaining love.

II
Why We Fall in Love with Particular People

It is tempting to describe our instinctive attractions to particular people as simply *mysterious*. It feels, as we put it tellingly, 'Romantic' *not* to analyse our feelings, and merely to follow their dictates with awe and abandon.

However, our feelings are not the mysterious yet intelligent lodestars we might wish them to be. They are, for the most part, plainly misleading. A sense of being in love with someone is seldom a prelude to long-term contentment. If we intend to get better at relationships, we must attempt to examine the calls of Romantic love rationally. This isn't a question of abandoning instinct, but of improving upon it.

The most notable aspect of our instinct in love is its *particularity*. We aren't capable of falling in love with just anyone; we are powerfully led by our 'types'. We may reject many good candidates who, on paper, could sound perfect. We may not be able to explain much more about their inadequacies other than to say weakly that they didn't 'feel right'. Alternatively, we can be powerfully impelled towards other candidates, this time less clearly suitable, for reasons wholly beyond our conscious command. We are extremely, fascinatingly *choosy*.

Why, then, do we fall in love with particular people and not others? Why do we have the types we do? What guides our attractions? We can identify three components:

1
An instinct for completion

One of the most powerful forces within love is the Instinct for Completion. All of us are radically incomplete: we lack a range of *qualities* in our characters, psychological but also physical. We might be missing calm, creativity, practical know-how, wit, strength or sensitivity. It is as if, somewhere within us, we recognise this incompleteness and experience an attraction whenever we enter the orbit of someone who possesses a complementary quality. Through love, we seek to make good a defect and to complete ourselves.

As all of us have very different kinds of incompleteness, it stands to reason that we will find very different people attractive. Certain candidates will have qualities that leave us cold, because we have these in spades already: we may not need, for example, someone who is as calm as we are. Things would threaten to get dangerously quiet. We might need an injection of creativity and irreverence instead. Our tastes will be as varied as our deficiencies.

This mechanism of attraction in love is similar to the mechanism of attraction we have around styles of architecture and design. When it comes to buildings and interiors, we also operate with an instinct for completion. The places we call 'beautiful' (like the people we call 'attractive') are often those that have qualities we want but don't yet have enough of. Consider these two very different buildings (right). We are most likely to be drawn to one or the other on the basis of a quality we don't feel we possess enough of in ourselves. People who feel a painful lack of exuberance, drama and extravagance, and are overwhelmed by drabness and sobriety might be drawn to Vienna's Peterskirche. Those who feel an anxious lack of calm, coherence and serenity, and have too much chaos, activity and intensity, might feel moved by the simplicity of the St Moritz Church in Augsburg.

TOP Peterskirche, Vienna, 1733

BOTTOM Baptism Chapel, St Moritz Church, Augsburg, 2008–2013

2
The instinct for endorsement

There is a second instinct that drives us in love: the Instinct for Endorsement. We have many issues and feelings that we are lonely with, misunderstood for and that most people don't get or are uninterested in: perhaps we dislike certain people who are generally popular; maybe we are anxious about things that others are robust around; we might have sorrows that no one else seems to share, or we could have excitements and interests that carry no echo in others.

We might then be powerfully attracted to people who seem to understand the lonely aspects of us. We love them for their ability to endorse fragile, isolated, offbeat traits. They 'get' us, in contrast to the legions of the insensitive who cannot.

When we are finally with the ideal endorsing candidate, we feel engaged in a small conspiracy against the rest of the world. We don't have to explain very much about ourselves. They just *know*. They 'get' things quickly, without us having to speak. They *read our souls*, so we don't have to spell out their contents in the normal, arduous way. Our love is a dividend of gratitude for their magical ability to understand.

Perhaps we really like doing jigsaw puzzles – an interest that our more intellectual friends scoff at. Or we have a sexual quirk that we have never dared to share with past partners. Or we have sympathy for a political figure that everyone else seems to despise. Or we really love but also feel suffocated by our mother, and that has always sounded odd to people. Or no one seems to understand and forgive us for just how stressed we get around administrative tasks. Or we used to love crawling under our bed when we were a child – and we still like that part of us but we don't find it easy to bring it into the open. All of this the ideal partner will – on their own – simply *know*.

3
The instinct for familiarity

The way we approach love as adults is highly shaped by how we experienced love as children. In adulthood we will be attracted to people who remind us – more or less unconsciously – of the people we loved as children. The idea seems unnerving because of a natural feeling of disgust around thinking of parental figures as sexual. But this is not the point. It isn't that we are attracted to people who are in every way like our parents. It's just that, with unnerving symmetry, some of the qualities we find most attractive in adults are those that were once manifest in our caregivers from childhood. The affection of our partners can end up tinged with a feeling of familiarity. In their arms, in an emotional sense, we come home.

And, without anyone giving the matter too much thought, they sweetly call us 'baby'.

III
Our Problems with the People We Are Attracted To

Our society encourages us not to probe our three Instincts (for Completion, Endorsement and Familiarity) too much. We are encouraged to 'go with our feelings' and to 'trust our instincts'.

However, a degree of wisdom begins with the knowledge that our instincts will at points be extremely misleading. This is a feature of all human instinct, not merely the affectionate kind. We need only study our instinct for food: half of the rich world's population is obese and addicted to excess fat, sugar and salt. We're not spontaneous experts in knowing what is good for us.

An instinct is not easy to discount or dislodge, but it is possible to improve upon it and train it towards maturity. We will always be creatures of instinct, but we can learn to manage our drives more effectively. By doing so, we will radically improve our chances of finding someone we can love successfully over the long term.

1
The problem with our instinct for completion

The Instinct for Completion drives us towards strengths in others that promise to compensate for weaknesses in our own natures. What this means in practice is that, in order to become complete, two things must happen: we need to be willing to *learn* things and our partner must be willing to *teach* us things. And vice versa. The success of love will depend on success at *learning and teaching.*

Unfortunately, we tend to fail badly in both areas. We can decide that we don't really want to be taught. We don't want to change; change is painful. So although we're attracted to strengths in others, we don't necessarily accept that we have to correct the weaknesses in ourselves that fired our attractions in the first place. We are asking, in effect, to be educated by the other but we don't factor in that we might be reluctant pupils. Close up, we resist the lessons that we were, from afar, drawn to – and end up feeling patronised, humiliated and 'got at' by our partner.

Furthermore, our partner may not always be the tolerant, wise teacher we might have needed. However patient they might be in other contexts, they will be at risk of getting scared and offended by our flaws. They may become intemperate teachers from an overwhelming fear that they have married an idiot and ruined their lives. No wonder they may deliver their lessons sarcastically or with humiliating menace.

2
The problem with our instinct for endorsement

The Romantic script of love tells us that a true lover will and must understand us *without us needing to speak*. They will endorse our lonely, confused, hard-to-reach aspects just by *intuition*.

This is very touching, but a huge problem in the long-term. It dissuades us from the difficult but necessary task of explaining ourselves: what we want, how we feel, why we are sad, what irritates us. We start to believe that a good lover should simply know the contents of our minds without us doing anything to share them. The fact that they understood *parts* of our minds so well, and so naturally, at one particular point leads to the counter-productive feeling that they should therefore understand the *whole* of our minds at all times – breeding a marked reluctance to explain (it doesn't feel very Romantic, we might say).

The background problem is that we are deeply complex creatures. Realistically, no human being will be able to feel their way intuitively into all areas of anyone else's mind. This means that in many situations that are very important to us, and in which we'd ideally like wordless understanding, we will not find rapid or easy endorsement from the person our instincts lead us to. In many cases, our unformulated needs will simply be met with deep, blank incomprehension or irritating error.

One of the great dangers of our Instinct for Endorsement is that it leads, when frustrated, to an outbreak of sulking. Sulking is a highly distinctive phenomenon within the psychology of love. Crucially, we don't sulk with just anyone. We reserve our sulks for people we believe should understand us but happen not to on a given occasion. We could explain what is wrong to them, of course, but if we did so, it would mean that they had failed to understand us intuitively and therefore that they were not worthy of love.

A sulk is one of the odder gifts of love. Our incensed background belief that a good lover should just know explains why on the evening when they unwittingly cause us offence at a party, we will sit quietly in the car on the way home and will reply with a simple 'Nothing' when they enquire if anything is up. When we get home, we'll disappear straight into the bathroom and bolt the door – and when they ask again, 'Please tell me what is wrong', we'll remain silent with our arms folded, for we implicitly believe that a true lover – someone really worthy of our affection – would be able to read our intentions through the bathroom panel, through our outer casing and into the caverns of our burnt and pained souls.

3
The problem with our instinct for familiarity

1. The Repetition Dynamic

We are led by instinct to potential partners who feel familiar. In many ways, adult love is a search for a rediscovery of emotions first known in childhood. In order to prove attractive, the partner we pick must re-evoke many of the feelings we once had around parental figures.

However, parental figures may not merely be associated with tenderness and understanding; they may have mixed up their love with a host of problematic components. For example, they might have been depressed, unreliable, humiliating or chaotic. These qualities may now be the very things we need to find present in someone before we can experience ourselves as 'in love' with them. We may reject candidates without particular flaws and not even know why, simply saying that they are 'too nice' or 'a bit boring'. These are code terms for: 'unlikely to bring me the sort of problems that feel necessary in their familiarity'; or 'unable to make me suffer in the ways I need to in order to love'.

We might go so far as to say that we don't primarily want to be happy with the partner we choose. We want a partner to feel *familiar* – and this may mean that we are driven to seek out unhappy circumstances, if the affection we knew as children was connected with certain sorts of pain.

Following patterns laid down in childhood, we might say: I feel I'm in a close relationship when the other person bosses me about a lot, doesn't pay me much attention and tends to withhold affection, gets irritated by minor things I do or don't do, feels intellectually superior to me and lets me know it, or makes me feel furtive and ashamed about my body.

The Repetition Dynamic is what we call the odd tendency in relationships where we repeatedly go for partners with a very flawed nature who don't allow us to flourish or find happiness. This tendency is very hard to see in oneself but far easier to spot in others. It seems like a mistake, but it's far more intentional than this. At an unconscious level, we have no option but to follow a path of unhappy love laid down in childhood.

There is no blame here. Many people who cared for us had problematic aspects that they didn't choose. If they caused us trouble, it wasn't because they meant to. Still, we have to deal with the legacy.

2. The Recoil Dynamic

Challenging past experiences can also shape our relationship instincts in a very different way. Instead of being drawn to an adult who reminds us of a parent, our instincts may turn emphatically in the opposite direction. Something in our younger experience was so difficult that *any sign of similarity* between a parent and a prospective partner becomes deeply off-putting. We call this the Recoil Dynamic.

The reason why this can turn into a problem is that almost all parents have good as well as bad sides. When we suffer from the Recoil Dynamic, we may want to escape the bad but, along the way, can end up developing allergies to a lot of what was good. Maybe a parent was deeply creative, *but had an appalling temper:* now we can't stomach anyone creative. Maybe a parent was very clever, *but humiliating:* now we can't stomach anyone clever. Maybe a parent was good at business, *but emotionally cold:* now we can't stomach anyone who succeeds in commerce.

We may therefore have no internal option but to end up with people who are without qualities that would actually have benefited us, that would have nurtured us and with which we are by nature in sympathy. Our friends can find this puzzling. They may ask how someone so creative – and whose mother was too – could be with a partner like that. Or how someone from such an economically competent family could have ended up with this kind of layabout. In such circumstances, we should look for tell-tale evidence of the Recoil Dynamic.

Good quality in a difficult parent	**Recoil requirement**
High economic competence	Very unimpressive around money
Ordered and punctual	Freewheeling and chaotic
Socially poised and polite	Blunt and uncouth
Obviously intelligent	Very unintellectual

IV
Improving Our Problematic Instincts

1
Improving the instinct for completion

We are not helpless before our instincts. By understanding the way they work, we can take steps to attenuate their worst consequences. We can learn to be intelligently suspicious of our first impulses, and submit them to reasoned examination before following their commands.

Not only do we need someone who possesses the qualities we need; we also require something else that our instinct fails to inform us about: a willingness in ourselves to hear the lessons and take the steps that will help us become the more rounded and balanced people we would like to be. The fact that the other possesses the relevant aptitude does not entail that we will be good at learning from them. Having the weakness doesn't mean we'll automatically be a willing and fast-learning pupil. We need to become better students of what we want the other to teach us.

Our instinct aims at completion but massively fails to register the difficulty of the process of being completed. Instinct might take us to someone who in principle has the strengths we're missing, but the relationship becomes an agony when we grow offended by the idea of learning. We (understandably, but unfairly) feel we've got together with an oppressive tyrant who only notices our failings and is constantly on at us.

It's not that instinct is stupidly wrong in the direction it points us to; it's just that it is radically insufficient on its own. It is a good instinct, but, taken alone, it creates immense opportunities for relationship sorrows.

A flourishing relationship should be a forum in which we teach each other many things and gracefully learn in turn. If we understand ourselves properly, we will know that there are many sides of us that need improvement. Love aims to be a safe arena in which two people can gently teach and learn how to grow into better versions of themselves. Teaching and learning does not symbolise an abandonment of love: it is the basis upon which we can develop into better lovers and, more broadly, better people.

2
Improving the instinct for endorsement

Our sulking and our belief in intuitive understanding has its touching side, evoking the enormous faith that we place in our partner's capacity to interpret us. But part of becoming an adult must be to believe that we cannot continue to expect others to read our minds if we have not previously laid out their contents through the (admittedly very cumbersome) medium of words. Even the most intelligent, sensitive lover cannot be expected to navigate around us without a lot of patiently articulated verbal indications of our desires and intentions.

Those charming early lucky guesses about what our lovers feel should not fool us for too long. Even in a very successful relationship, there is only a tiny amount that a lover should be expected to know of their beloved without it having been explained in language. We should not become furious when our lovers don't guess right. Rather than bolting our mouths and retreating into a sulk, we should have the courage to try to explain; to teach them calmly.

3
Improving the instinct for familiarity

I. The Repetition Dynamic

The Instinct for Familiarity leads us to two kinds of difficult types: people who have the same bad qualities as parental figures, and people who have none of the bad qualities as parental figures, but none of their good qualities either.

Two responses to these problems are often suggested by outsiders: that we should leave a troubling person, or that we should change our types. Both of these are very hard. At The School of Life, we are pessimistic about whether human beings can ever completely change the types of people they are attracted to.

Therefore, we offer a different solution: we believe that we should direct our efforts *to changing the way we characteristically deal with the difficulties we are attracted to*. At present, the way we tend to deal with the difficulties we are attracted to is *in the manner of the children we once were*. Our pattern of response is riddled with some of the problems that a young person might make. For example: we over-personalise issues that we are not principally responsible for; we don't explain our distress; we panic; we retreat into silence; we sulk.

In other words, there is an enormous opportunity to move from a child to an adult pattern of response in relation to the difficulties we are attracted to. What may be making our relationships awful is not simply that (for instance) we're attracted to someone who is a bit fiery, distant or manically busy, but that we continue to react to these issues as we did when, long ago in childhood, we first met with them. There is a properly grown-up – less agitated, less fragile – response that in principle we could have and that would make almost all the difference.

For most tricky characteristics to which we might instinctively be drawn, we can distinguish a child's reaction and an ideal adult response.

Our past may have assigned us an instinctive draw towards tricky people. But how we deal with them, once we're together, is open to revision. It makes all the difference whether we can move from column B to column C.

A: Tricky behaviour	**B: Child reaction**	**C: Ideal adult reaction**
Shouting	*'It's all my fault…'*	*'It's something in them.'*
Crushing intelligence	*'I'm stupid.'*	*'That's interesting…'*
Depressed	*'I have to fix you.'*	*'I'll do my best, but I'm not ultimately responsible for your mindset…'*
Frightening	*'I deserve this.'*	*'I'm not intimidated by you.'*
Distracted, preoccupied	Attention-seeking: *'Notice me'.*	*'You're busy; I'm busy, that's OK…'*

2. The Recoil Dynamic

In the Recoil Dynamic, a pattern of behaviour has been experienced as so dangerous that one seeks its opposite as the natural escape. They were horrible and also scholarly, well organised, polite, creative or rich, so the latter attributes become toxic. We feel that everyone who doesn't have those attributes will be nice: we look for recoil qualities that are directly the opposite of the toxic qualities.

The trouble is that, with time, the recoil qualities tend to annoy us too. At first, it's a relief to be with someone who doesn't have the characteristics we've grown allergic to. Then we start to criticise our partners for the very qualities our instincts sought them out for. It's not surprising we do this, because we've been taught by experts (in childhood) how to put down these kinds of people.

Our difficult parent not only made their own merits toxic, they

A: **Types we're drawn to**	**B:** **What we know well how to say**
Non-intellectual	*'You're a fucking idiot.'*
Relaxed, disorganised	*'Get your shit together.'*
Socially modest	*'You're vulgar.'*
Shy	*'You're so boring.'*
Economically unimpressive	*'You're so poor.'*
Uncomplaining, unassertive	*'You're a wimp.'*

simultaneously taught us how to criticise those who lacked those merits. Our memories retain a clear education in how to attack the very thing we're drawn to in recoil. We are highly skilled at being crushing: we were taught by world experts from the earliest age!

One suggestion is just to stop dating Recoil people. The advice is to transform our instincts (or dramatically override them) and learn to be attracted to people who have the good qualities of parental figures, but – by good fortune – not their problematic sides. But this is hard. A more realistic goal is to accept that we're probably always going to be drawn to Recoil qualities, but we can learn to manage them less aggressively and with a greater degree of forgiveness.

We could learn to feel rather differently about people who possess Recoil qualities, because the rebound qualities aren't bad in themselves.

We have trouble with our partners not because they are so awful, but because we've learned to respond to their Recoil qualities in a punitive manner. There is another way of handling them. The first thing is to keep clearly in mind that our partner is doing us a favour: for example, the unintellectual person is sparing us the traumatic humiliation we would have around a scholarly type. The rather disorganised person is protecting us from the distress we would feel if we were with someone highly methodical and organised. We should keep reminding ourselves of the awkward truth that certain qualities are difficult for us. It's not a mistake that we've been drawn to this person. We should remind ourselves that our room for manoeuvre is limited. The task is not to hate a partner for their deficiencies; it is to get interested, in a kindly way, in their development.

Qualities of a difficult parent that became toxic	**Recoil qualities we like**	**Critical things we say**	**Nicer things we could say**
Highly intelligent	Non-intellectual	*'You're a fucking idiot.'*	*'Many important things aren't complicated.'*
Driven, very organised	Relaxed, a bit disorganised	*'Get your shit together.'*	*'So what? You can be you.'*
Socially modest, shy	Gregarious, socially ambitious	*'You're a snob; you're pretentious.'*	*'You're confident and friendly and we don't have to do everything together.'*
Powerful personality	Slightly shy	*'You're so boring.'*	*'You are a calming presence in my life.'*
Rich	Economically unimpressive	*'You're so poor.'*	*'Money isn't everything.'*
Strong-willed	Compliant	*'You're a wimp.'*	*'You're sweet.'*

V
Obstacles to Finding Love

1
The challenge of reciprocation

Ostensibly, we all want love – but when love actually starts to be reciprocated, it may prove intensely alarming. We can start to think very badly of the person we liked only a little time before. We typically accuse the now-reciprocating lover of two things.

We feel they are naive in finding us wonderful. They like us only because they don't know how to read human nature. They are gullible and too easily taken in by people. It's hard to respect seducers who are so psychologically unastute. They are too intellectually limited to 'read' us properly. They don't perceive the less appealing, more disturbed, darker aspects of who we are. Their affections therefore seem precarious and dangerous: they would surely cool if they discovered the truth about us, which is frightening. Therefore, we take extra care to give little away. We feel lonely because, despite the love, big parts of us aren't in any position to be acknowledged.

Also, we accuse these partners of being 'needy'. They start to rely on us and want us a lot – and, in the process, appear weak and not quite grown up. We wonder why they can't stand on their own two feet, like a normal adult.

We're accusing the lover of being in the wrong. But really, the problem almost certainly lies with us. We should consider what is causing us to resort to the words 'naive' and 'needy'. Their alleged naivety is our doing. They think us wonderful, but only because this is the way we have presented ourselves. We have been extraordinarily successful at hiding all our shadow sides from them. It is not they who are naive, it's we who are good liars. It is normal, during seduction, to throw the light on the more positive aspects of our characters, but there is a phenomenon that goes beyond this, an extreme seduction, where we assiduously hide everything problematic in our characters. What lies behind extreme seduction is self-hatred. We think that, at heart, we are unacceptable people, that no one could really love us if they saw our true selves, and therefore we develop great skill at camouflaging ourselves. This works, at a price of devastating loneliness.

The solution isn't to blame the other person for naivety; it is to learn to show others who we truly are, on the basis of loosening our suspicion of ourselves. We need to make the initially implausible leap of faith that we might be acceptable to someone else who knew us more completely; we don't necessarily have to lie in order to deserve love. Furthermore, perhaps the lover isn't naive at all. They can see us for what we are: they have noticed the nervous efforts at seduction, the manic attempts to please, the shame about our true nature. And they don't mind; they know we're not quite who we say we are, but they know we're not so bad either – and the reality is, they aren't wrong. So it's not that they are naive about us, but that we're naive about them; they're not the simpletons we judged them to be. They know human nature. They know that, of course, everyone has shadow sides. They've made their peace with theirs. They would like us to make peace with ours. Ahead of us, they understand that both they and we are worthy of love. We give up on extreme seduction and learn the art of intelligent self-revelation: the art of gradually and honestly unfolding our complex humanity to a generous witness.

As for 'neediness', the term can all too quickly summon up an image of disreputable figures with a lack of boundaries and an insatiable, unwarranted appetite for our time. Perhaps they call us three times an hour to 'check in' or get nervous if we go into the next room. There are, of course, a few pathologically dependent people at large, but a lot of the time – far more than is generally accepted – the person who has the problem isn't the 'needy' person, it is us: the ones who are doing the accusing.

We will feel that someone is sickeningly 'needy' when we don't see ourselves as appropriate targets of someone else's need. Somewhere inside, we don't trust that we are reliable, strong, dependable, admirable or decent; we aren't quite grown-up – and so those who need something from us therefore come across as deranged and fitting targets for mockery. At the first sign that someone is becoming reliant on us, we flinch. We suspect that someone who needs us enough to depend on us for a pleasant weekend or a Tuesday evening must be diseased.

However, the solution isn't necessarily to try to change the lover by telling them to stop asking so much. They most probably aren't asking too much at all; they are just strong enough to reveal that they aren't invulnerable. Showing need is a precondition of strength rather than weakness. We should revise our view of ourselves, to see ourselves as more or less plausible people for someone else to stand in need of. The fear of 'needy' people is only a species of self-hatred rippling outwards to tar our lover.

A reduction of self-hatred does not depend on self-boosterism (telling ourselves how great we are). We should learn to tolerate ourselves, not by believing we are wonderful, but via a secure realisation that everyone is both OK and sometimes a bit awful. We can be cured of our uncommonly vicious self-suspicion by a more accurate vision of what constitutes normality. Of course we are a bit weak, a bit sly and a bit foolish, to put it gently. But so is everyone. We are no more idiotic or wayward than the next person. We can embrace a person's hopes for a close and deep relationship with us simply on the basis that we are all a bit odd and broken. The need that the lover has of us is not delusional; it is an accurate request that any flawed human might make of another comparably damaged example.

To cope better with the challenges of reciprocated love, we need to nuance what we believe love means. We are appalled by reciprocated love when we operate with a background idea of sentimental love. This states that loving ourselves is what we can do *only* when we are totally pure, and that loving another is what we can do *only* when someone is perfect. Yet we are, of course, all deeply flawed.

The origins of a sentimental interpretation of love usually lie with parents who could not tolerate their children's shadow sides. Somewhere in the past, a child had to be perfect in order to deserve affection. Tantrums, bad habits and nasty thoughts had to be banished. The child became outwardly 'good' and inwardly ashamed and lonely. We need to move towards a more humane and mature model of complex love; a love that tolerates imperfection and ambivalence, that accepts that we can have faults *and* love ourselves and can see the faults of another person *and* still love them.

2
The fear of happiness

It is normal to expect that we will always – almost by nature – actively seek out our own happiness in love.

It is therefore odd and a little unnerving to find how we can in love sometimes act as if we were deliberately trying to ruin our chances of getting what we wanted. When going on dates with candidates we are keen on, we may suddenly lapse into unnecessarily opinionated and antagonistic behaviour. Or when we are in a relationship with someone we love, we may drive them to distraction through repeated unwarranted accusations and angry explosions – as if we were somehow willing to bring on the sad day when, exhausted and frustrated, the beloved would be forced to walk away, still sympathetic but unable to take our elevated degree of suspicion and drama.

Such behaviour can't be put down to mere bad luck. It deserves a stronger, more intentional term: self-sabotage. We are familiar enough with the fear of failure, but it appears that success can bring about as many anxieties, which may culminate in a desire to scupper our chances of happy love in a bid to restore our peace of mind.

There is a basic truth at the heart of this worry: when we love someone, we risk loss. They could turn against us, succumb to a rare illness, or turn their attentions elsewhere. There is no way these possibilities can ever be entirely eliminated. What is distinctive about the self-saboteur is not that they are aware of the possibilities of loss, but that these possibilities affect them so acutely.

As ever, an explanation has to start with childhood. The self-saboteur is one who has grown to find the price of hope too high to pay. We may, when we were younger, have been exposed to brutal disappointments at a time when we were too fragile to withstand them. Perhaps we hoped our parents would stay together and they didn't. Or we hoped our father would eventually come back from another country and he stayed there. Perhaps we dared to love an adult and, after a period of happiness, they swiftly and oddly changed their attitude and let us down. Somewhere in our characters, a deep association has been forged between hope and danger, along with a corresponding preference to live quietly with disappointment, rather than more freely with hope.

The solution is to remind ourselves that we can, despite our fears, survive the loss of hope. We are no longer those who suffered the disappointments responsible for our present timidity. The conditions that forged our caution are no longer those of adult reality. The unconscious mind may, as is its wont, be reading the present through the lenses of decades ago, but what we fear will happen has, in truth, already happened; we are projecting into the future a catastrophe that belongs to a past we have not had the chance to fathom or mourn adequately. We are suffering from a localised immaturity: an archaic part of us remains as it was when we were a child. It has not been able to grow and shed its terrors. The intensity of the fear is based on the idea that we can only bring childhood resources to the problem. We still feel the same age as we were when we met a horrendous loss.

But, in fact we're big now. We have the capacity to cope very well. Should this relationship fail, we'll be sad for a while but won't actually be destroyed. We are not in as much danger as the primitive part of the mind thinks – and as we once were. We are no longer the children for whom loss was unbearable.

3
Fixation

One of the key things that can go wrong in our search for love is that we get fixated on a particular person who turns out not to be a promising or realistic option. It may be that the person is in another country, with someone else, definitely not interested in us – or even dead.

Fixation is the conviction that there is only one person we can genuinely love, even if we can't actually have a relationship with them. When a new person comes along who might potentially be a good partner for us, we reject them. We feel it would be disloyal to the individual we are fixated upon, even though they may neither know nor care about this.

Fixation disguises itself as a very Romantic attitude. Our love is unrequited, impossible – yet also seems especially intense and pure. The most famous love story of the 18th century, Goethe's *The Sorrows of Young Werther* (1774), is about a fixation in love. Werther falls passionately in love with Charlotte, who likes him but doesn't love him back – and soon gets married to someone else. There are plenty of other nice women around who are single, attractive and interested in Werther. But Werther has no time for them. The only one he cares for is Charlotte, the one who can't care for him.

This sounds Romantic, but to loosen ourselves from the grip of our fixations, we should realise that a devotion to an unrequited situation is in essence a clever way of ensuring we won't end up in a relationship at all. Fixation is really a fear of love.

The fear may be motivated by a dread of possible loss, self-hatred or a fear of self-revelation: a reluctance to let anyone into the secret parts of ourselves. These are the issues we have to grapple with, rather than the surface matters we endlessly discuss (how to persuade the uninterested lover to love us; and how, despite their rejection, they are so perfect).

Once we see fixation for what it really is, the idea that a particular person could be so important stops looking like a great act of love and devotion. Fixation is not a manifestation of love; it is a calculated commitment to an obstacle to finding love.

Another move to unfixate ourselves is not to tell ourselves that we don't like this person or to attempt to forget how much we are attracted to them. It is to get very serious and specific about what the attraction is based on, and then to realise that the qualities we admire exist in other people who don't have the problems that are currently making a fulfilling relationship impossible. The careful investigation of what we love about one person shows us – paradoxically but liberatingly – that we could also love someone else.

Understanding what we like in a person – what gives us pleasure – is therefore a central anti-fixation move. By strengthening our attachment to qualities, we are weakening our attachment to specific individuals. When we properly grasp what draws us to one lover, we necessarily identify qualities that are available in other lovers too. What we really love isn't this specific creature, but a range of qualities we located in them first, normally because they were the most conspicuous examples of a repository for them. This is where the problem started, because over-conspicuous people tend to attract too much attention, get over-subscribed and are then in a position to offer only very modest reciprocation.

Yet in reality, the qualities can't exist only there. They are necessarily generic and will be available under other, less obvious, guises – once we know how to look. This is not an exercise in getting us to give up on what we really want. The liberating move is to see that what we want exists in places beyond the pain-inducing characters we have already identified it in.

4
The inability to leave someone

For many of us, a major obstacle to getting into a good relationship is an inability to leave an unfulfilling one to which we are deeply but unhappily committed. Although we may long to flee, we don't feel ruthless enough to break away. Our present lover seems so content with us; they have emitted so many signals of their trust and investment in our future; they are so vulnerable in front of us, that we can't bring ourselves to be the bearers of terrible news. We fear two things above all: that they will collapse without us and never find happiness again, and that our rejection will render them immensely furious and vengeful. We are at once concerned and scared.

Almost always, our fears are unrealistic. People leave each other all the time, almost always without anything properly horrible happening. What is striking, then, is why some of us can be so afraid of upsetting someone, projecting onto another a degree of extreme fragility that they are unlikely to have. Of course they will be furious and upset for a while, but they will, most likely, survive.

It is not so much the idea that they won't be able to cope that holds us back; it's the feeling that we won't be able to cope with upsetting them. We have become people for whom the thought of upsetting another person (even for very good reasons) has become intensely troubling.

As ever, we can look to childhood for answers. We are likely to have experienced moments when adults around us seemed unable to take bad news, be it from us or from others in their lives. They slammed doors, screamed, threatened to kill themselves, threw things at us... There was no room for us to bring our problems to the table. The parents seemed agitated and unhappy enough as it was. 'Do you want to kill me or something?' a parent might have shouted, the day we got caught stealing a ball or had a nosebleed over the carpet. We took care never to do that, or anything else like it, again. Perhaps the reality was not as bad as it seemed to a 5-year-old child, but that is the point: children are unable to sense the difference between catastrophe and an evening of deep but passing upset in an easily agitated adult. The two merge into one another and create a confusion – which can survive deep into adulthood – between unhappiness and suicidal grief. A traumatic encounter with fragility may leave us feeling that we must never, at any cost, be the bearers of terrible news. We strive to be people-pleasers. However, in the realm of love, politeness about the future ruins lives.

The truth is that our lingering childhood fears are likely to be phantasms. Certainly there will be some momentary drama. The news will be very shocking. There will be tears. There could be screaming. Something might be thrown and broken. But humans can survive a night of hysterical crying. It won't be the end of the story. The novel of the rejected partner's life, which on the night of the break-up will look as if it had ground to an appalling end amid damp tissues and vows never ever to love again, will of course carry on. The sun will rise again. The next chapter might read something like this: *'After Nabil told her it was over, Mel cried for a month. She could barely get out of bed. She ate almost nothing. She told friends that her life was over and that she would never,*

ever get through this. Once she called up Nabil to beg him to come back. He was very accommodating and embarrassed – but didn't. Then, as spring came around, work got busier and Mel started to feel better. A few weeks into April, she had a drink with Nick, a friend of a colleague at work. He was lovely and invited her to the cinema the following weekend...'

We are inclined to forget, too, that there are many forms of harm. We don't only harm by being brutal with others; we can as easily – and perhaps more deeply – harm someone by seeming very nice to them, while wasting their years in a union to which we know all along we don't feel committed. Part of properly growing up is knowing the difference between seeming nice and being nice – the latter requiring one to do things to a lover that will for a time enrage and devastate them. For real kindness, we need to have the courage to allow ourselves to be hated. The psychological imperative to appear nice at all costs will guarantee that we'll be nothing other than quietly, exceptionally cruel. We owe it to those we no longer love to kill all hope and allow them to hate us, confident that we can withstand their anger. In the end, that is true kindness.

5
A lack of confidence in seduction

The need to seduce prospective lovers into our beds and lives is fraught with the dangers of humiliation. But how afraid we are of humiliation depends on one thing in particular: how attached we are to our own dignity.

There's a kind of underconfidence that can afflict us in seduction when we grow too keen never to appear ridiculous. It is impossible to seduce someone and not run a serious risk of looking absurd: they may have a partner already; they may think we're repulsive; they may not show up at the restaurant; they might say 'Don't be so silly!' when we touch their hand. If we are desperate never to look foolish, we can't dare to do very much and thereby, from time to time, miss out on the best opportunities of our lives.

At the heart of our underconfidence in seduction is a skewed picture of how dignified a normal person can be. We imagine that it might be possible, after a certain age, to place ourselves beyond mockery. We trust that it is an option to lead a good love life without regularly making a complete idiot of ourselves. It isn't.

The way to greater confidence isn't to reassure ourselves of our own dignity; it's to grow at peace with the inevitable nature of our ridiculousness. We are idiots now, we have been idiots in the past, and we will be idiots again in the future – and that is OK. There aren't any other options available for human beings.

Once we learn to see ourselves as already, and by nature, foolish, it doesn't matter so much if we do one more thing that might look quite stupid. The person we try to kiss could indeed think us ridiculous. But if they did so, it wouldn't be news to us; they would only be confirming what we had already gracefully accepted long ago: that we, like them – and every other person on the earth – are a nitwit. The risk of trying and failing would have its sting substantially removed. The fear of humiliation would no longer stalk us in the shadows of our minds. We would grow free to give things a go by accepting that failure was the norm. And every so often, amid the endless rebuffs we'd have factored in from the outset, it would work: we'd get a kiss, we'd make a friend, we'd get married...

It's important to recall another point to give us confidence: if we did kiss, make a friend and marry, we'd almost certainly be quite unhappy with this partner a lot of the time. Our intimidated feelings before a prospective lover stem from a melodramatic sense of how much is at stake. We hesitate to ask for a number or go out for dinner because we feel we are in the presence of an exalted being who appears to have no ordinary frailties and potentially holds the keys to earthly satisfaction in their hands. No wonder we may be too shy to speak or stumble over our words when we do so. The wiser response is to remember that this paragon of apparent beauty and perfection will, with time, prove to be much more complicated than they appear and will at points be heart-wrenchingly disappointing and maddening. This dark knowledge should relax us as we struggle to speak to them: we are not, in fact, faced with a divine being balancing our fate in their well-formed hands. They are an ordinary creature beset with all the tensions, compromises and blind spots we know from our own selves. We can approach our date with the down-to-earth confidence of one misery-inducing human reaching out to another to start a relationship that will, in time, at many points, feel like an enormous mistake. We can import into the seduction phase some of the (usefully relaxing) ingratitude that we naturally experience once a relationship has started – and use it to get love going.

The road to greater confidence in seduction begins with a ritual of telling oneself solemnly every morning, before heading out for the day, that one is a muttonhead, a cretin, a dumbbell and an imbecile, rarely capable of being happy for longer than fifteen minutes. One or two more acts of folly should, thereafter, not matter very much.

6
Impatience

One of the most important principles for choosing a lover sensibly is not to feel in any hurry to make a choice. Being satisfied with being single is a precondition of satisfactory coupledom. We cannot choose wisely when remaining single feels unbearable. We have to be at peace with the prospect of many years of solitude in order to have any chance of forming a good

We should strive to make ourselves as much at peace as we can be with the idea of being alone.

relationship, or we'll love no longer being single rather more than we love the partner who spared us being so.

Unfortunately, after a certain age, society makes singlehood feel dangerously unpleasant. Communal life starts to wither. People in couples are too threatened by the independence of the single to invite them around very often – in case they are reminded of something they might miss. Friendship and sex are, despite all the gadgets, remarkably hard to come by. No wonder then, that when someone even slightly decent comes along we cling to them, to our eventual enormous cost.

When sex was only available within marriage, people recognised that this led people to marry for the wrong reasons: to obtain something that was artificially restricted in society as a whole. Sexual liberation was intended to allow people to have a clearer head when choosing who they really wanted to be with. But the process remains half-finished. Only when we make sure that being single can be potentially as secure, warm and fulfilling as being in a couple will we know that people are choosing to pair up for the right reasons. It is time to liberate 'companionship' from the shackles of coupledom, and make it as widely and as easily available as sexual liberators wanted sex to be.

In the meantime, we should strive to make ourselves as much at peace as we can be with the idea of being alone for a long time. Only then do we stand a chance of deciding to be with someone on the basis of their own merits.

VI
Conclusion: Realism

1
Difficulty and imagination

We often tell ourselves that we keep meeting no one with whom we could possibly go out. Even if we live in a city of millions and have access to billions more on our devices, we are clear about our situation: *there is no one out there for us.*

We here allege a different thesis. There are plenty of people out there for us, and we have already encountered a range of candidates it would be entirely plausible for us to be with; it's just that we are unable to see the opportunities. More particularly, we believe – rather wrongly – that there is no one out there 'good enough' for us. We feel we could do better, and yet – tellingly – we never do. To shake us from our proud and unhelpful assumption, there are two moves we can make.

Firstly, we should take an honest look at ourselves and wonder whether we really are such deserving, special beings. Our sense of how much of a prize we are often depends on a sense of our pleasing looks or our high status. Here, indeed, we may have a lot to be proud of. But a more fruitful kind of humility – and therefore gratitude and generosity towards our dates – might emerge from considering our personalities. Here there tends to be a veil of silence around our difficult sides. It is in few people's interests to inform us of quite what tricky types we are. Our parents are too kind, our friends lack an incentive, and our ex-lovers are more likely to have left us with a blithe claim that they needed more 'space' or were going to India, rather than explaining how nightmarish we could be. We therefore sally forth with a confident sense of our power to contribute a lot to any relationship and expect to receive ample gratitude from others just for looking their way. We can't tell that we are, in many ways, real trouble to be with.

We might be a proper pain in a range of ways: we don't like doing things differently; we don't like having to back down when we've decided on something; we don't listen very well to what the other person is saying; we struggle to share responsibility; we are demanding, but not good at explaining why certain things are so important to us; we work too much, we have a tendency to scold rather than gently teach; we get worked up about things that other people don't care about (but don't seem to notice their boredom).

Excessive self-hatred is a great enemy of relationships, but so too is excessive self-love. Only by realising that we're not perfect in certain hard-to-see areas can we be liberated to get together with people who are not perfect either; the only kind of people we are ever going to meet.

Realism about oneself leads to a more realistic engagement with others. It helps us compromise constructively around our ideas of who might be good enough for us. Of course, we have got a lot of merits, but we need to compromise because we're difficult people to be with. We will be a challenge for anyone.

A broadening of options emerges not only from realising our flaws; it also comes from taking a second, more imaginative, look at the litany of flawed potential partners whom we have grown used to dismissing so quickly and ruthlessly. We need to rediscover the role of the imagination in the genesis of love. When our imaginations are switched off, we judge people on the very obvious things about them. We meet someone who is quite nice, but their nose is big. That's a no. Or they are an engineer, and engineers are unsophisticated. So that's a no. Maybe they are rich, and rich people are snobs. A no too. Perhaps their hair is thinning and bald people aren't our thing. No. Or their wrists are knobbly; no. When we're in an unimaginative mode, we strike many people off the list of possibles very quickly. In this frame of mind, we have a relatively brief tick-list of things that interest (or repel) us. We feel it only takes a moment or two to sum someone up – and fire them.

But what we call imagination means sensitivity to the less obvious things. One scans past the surface and wonders about what else might be going on in a person. They *look* conventional and a bit formal, but they could turn out to have playful and wild sides too. They *look* mousey, but maybe they are also very witty around people they know well. They *do* have a slightly wonky nose, but their eyes are very tender and their lips surprisingly sensual. They have a job that sounds unimpressive, but their interests are very broad and they might be the ideal person to go round an antiques market with. With the help of imagination, we start to engage with quieter virtues that we can't see if we look head on. Practising imagination is a key to love. In a way it *is* love, for we all ultimately have to be considered imaginatively in order to be tolerated and forgiven over the long term. By thinking imaginatively, we're not being disloyal to the true ambition of love; we're stumbling on the essence of what love involves.

2
'Good enough' and obviously terrible

One of the factors that holds us back from committing to a partner is a feeling that it isn't normal for there to be certain areas of problems and compromise. We reject a situation from a background impression that, on the whole, love is said (especially in art) to be far better than this. Our ideals crush the available realities. But maybe what we're encountering isn't a bad relationship, just a normal one.

In the mid-20th century, the English psychoanalyst Donald Winnicott (1896–1971) coined a phrase to help anxious parents doing their best but constantly worried that they were falling short of being perfect parents. The real goal, Winnicott said, wasn't to be ideal in every way, just to be 'good enough'. A child doesn't need a perfect parent. They need an ordinary, somewhat flawed, well-intentioned parent who will make mistakes, have regrets, worry, get cross, then apologise; someone who will have other demands in their life that will sometimes have to take precedence, but who will still love and be kind and fulfil many of their needs. They will be 'good enough'. Winnicott was reassuring parents tortured by an unattainable ideal: people who judged their lives and themselves harshly by standards they could never reach. Ironically, these types risked being less warm and natural parents because they were constantly anxious about not being perfect. Human relationships, Winnicott was saying, can look quite bad and yet we're actually doing OK, considering the norm. This is a useful attitude to bring to our loves, for they too are unlikely to be perfect. But they are likely to be, in their way (and far more than we sometimes allow), acceptably 'good enough.'

There's a darker version of this move from the early 19th-century Danish philosopher Søren Kierkegaard (1813–1855). Kierkegaard was especially interested in the enormous choices humans constantly have to make and the paralysis that can ensue. We have to decide to get together with someone, possibly for the next fifty years. How to take on such a burden? How can we ever decide and move forward? In Kierkegaard's eyes, we can get stuck choosing because of one reason: we are so hopeful that we can choose well. We are convinced that there is one potentially very right choice and lots of very bad ones. That is why we are so careful, so choosy and so worried. Actually, Kierkegaard insists, we exaggerate the difference. We don't face a perilous moment of decision between an excellent path and a dark one, because everything we choose is going to be fairly grim in certain ways, because life is necessarily rather than incidentally awful. We are only ever faced with bad options – which is at once tragic and beautifully liberating. We don't need to be so fastidious about the business of choosing. Hence Kierkegaard's playfully, bleakly exasperated outburst from his book *Either/Or:*

> Marry, and you will regret it; don't marry, you will also regret it; marry or don't marry, you will regret it either way. Laugh at the world's foolishness, you will regret it; weep over it, you will regret that too; laugh at the world's foolishness or weep over it, you will regret both. Believe a woman, you will regret it; believe her not, you will also regret it... Hang yourself, you will regret it; do not hang yourself, and you will regret that too; hang yourself or don't hang yourself, you'll regret it either way; whether you hang yourself or do not hang yourself, you will regret both. This, gentlemen, is the essence of all philosophy.

In other words, whatever we choose will be a bit wrong, so we shouldn't agonise too much about any one choice we make. The real skill is not always to strive to make better choices; it's to know how to make our peace with our necessarily bad choices. We keep on supposing that our lives would turn out well if only we could somehow make an ideal right decision. But Kierkegaard is firmly opposed to this naive error. We should with cheer accept that we never had ideal options in the first place. This is not a curse on us: the same difficult truth has to be faced by everyone.

Both Winnicott and Kierkegaard are saying that there will always be something wrong around relationships. It sounds as if this might be a depressing message, but its effect is the reverse. If things are a bit bad, it's probably because we're doing it right. These thinkers are backing us away from an unhelpful ideal. They are inviting us to be more modest in our expectations of relationships, not to make us unhappy, but in order to help us make our peace with the only thing that is actually on offer: a radically imperfect but genuine love for another flawed person and a necessarily troubled but still valuable shared life beside them.

The Sorrows of Love

I
Introduction

We expect love to be the source of our greatest joys. But, in practice, it is one of the most reliable routes to misery. Few forms of suffering are ever as intense as those we experience in relationships. Viewed from outside, love could be mistaken for a practice focused almost entirely on the generation of despair.

We should try to understand our sorrows. Understanding does not magically remove problems, but it sets them in context, reduces our sense of isolation and persecution, and helps us to accept that certain griefs are highly normal. The purpose of this essay is to help us develop an emotional skill that we term 'Romantic Realism'. This can be defined as a correct awareness of what can legitimately be expected of love and the reasons why we will, for large stretches of our lives, be disappointed by it, for no especially sinister or personal reasons.

The problems begin because, despite all the statistics, we are inveterate optimists about how love should go. No amount of information seems able to shake us from our faith in love. A thousand divorces pass our doors; none seem relevant to us.

We see relationship difficulties unfold around us all the time, yet we still retain a remarkable capacity to discount negative information. Despite the evidence of failures and loneliness, we cling to some highly ambitious ideas of what relationships should be like – even if we have never seen such unions in real life.

The ideal relationship is the equivalent of the snow leopard; our loyalty to it as a realistic possibility cannot be based on the evidence of our own experience. Instead it derives from a range of reckless ideas circulating in our societies about what sharing a life with another person might be like. The

Once we understand the true nature of love, sorrows will move from being symptoms of a personal curse to simply being facts of life.

problem starts with the wedding. In a wiser world than our own, our marriage vows would set the tone from the outset.

A wedding day signals a commitment by two deeply imperfect people to endure a range of arduous difficulties until the end. It is a vow to be pretty unhappy together for much of the time without blaming one another unfairly. The family and friends gathered will be aware of their own relationship sufferings, will admire the couple's courage and wish them luck – while worrying (and knowing) that a rocky – and in many ways, devastating – experience lies ahead of the couple.

How happy we are depends to a large extent on whether we judge certain problems to be normal or not. Because our societies have failed to normalise and speak honestly about a great many issues in love, it is easy to believe ourselves uniquely cursed. We not only feel unhappy; we feel unhappy that we are unhappy. When difficulties strike, we start to feel that we are going out with a particularly cretinous human. The sadness must be someone's fault; naturally enough, we conclude that the blame lies with our partner. We avoid the far truer and gentler conclusion: that we are trying to do something very difficult at which almost no one succeeds completely. At an extreme, we exit the relationship too early. Rather than adjust our ideas of what relationships are generally like, we shift our hopes to new people who won't share the irritating problems we experienced with the last partner. We blame our lover in order not to blame love itself, the truer but more elusive target.

We would be wiser to follow Romantic Realism in trusting that love will prove challenging for us, not for accidental or unique reasons, but for structural and intractable ones. Paradoxically, Romantic Realism is not the enemy of love; it is one of the attitudes that best contributes to the flourishing and survival of relationships in the long term.

Once we understand the true nature of love, sorrows will move from being symptoms of a personal curse to simply being facts of life. Realising this will already bring significant and consoling progress, which this book hopes to hasten and develop.

II
The Sorrows

1
I've become a monster

The Romantic ideal states that we will be nicer to our partner than to anyone else in the world. We selected them because we liked them so much and will therefore bring our kindest and most gentle sides forward in the relationship. We'll be a lot nicer with them than with any of our friends, for example. We like the latter; we love the former.

But the reality is intriguingly and soberingly different. If things go to plan, we tend to become something akin to monsters in love. As Romantic Realism attests, we are likely to be significantly less kind to our partner than to almost any other human on the planet.

What explains our bad behaviour? Firstly, there is so much at stake. Our whole life is on the line. Friends are with us just for the evening; our mutual challenges may go no further than the need to locate a half-decent restaurant. But if things go well, the person we love becomes involved in some of the grandest and most complex matters we ever undertake: we ask them to be our lover, our best friend, our confidant, our nurse, our financial advisor, our chauffeur, our co-educator, our social partner and our sex mate. With them, we set up a house, raise a child, run the family finances, nurse our elderly parents, manage our careers, go on holiday and explore our sexuality. The job description is so long and so demanding, no one in the standard employment market could conceivably deliver on even a fraction of the demands. The good lover needs to be a blend of therapist, PA, teacher, host, chef, nurse and escort. Asking someone to marry us turns out to be an impossibly demanding and therefore pretty mean thing to suggest to anyone we really want the best for.

Furthermore, it is the precondition of any long-term relationship that we cannot easily fire the partner and flee when issues arise. Many frustrating situations are rendered a great deal more bearable with the thought that we can escape them without too many penalties. But within long-term love, an irritant that exists now may have to be endured for many decades. A problem that would not have to be maddening in itself (a towel on the floor, a delay in answering, a chewing sound) can unleash catastrophic anxiety when we feel that this may be a more or less permanent feature of the one life we have been granted on this earth. At the backs of our minds, driving our agitation during domestic struggles, is a simple, explosive thought: that the other person hasn't just done this or that thing that we find problematic; rather, they have ruined our lives.

We aren't monsters with our friends because they do not have the capacity to do us much damage. We might only spend a few hours a month with them. We don't care about them enough to be anything other than sweet with them. We need to care a lot about someone before we will be motivated to scream at them, slam doors on them, and call them a fucking cunt.

What further makes us monsters is that, in our agitated state, we don't say clearly and calmly what might be wrong. Instead, we lose our composure and scream, sulk and get bitter. We should, ideally, teach our partners how we feel and convey precisely why we have certain ideas in mind. But teaching requires a degree of calm indifference, which is in short supply amid the panic unleashed by the idea that our partner has ruined our lives. We end up far too anxious about our problems to begin to know how to fix them.

We are monsters too because we labour under the illusion that, on the whole, we are quite easy to live with – and, under such illusions, don't prepare our partners for the struggles they will have with us, or apologise readily enough for the damage we cause. We fall prey to a belief in our own normality because, when we are single, it can be hard to see where our crazy sides are located. When alone, at moments of fury, we don't shout, as there's no one there to listen – and therefore we overlook the true, worrying strength of our capacity for anger. Or we work all the time without realising how manically we use work to gain a sense of control over life, because there's no one calling us to come for dinner – and how we might cause hell if anyone tried to stop us.

It is only in close long-term relationships that problematic sides of us come into contact with, and clash against, the needs and expectations of another person – at which point it feels natural to blame the partner for being uncommonly tricky. We labour under the self-righteous belief that we are relatively reasonable and sound people to be with, if only we could find the right person.

Another alarming reason why we are mean to our partners is that we feel safe enough to be horrible to them. If we were so intemperate with our friends, they would soon make excuses to stop seeing us. But with a partner, we are – below the surface – confident that they won't run away despite our tetchiness. Their loyalty makes them a safe target for our more distressed and desperate emotions. Love lends us the safety to show a partner who we really are – a privilege we would in truth be wiser and kinder never to share fully with anyone.

To edge us away from self-righteousness and fury, we should accept that we haven't come together with someone unusually incompetent; we're trying to do something unusually hard. We should blame the task, not our colleague.

We should cease, too, to be so priggish about our own characters. We are, naturally, appallingly difficult to live with. It's just that no one ever cared enough about us to tell us; our friends couldn't be bothered; our exes wanted to be rid of us without hassle; our parents were blind to our faults. But that doesn't mean we are paragons of virtue; we are necessarily offensive to anyone who has to experience us closely.

Fortunately, perfection is no requirement for love. We just need to be able to explain our imperfections in good time, without pomposity, before we have hurt the other person too much with our madness. It is not an option for any of us to be more than mediocre. Acting foolishly and not-so-nicely is what we do for much of the time. By behaving badly, we are not deviating from the course; we are confirming our membership of the human race.

2
They're not who they at first seemed to be

For many of us, love starts very quickly, often at first sight: with a sudden overwhelming impression of the other's loveliness. This phenomenon – the crush – goes to the heart of the modern understanding of love. It could seem like a small incident, a minor planet in the constellation of love, but it is in fact the underlying secret central sun around which our notions of the Romantic revolve. A crush represents in pure and perfect form the essential dynamics of Romanticism: the explosive interaction of limited knowledge, outward obstacles to further discovery and boundless hope.

We wouldn't be able to develop crushes if we weren't so good at allowing a few details about someone to suggest the whole of them. From a few cues only – the depth of their eyes, their handsome brow or a handful of funny comments – we rapidly start to anticipate an intense connection and years of happiness, buoyed by profound mutual sympathy and understanding. We have a proclivity for developing life-long certainties in an instant.

We pay dearly for our haste as any relationship progresses. We are all, of course, a perplexing and boundless mixture of good and bad. The primary error behind our passionate early feelings is that we overlook a central fact about people: everyone has something substantially wrong with them once their characters are fully known.

The facts of life have deformed all of our natures. No one has come through unscathed. We all lack courage, preparation, confidence and intelligence. We don't have the right role models; we were (necessarily) imperfectly parented; we fight rather than explain; we nag rather than teach; we fret instead of analysing our worries; we have a precarious sense of security; we can't understand either ourselves or others well enough; we don't have an appetite for the truth, and suffer a fatal weakness for flattering denials. The chances of a perfectly good human emerging from the perilous facts of life are nonexistent. Our fears and our frailties play out in a thousand ways. They can make us defensive or aggressive; grandiose or hesitant; clingy or avoidant. Unfortunate tendencies exist in us all, and will make everyone much less than perfect and, at times, extremely hard to live with.

Every human can be guaranteed to frustrate, anger, annoy, madden and disappoint us – and we will do the same to them. There can be no end to our sense of emptiness and incompleteness. This is a truth chiselled indelibly into the script of life. Choosing who to marry or commit ourselves to is therefore merely a case of identifying a kind of misery we can bear rather than an occasion miraculously to escape from grief altogether.

We should enjoy our crushes. The person on the train probably does have a beguiling air of self-deprecation in their eyes. The person glimpsed by the fresh fruit counter really does promise to be a gentle and excellent parent, friend and lover. But these characters will, just as importantly and inevitably, also be sure to frustrate our lives in key ways if ever we begin to know and love them.

Every human can be guaranteed to frustrate, anger, annoy, madden and disappoint us – and we will do the same to them.

Romantic Realism simply takes it for granted that one person should not be asked to be everything to another. With this truth accepted, we can look for ways to accommodate ourselves as gently and as kindly as we can to the awkward realities of life beside another fallen creature: never feeling betrayed by, or furious about, their imperfections and apologising heartily, early and constantly for ours.

If we do start a relationship, we should never blame our one-time angel for not really being who they seemed at the start. It is just that we decided who they were without checking. They haven't become awful. They were just always tricky, as we all are. In a wiser culture than our own, those who fell in love would be immediately judged as suffering from a passing mental disease and their opinions handled with extreme caution, rather than being anointed courageous visionaries able to perceive something important about another person.

The only people we can think of as amazing are those we don't yet know very well. However, accepting that everyone is maddening is no reason to give up on relationships; it is simply a sign that we are finally getting to know human nature.

3
I didn't make the right choice

At times of trouble, we can be haunted by a searing, devastating thought: that we made the wrong choice. We shouldn't tell ourselves that we haven't; we should learn to see and sympathise with the many solid reasons why we did so. We should graciously accept that we didn't stumble into error by chance. We made a mistake because we were very lonely – and this can be exceptionally hard to admit to. We weren't calmly choosing from dozens of candidates, as we might be when buying a fridge or a computer. We were struggling to fill an urgent need with whomever we could find.

We would have needed to be utterly at peace with the prospect of many years of solitude in order to have any chance of choosing with the requisite pickiness and wisdom. But most of us hate being single even more than we love the partner who eventually spares us being so. We shouldn't kick ourselves. After a certain age, society makes singlehood unbearably unpleasant. Communal life starts to wither, and couples become too threatened by the independence of the single to invite them round very often. Celibate life becomes a nightmare. When sex was only available within marriage, people recognised that this led many types to settle down for the wrong reasons: to obtain something that was artificially restricted in society as a whole. They grasped that lovers would be free to make much better choices about who they united with when they were not simply responding to a desperate desire for sex. We may have solved that issue, but we still haven't found a way of making companionship freely available, and so avoiding unfortunate unions formed under the unfair pressure of our vexing solitude.

There is a psychological reason too for our poor choices: we feel actively drawn to the wrong people. We believe we seek happiness in love, but actually what we often seek is familiarity – which may complicate any plans we might have for happiness. We long to recreate in adult relationships some of the feelings we knew in childhood. It was as children that we first came to know and understand what love meant. But, unfortunately, the lessons we picked up may not have been straightforward. The love we knew then may have come entwined with other, less pleasant, dynamics: being controlled, feeling humiliated, being abandoned, never communicating; in short: suffering. As adults, we may reject certain healthy candidates, not because they are wrong, but because they are too well balanced (too mature, too understanding, too reliable), and their rightness feels unfamiliar and oppressive. We call these kind of people 'boring' or 'unsexy' and instead head towards candidates who, our unconscious tells us, will frustrate us in familiar ways. We make mistakes because we don't associate being loved with feeling satisfied.

Knowing that we don't choose our partners freely – from either a psychological or a practical point of view – helps to dampen our anger with those we've ended up with. We weren't merely stupid; we were constrained, as much by the difficulty of finding anyone as by the warps in our own nature. We can be reassured that being with the wrong person was profoundly necessary for us. It was the price we needed to pay for being in a relationship at all.

4
I wish I were still single

One of the haunting thoughts that can make us especially snappy and bitter is the idea that we would be a lot happier if only we were single. We can be so conscious of the troubles of our present lives that we are naturally drawn to look back and remember the nicer aspects of solitude. We remember being able to get up whenever we wanted; we recall not having to fret about where we threw things. We remember how inoffensive our own bad habits were when we were the only ones to witness them. We recall not having to justify our meal choices, however eccentric; we could go out somewhere and never tell anyone; we could work through till 2 a.m. when we felt like it without being accused of being obsessive or cold. Although we were sometimes sad, we could at least always hope for a better future. It was so fulfilling in comparison with the life we lead now.

But memory is a hugely unreliable and therefore reckless instrument – which isn't a minor point, for our powers of recall have a huge impact on how we assess our lives in the present. We know just enough about how to romanticise our single days in order to poison our conjugal ones.

Some of our ingratitude might be eroded if, long before we met anyone, a talented film-maker were charged with making a close observational documentary about our lives as single people. They'd capture our face at 5.30 p.m. on a winter Sunday afternoon, as the sun was setting and we knew we'd be alone till we reached the office on Monday morning. They'd observe us looking across the room at someone at a party, longing for their kindly face, but lacking any courage to go up and address them. They'd capture us spending a lot of time at our parents' house, growing increasingly tetchy in their company. They'd show us struggling to know what to do when the fridge stopped working or we felt a terrible pain in the middle of the night.

We would be required to view this documentary at regular intervals just after bruising fights with our partners. It would provide crucial evidence of how less than ideal the single state can be, which our own memories are so good at strategically omitting. We would realise that, although we are sad now, we were also very sad then. We would accept, with good grace and a touch of dark humour, that life simply gives us few opportunities to be content.

5
There's so much laundry

In the history of Western literature, in hundreds of poems and novels, no Romantic hero or heroine has ever ironed their own underpants. This may seem like a trivial point, but it is a crucial and urgent fact, because it signals that we have taken our cues about what belongs to love from a societal narrative that is radically incomplete and misleading in nature.

Romantic culture takes no interest in the myriad of challenges that fall within the realm of the 'domestic' – a term that captures all the practicalities of living together, extending across a range of small but crucial issues, including who one should visit on the weekend, when to empty the bins, who should clean the oven and how often to have friends over for dinner.

From the Romantic point of view, these things cannot be serious or worth the attention of intelligent people. Relationships are made or broken over grand, dramatic matters: fidelity and betrayal; the courage to face society on one's own terms, or the tragedy of being ground down by the demands of convention. The day-to-day minutiae of the domestic sphere seem unimpressive and insignificant by comparison.

Partly as a result of this neglect, we don't go into relationships ready to perceive domestic issues as important potential flashpoints to look out for and devote sustained attention to. We don't acknowledge how much it may end up mattering whether we can maturely resolve issues around how to clean the kitchen floor or the conundrum of whether it is stylish, or a touch pretentious, to give a cocktail party.

When a problem has high prestige, we are ready to expend energy and time trying to resolve it. This has often happened around large scientific questions. It was understood that mapping the human genome would be enormously difficult, as well as hugely beneficial. It is taken for granted that developing a commercially viable driverless car is a monstrously difficult puzzle, but one worth devoting great resources to. This respect leads to an unexpected but crucial consequence. We don't panic around the challenges, because we understand the difficulty of what is being attempted. We are much calmer around prestigious problems. It is problems that feel trivial or silly and yet that nevertheless take up large sections of our lives that drive us to heightened states of agitation. Such agitation is precisely what the Romantic neglect of domestic life has unwittingly encouraged: its legacy is over-hasty conversations about the temperature of the bedroom and curt remarks about the right channel to watch on TV, matters that can – over many years – contribute to a critical erosion of our power to love.

When there are tensions we refuse to budget for, we readily fall into the roles of the nagger and the shirker. The nagger is trying to influence the other's behaviour, but they have given up trying to explain their desire rationally. They simply deploy a tactic of prodding, cajoling and insisting instead. The nagger has abandoned explanation; it's what we do when we don't think a topic is worth much attention. The shirker simply avoids doing what's being suggested, but they don't gift the nagger a serious and compelling explanation for their disagreement. From each side it feels obvious that the struggle isn't worth having, which still doesn't prevent it from occurring.

But if we admit that sharing a space and a life is very difficult – and yet very important and worthwhile – we come into conflict with a very different attitude. We might still argue about who puts out the bins, who gets more duvet and what to watch on TV, but the nature of the struggle will change. We won't necessarily get so impatient and so rude; we won't necessarily nag and so we won't shirk. We will have the courage of our dissatisfactions – and patiently sit with our partners elucidating the issues between us.

We might argue that part of the reason our relationships end up being fractious is that prestige has been distributed in the wrong places. Those obliged to do practical tasks are highly likely to resent them and feel that something has gone wrong with their lives for having to involve themselves so closely with them. And yet these tasks are truly 'romantic' in the sense of 'conducive to and sustaining of love'. They should be interpreted as the bedrock of a successful relationship, and accorded all the prestige currently given to other activities in society, like mountain climbing or motor sport. As people, we are not against trivia per se, just against having to do small things that lack a sense of dignity.

At certain points in history, artists have attempted to correct the distribution of prestige. In the 17th century, the Dutch painter Pieter de Hooch (1629–1684) specialised in portraying high-status, interesting-looking people engaged in domestic chores. He wanted to show the relevance of such activities to having a good life and to convey that these were not in any way

Pieter de Hooch, *Interior with Women beside a Linen Cupboard*, 1663
De Hooch beautifully rendered the minutiae of domestic life, gracing it with dignity and importance.

degrading or unworthy tasks. Organising a linen cupboard was, de Hooch proposed, no less worthwhile a task than checking the accounts of a major corporation or making sure that a load-bearing wall was sufficiently strong to support the weight of an attic storey.

Domestic preoccupation is not a sign of the death of love; it is what we start to get involved with when love has succeeded brilliantly. We will be reconciled to the reality of love when we can accept without rancour the genuine dignity of the ironing board.

6
It was supposed to be nicer

Often, our partner isn't necessarily being terrible in any overt way, but we feel a growing sadness about the character of our relationship: they are not as focused on us as we had hoped; there are often times when they don't understand us properly; they are often busy and preoccupied; they can be a bit offhand or abrupt; they are not hugely interested in the details of our day; they call their friends rather than talk with us. We feel disenchanted and let down. Love was supposed to be lovely. But, without any one huge thing having gone wrong, it doesn't much feel that way day-to-day.

This sorrow has a paradoxical source: we are upset now because at some point in the past we were really rather fortunate. We are sad because we have been lucky. To explain this seeming paradox we need to look at the intimate origins of love.

Our idea of what a good, loving relationship should be like (and what it feels like to be loved) never comes from what we've seen in adulthood; it arises from a stranger, more powerful, source. The idea of happy coupledom taps into a fundamental picture of comfort, deep security, wordless communication and of our needs being effortlessly understood that comes from early childhood.

Some of the most popular pictures in the world show a mother tenderly holding a small child, with an expression of complete devotion and love on her face. Officially, these are pictures of one very specific and unusual child and one very holy and good mother. But the religious background to the mother-and-child images isn't the key to their appeal. We are moved because we recognise a paradisiacal moment in our own personal story; we're being brought into semi-conscious contact with a delightful memory of how we were once cared for.

At the best moments of childhood (if things went reasonably well), a loving parent offered us extraordinary satisfaction. They knew when we were hungry or tired, even though we couldn't explain. We did not need to strive. They made us feel completely safe. We were held peacefully. We were entertained and indulged. Even if we don't recall the explicit details, the experience of being cherished has made a profound impression on us; it has planted itself in our deep minds as the ideal template of what love should be.

As adults, without really noticing, we continue to be in thrall to this notion of being loved, projecting the best experience of our early years onto our present relationships, and finding them sorely wanting as a result – a comparison that is profoundly corrosive and unfair.

The love we received from a parent can never be a workable model for our later, adult, experience of love. The reason is fundamental: we were a baby then, we are an adult now – a dichotomy with several key ramifications.

For a start, our needs were so much simpler then. We needed to be washed, amused, put to bed. We didn't need someone to trawl intelligently through the troubled corners of our minds. We didn't need a caregiver to understand why we prefer the first series of a television show to the second; why it is necessary to see our aunt on Sunday; or why it matters to us that the curtains harmonise with the sofa covers or that bread must be cut with a proper bread knife. The parent knew absolutely what was required in relation

Sandro Botticelli, *Virgin and Child with an Angel*, 1475–1485
The template for our idea of perfect love tends to stem from the tender selflessness of a parent, which doesn't always translate well into adult relationships.

to our basic physical and emotional requirements. Our partner is stumbling in the dark around needs that are immensely subtle, far from obvious and very complicated to deliver on.

Secondly, none of this relationship was reciprocal. The parent was intensely focused on caring for us, but they knew and totally accepted that we wouldn't engage with their needs. They didn't for a second imagine that they could take their troubles to us or expect us to nurture them. They didn't need us to ask them about their day. Our responsibility was blissfully simple: all we had to do to please them was to exist. Our most ordinary actions – rolling over on our tummy, grasping a biscuit in our tiny hand – enchanted them with ease. We were loved, but we didn't have to love: a distinction between kinds of love that language normally artfully blurs, shielding us from the difference between being the privileged customer of love, or its more exhausted and long-suffering provider.

Furthermore, our parents were probably kind enough to shield us from the burden that looking after us imposed on them. They maintained a reasonably sunny façade until they retired to their own bedroom, at which point the true toll of their efforts could be witnessed (but by then we were asleep). They did us the honour of not quite showing us what looking after us cost them. This was immensely kind, but did us one lasting disservice: it may unwittingly have created an expectation of what it could mean for someone to love us that was never true in the first place. We might in later life end up with lovers who are tetchy with us, who are too tired to talk at the end of the day, who don't marvel at our every antic, who can't even be bothered to listen to what we're saying – and we might feel (with some bitterness) that this is not how our parents were. The irony, which has its redeeming side, is that this is exactly how our parents were, just up in their bedroom when we were asleep and realised nothing.

The source of our present sorrow is not, therefore, a special failing on the part of our adult lovers. They are neither tragically inept nor uniquely selfish. It is rather that we judge our adult experiences in the light of a very different kind of childhood love. We are sorrowful not because we have landed with the wrong person but because we have (sadly) been forced to grow up.

7
I can't tell my partner everything

Many relationships begin with a deeply misleading but charming sense that we can tell a partner everything. At last, there is no more need for the usual hypocrisies. We can come clean about so much that we had previously needed to keep to ourselves: our reservations about our friends; our irritation over small but wounding remarks by colleagues; our interest in less-often-mentioned sexual practices. Love seems founded on the idea of an absence of secrecy.

Then, gradually, we become aware of so much we cannot say. It might be around sex: on a work trip we kissed a colleague and nearly went to bed with them; we discovered a porn site that beautifully targeted a special quirk of our erotic imagination; we find our partner's sibling very alluring. Or the secret thoughts can be more broad-ranging: the blog they wrote for work, about their experience in client care, was very boring; the dark green scarf they so love wearing is hideous; their best friend from school, to whom they are still very loyal, is (in our view) silly and dull; in the wedding photo of their parents (lovingly displayed in a silver frame in the living room) their mother looks unbearably smug.

Love begins with a hope of – at last – being able to tell someone else everything about who we are and what we feel. The relief of honesty is at the heart of the feeling of being in love. But this sharing of secrets sets up in our minds – and in our collective culture – a powerful and potentially problematic ideal: that if two people love one another, they must always tell each other the truth about everything.

The idea of honesty is sublime. It presents a deeply moving vision of how two people can be together, and it is a constant presence in the early months. But in order to be kind, and in order to sustain love, it ultimately becomes necessary to keep a great many thoughts out of sight.

Keeping secrets can seem like a betrayal of the relationship. At the same time, the complete truth eventually appears to place the union in mortal danger.

Much of what we would ideally like to have recognised and confirmed might be genuinely disturbing even to someone who is fond of us. We face a choice between honesty and acceptability and – for reasons that deserve a great deal of sympathy – mostly we choose the latter.

We are perhaps too conscious of the bad reasons for hiding something; we haven't paid enough attention to the noble reasons why, from time to time, true loyalty may lead us to say very much less than the whole truth. We are so impressed by honesty that we have forgotten the virtues of politeness – this word defined not as a cynical withholding of important information for the sake of harm, but as a dedication to not rubbing someone else up against the true, hurtful aspects of our nature.

It is ultimately no great sign of kindness to insist on showing someone our entire selves at all times. Repression, a certain degree of restraint, and a dedication to editing our pronouncements belong to love as much as a capacity for explicit confession. The person who cannot tolerate secrets, who in the name of 'being honest' divulges information so wounding it cannot be forgotten, is no friend of love. Just as no parent should ever tell a child the whole truth, so we should accept the ongoing need to edit our full reality.

8
I'm so lonely in my relationship

It is hard to admit to feeling lonely within a relationship. The basic assumption is that no respectable person could ever feel isolated unless they were outside of a couple. Yet in truth, a high degree of loneliness is an inexorable part of being a sensitive, intelligent human. It is a built-in feature of a complex existence, whatever our relationship status. It is impossible that another person could ever have had all the key background experiences that would be necessary to understand and sympathise with our situation.

Even a partner who is quite well aligned with us in principle is unlikely to be in exactly the same mood at the same time. They won't necessarily be thinking just the same thoughts as us on coming out of the cinema. And looking out at the night sky, just when we want them to say something highbrow and beautiful, they will perhaps be remembering a painfully banal and untimely detail from an area of domestic life (or vice versa). It is – almost – comic.

It is profoundly gratifying to be deeply understood. But a lot of other factors take us into relationships. Our partner may be great around money, or we may find them very alluring sexually. They may excel at arranging interesting weekends, or have a lovely way of being cosy and relaxed. We may have been drawn to them for some very sensible and good reasons other than their ability to have conversations in which they delicately tease out the troubles of our souls.

We must all die alone, which really means that many of our pains are for us to endure alone. Others can throw us words of encouragement, but in every life, we will at points be out on the ocean drowning in the swell while others, even the nicest ones, are standing on the shore, waving encouragingly.

The problem is sure to get worse the more thoughtful and perceptive we are. There will simply be fewer people like us around. This isn't a Romantic myth: loneliness truly is the tax we have to pay to atone for a certain complexity of mind. In other words, there are areas of what might be (grandly but accurately) called metaphysical loneliness that no other person, however well intentioned, can assuage.

At an exasperated moment, near the end of his life, the German writer Johann Wolfgang von Goethe (1749–1832), who had a lot of interesting friends and a very active social life, exploded bitterly: 'No one has ever properly understood me, I have never fully understood anyone; and no one understands anyone else.' There are – he was saying – irremovable barriers between the souls of individual people. It is impossible (and wholly normal) not to feel a bit lonely.

9
Sex is a letdown

At the centre of modern attitudes to relationships lies an ambitious three-fold hope: to have a great sex life, to have it with someone we love and to maintain it for as long as we live.

These hopes are not new. Throughout the ages, people have wanted to have great sex, they have wanted to love a special person, and they have been interested in the long term. What is distinctive and deeply problematic is the contemporary idea that we should and could secure all three ingredients at the same time; this is the distinctive ambition – and pain-inducing folly – of Romantic love.

Previous generations were wiser in assuming that only two of the three options could ever coexist. We could, for example, have great sex with someone we loved – but only in the short term, perhaps over a few weeks in the summer of our eighteenth year. Or we would find a partner with whom to have

A high degree of loneliness is an inexorable part of being a sensitive, intelligent human.

regular great sex over the long term, but this wasn't expected to be a person we were in love with; the European and East Asian aristocracies had a subtle understanding of the legitimate role of the lover, the concubine, the mistress and the gigolo. Or, we could find someone we loved and could marry, but it was clear that, after the children were born, sex would stop almost entirely. In other words, the pre-Romantic view starkly – but in the end kindly – asked us to choose which of three varieties of suffering we might prefer:

1. An intense, loving but brief sexual relationship.
2. Long-term sex, but without real love.
3. Cosy long-term love, but without great sex.

In our own age, the sense of an incompatibility between sex and long-term love is a discovery that for most couples is accompanied by acute shame, loneliness and a sense of blame and responsibility. Yet in truth, there are a host of entirely forgivable and ineluctable reasons why love and sex simply won't be an ongoing option. Despite the Romantic narrative, spousal values (the things that make a relationship loving) are in multiple ways fatally at odds with erotic values (the things that make sex fantastic).

In daily life within relationships, we have to stand our ground; we soon realise that we can't let the other person walk all over us. We must stand firm during bargaining over how money is spent or how the holidays should unfold; who should pick up the children or what colour the sofa should be. Satisfactory sex, on the other hand, requires a mindset of surrender and vulnerability: we may need to tell the partner a fantasy that exposes us acutely or ask them to do things to us or with us that could open us to ridicule. There might be small resentments and aggressions within the relationship that render us unwilling to grant the partner the pleasure they seek. Or we might feel that the decadence and debauchery of good sex runs counter to the demands of childcare; sex can seem impossibly selfish when others need us so much.

Furthermore, and more peculiarly, we all first learnt about love in childhood from people we were resolutely not meant to have sex with. Deep in our minds, being loved and being sexual may have grown fundamentally opposed. As children, without us quite understanding, we felt it was exciting to see our parents in the bathroom; it was lovely to clasp their legs, cuddle into their bed or stroke their hair. But it was equally important that any sexual implication be rigorously suppressed by these parents. They had to signal that these intimate things were emphatically asexual, that love did not imply an erotic component.

At this crucial stage of development, we learnt a necessary lesson that can have painful consequences in adult life: that sex and love are enemies; that those whom we love and those with whom we can have uninhibited sex need to be different. The more we grow tender towards our adult lovers, the more we re-engage some of the feelings of loyalty and cosiness we knew in childhood, and the more implausible sex with them can seem. No wonder if, after a while, most couples find it easier to imagine and have vivid sex with someone other than the person they face every day over the breakfast table.

At this point, some will argue the case for open relationships. Polyamory certainly sounds a mature solution to many of the tensions at stake. Perhaps sex and love really can be thought of as radically distinct entities with an almost accidental and unimportant connection. A fling (or a series of them) might go alongside a central loving long-term relationship. Yet this comfortingly wise philosophy forgets how nice it is when something is fully ours, and how worrying it is when we cannot make any claim on the person we have learnt to trust. As children, we probably never liked letting others use our toys, although borrowing those of others was always nice. A disavowed possessive streak runs deep in most of us. It remains extremely challenging when, at an orgy, our partner gives us a wink as they disappear into a softly lit bedroom with two strangers. Hearing the one we love orgasm at the hands of another is a complex experience.

Given the drawbacks, we may seek to reassure ourselves that life-long loyalty must be a decent enough answer. When things become stale, we can buy scented candles for the bedroom and book weekend breaks in country hotels. But this rosy picture presents an equally – though differently – sentimental and sanitised story. It is deluded to suppose that, by sleeping with only one person, we won't be missing out on some of life's greatest and most important pleasures. We may, as loyal partners, be spared jealousy and fears of abandonment, but we will also, quite a lot of the time, rightfully feel wistful and suffocated.

Ultimately, there is no answer, if by 'answer' we mean a pain-free solution. We cannot have love, great sex and a long-term arrangement. There is only one answer of sorts, and it can be called the Melancholy Position, because it confronts the tear-stained truth that, in certain key areas of human existence, there are simply no good solutions. Our sex lives never allow us to escape sadness altogether; they merely force us to make peace with one of its more bearable kinds.

10
This is such hard work

At tricky points in our relationships, we often complain that love has turned out to be 'too hard'. Perhaps we are repeatedly arguing over minor domestic details, and maybe it's been a long while since there was any uninhibited fun and delight. The difficulties not only distress us in and of themselves; they can also feel illegitimate, contrary to the rules of love, and a sign that the relationship itself must be an error.

This, too, is a legacy of Romanticism, an ideology that lulls us into the unhelpful belief that love is not something to be worked at, because it is a feeling and not a skill. We need only surrender to our emotions and our relationships will thrive. But we might be wiser to embrace a notion that love is inherently hard, and that if it feels too hard, this is only because we don't possess the right set of skills to cope with its arduousness.

Romantic Realism proposes that relationships are not fundamentally different from any other area of human activity in which we must develop expertise. It argues that it is no less peculiar to imagine that we might be able to love without an education than that we would be able to land a plane or perform brain surgery without one. It seeks successful love as a skill that can be dissected and systematically learnt, and suggests that we should find nothing cold or eerily rational about such calculated preparation. Romantic Realism insists that it is intuition, and not reason, that is the enemy of successful love.

In order to love, we must learn to grasp the role of our past in our selection of partners, to forgive failure rather than merely admire strength, to determine the other's distinctive manner of needing love, to cope with laborious, pedantic domestic issues, to acknowledge the difficulties of admitting to our needs and to accept the nature and drawbacks of our sexuality.

We will be ready for relationships when we accept that our chances of contentment depend on our willingness to go back to a school we were never, sadly, taught that we needed.

III
Conclusion: Stay or Leave?

Mastering the sorrows of love should not be taken to imply that no relationship, however miserable, could ever be worth leaving – or that being in a relationship must be the only state worth valuing. On the contrary, success at relationships is critically dependent on an awareness of when it might be wise to quit and an honest assessment of whether relationships are even an arrangement to which we are psychologically suited.

Our age does us a huge disservice in this area by so rigidly equating normality and happiness with membership of a couple. We are made to feel as if there could be no sane alternative to a life-long partner, as if every other possible arrangement would indicate a pernicious flaw in our character.

Other eras have not been as prescriptive. For most of the history of humanity, it was uncomplicatedly accepted that conjugal life would not suit everyone and that certain individuals would need to remain single in order to make the most of their lives. Perhaps one was too taken up with work or had no interest in children, needed a lot of time on one's own or got tetchy around large groups, was unusually devoted to God or liked to express oneself sexually outside of a loving union – in short, the best sides of oneself could not emerge from being with someone else all the time.

The name given to this choice was celibacy. The word is now often confused with chastity (the deliberate renunciation of sex), although it is quite different, indicating merely a decision not to entangle oneself emotionally with another, while otherwise remaining open to sexual existence. It is not so much that celibacy is forbidden in our society as that it is frowned upon. Some people live alone, of course. But the default assumption is that they would ideally like to be with someone – or should want to, were they not somehow mad or mentally unwell.

Two hugely unfair and negative images accompany the term 'celibate' in the cultural imagination: that of the spinster, the woman who no one wanted to marry, and the 'confirmed bachelor', the closet weirdo who is imagined as wanting to be with someone but prevented from finding fulfilment in a couple by social prejudice. The idea that someone might be perfectly capable of establishing a relationship and yet deliberately chooses to live by themselves appears deeply frightening to our age – perhaps because we unconsciously sense in celibacy a freedom of which we are profoundly jealous.

A truly evolved society would not be so aggressive in forcing its cohorts into couples. Only when being single truly has equal status with being in a couple can we be sure that people pair up for the right reasons; that is, on the ground of mutual attraction and psychological affinity, rather than in order to escape from social opprobrium. For all the vaunted liberations of our time, we need to liberate one last category, the celibate, from the weight of unfair prejudice and stigma. We need to offer closet celibates the chance to acknowledge and feel pride in their distinctive characters from the earliest age, so that they and their unlucky partners can avoid the unnecessary sufferings and recriminations of that deeply outmoded trap: the sham marriage.

Furthermore, although we need to be more determined and skilful about staying in relationships, we also need to become a good deal more strategic and intelligent about knowing when to leave them.

Wondering whether to stay in or leave a relationship is a regular daydream of almost all committed people. It could not be otherwise, given the multiple sorrows to which love exposes us. In deciding how to answer the matter, the issue is not whether we are suffering or not. As we have seen, sorrows belong to the lives of all couples, even the best-suited ones. The fact that we have many regrets – and we have considered at least ten here – should never in itself be a reason to end a relationship. Feeling furious and betrayed, shouting, resenting the laundry, fantasising sexually about other people, resenting that we're not loved enough, rarely having sex... all of these are elements that belong to highly workable and legitimate unions.

The moment to leave isn't when we're sad; it's when we identify that our lover is contributing sorrows above and beyond those that belong to love in general, when aspects of their character are embittering life far more than the normal rules of relationships mandate, and when we can see that the hurts we are facing don't belong anywhere even on the dark and long list of woes provided by the Romantic Realist. It is then that we should accept that we aren't simply being mature; we are unnecessarily ruining our lives.

Yet if, after an honest audit of our troubles, we come to suspect that our many griefs simply cannot be laid at the door of our partner but are the work of that less blameful entity, life itself, we should make our peace and stay put. We will know that we are encountering the misery of existence in the company of one particular person, but not – as it is so easy to presume – because of another person.

We will know we are sad not because love has gone wrong, but because it has gone exactly as it was always meant to go.

Why You Will Marry the Wrong Person

I
Why You Will Marry the Wrong Person

Anyone we might marry could, of course, be a little bit wrong for us. We don't expect bliss every day. We know that perfection is not on the cards. Nevertheless, there are couples who display such deep-seated incompatibility, such heightened rage and disappointment, that we have to conclude that something else is at play beyond the normal scratchiness: they appear to have married the wrong person.

How do such errors happen in our enlightened, knowledge-rich times? We can say straight off that they occur with appalling ease and regularity. Academic achievement and career success seem to provide no vaccines. Otherwise intelligent people daily and blithely make the move.

Given that it is about the single costliest mistake any of us can make (it places rather large burdens on the state, employers and the next generation too), there would seem to be few issues more important than that of marrying intelligently.

It's all the more poignant that the reasons why people make the wrong choices are rather easy to lay out and unsurprising in their structure. We ruin our lives for reasons that can be summed up in an essay. They tend to fall into some of the following basic categories.

1
We don't understand ourselves

When first looking out for a partner, the requirements we come up with are coloured by a beautifully non-specific sentimental vagueness: we'll say we really want to find someone who is 'kind' or 'fun to be with', 'attractive' or 'up for adventure'.

It isn't that such desires are wrong; they are just not remotely precise enough in their understanding of what we in particular are going to require in order to stand a chance of being happy – or, more accurately, not consistently glum.

All of us are crazy in very particular ways. We're distinctively neurotic, unbalanced and immature, but don't know quite the details because no one ever encourages us too hard to find them out. An urgent, primary task of any lover is therefore to get a handle on the specific ways in which they are mad. They have to get up to speed on their individual neuroses. They have to grasp where these have come from, what they make them do – and, most importantly, what sort of people either provoke or assuage them. A good partnership is not so much one between two healthy people (there aren't many of these on the planet), it's one between two demented people who have had the skill or luck to find a non-threatening accommodation between their relative insanities.

The feeling that we might not be too difficult to live with should set off alarm bells. The only people we can think of as normal are those we don't know very well. The question is just where the problems will lie: perhaps we have a latent tendency to get furious when someone disagrees with us, or we can only relax when we are working, or we're a bit tricky around intimacy after sex, or we've never been so good at explaining what's on our minds when we're worried. It's these sorts of issues that – over decades – create

A standard question on any early dinner date should be quite simply: 'And how are you mad?'

catastrophes and that we should ideally therefore need to know about way ahead of time, in order to look out for people who are optimally designed to withstand them. A standard question on any early dinner date should be quite simply: 'And how are you mad?'

The problem is that knowledge of our own neuroses is not at all easy to come by. It can take years and situations we have had no experience of. Prior to marriage, we're rarely involved in dynamics that properly hold up a mirror to our disturbances. Whenever more casual relationships threaten to reveal the 'difficult' side of our natures, we tend to blame the partner – and call it a day. As for our friends, they predictably don't care enough about us to have any motive to probe our real selves. They only want a nice evening out. Therefore, we end up blind to the awkward sides of our natures. On our own, when we're furious, we don't shout, as there's no one there to listen – and therefore we overlook the true, worrying strength of our capacity for fury. Or we work all the time without grasping, because there's no one calling us to come for dinner, how we manically use our jobs to gain a sense of control over life – and how we might cause hell if anyone tried to stop us labouring. At night, all we're aware of is how sweet it would be to cuddle with someone, but we have no opportunity to face up to the intimacy-avoiding side of us that would start to make us cold and strange if ever it felt we were too deeply committed to someone. One of the greatest privileges of being on one's own is the flattering illusion that one is, in truth, really quite an easy person to live with.

With such a poor level of understanding of our characters, no wonder we aren't in any position to know whom we should be looking out for.

2
We don't understand other people

This problem is compounded because other people are stuck at the same low level of self-knowledge as we are. However well-meaning they might be, they too are in no position to grasp, let alone inform us, of what is wrong with them.

Naturally, we make a stab at trying to know them. We go and visit their families, perhaps the place they first went to school. We look at photos; we meet their friends. All this contributes to a sense that we've done our homework. But it's like a novice pilot assuming they can fly after sending a paper plane successfully around the room.

In a wiser society, prospective partners would put each other through detailed psychological questionnaires and send themselves off to be assessed at length by teams of psychologists. By 2100, this will no longer sound like a joke. The mystery will be why it took humanity so long to get to this point.

We need to know the intimate functioning of the psyche of the person we're planning to marry. We need to know their attitudes to, and stance on, authority, humiliation, introspection, sexual intimacy, money, children, ageing, fidelity and a hundred things besides. This knowledge won't be available via a standard chat. We need a level of insight currently generally only available to psychological professionals at the PhD level.

In the absence of this, we are led – in large part – by what they look like. It matters immensely, of course. We keep thinking how beautiful they look. There seems to be so much information to be gleaned from their eyes, nose, shape of forehead, distribution of freckles, smiles... But this is about as wise as thinking that a photograph of the outside of a power station can tell us the essentials of nuclear fission.

Henri Matisse, *Bust of a Woman with Her Head Resting on Her Hand*, 1935

We 'project' a range of perfections onto the beloved on the basis of only a little evidence. In elaborating a whole personality from a few small – but hugely evocative – details, we are doing for the inner character of a person what our eyes naturally do with the sketch of a face.

We don't see this picture by Henri Matisse (1869–1954) as a depiction of someone who has no nostrils, eight strands of hair and no eyelashes. Without even noticing that we are doing it, we fill in the missing parts. Our brains are primed to take tiny visual hints and construct entire figures from them – and we do the same when it comes to the character of our prospective spouse. We are – much more than we give ourselves credit for, and to our great cost – inveterate artists of elaboration.

The level of knowledge we need for a marriage to work is higher than our society is prepared to countenance, recognise and accommodate – and our social practices do nothing to prevent us slipping off the precipice. We are collectively a great deal more interested in a beautiful wedding than a tolerable marriage.

3
We aren't used to being happy

We believe we seek happiness in love, but it's not quite that simple. What at times it seems we actually seek is *familiarity* – which may well complicate any plans we might have for happiness.

We recreate in adult relationships some of the feelings we knew in childhood. It was as children that we first came to know and understand what love meant. But unfortunately, the lessons we picked up may not have been straightforward. The love we knew as children may have come entwined with other, less pleasant dynamics: being controlled, feeling humiliated, being abandoned, never communicating – in short: suffering.

As adults, we may then reject certain healthy candidates whom we encounter, not because they are wrong, but precisely because they are too well-balanced (too mature, too understanding, too reliable), and this rightness feels unfamiliar and alien, almost oppressive. We head instead to candidates whom our unconscious is drawn to, not because they will please us, but because they will frustrate us in familiar ways.

We marry the wrong people because the right ones feel wrong – undeserved. We marry wrongly because we have no experience of health and because we don't – whatever we may say – ultimately associate being loved with feeling satisfied.

4
Being single is so awful

One is never in a good frame of mind to choose a partner rationally when remaining single has come to feel unbearable. We have to be utterly at peace with the prospect of many years of solitude in order to have any chance of forming a good relationship. Or we'll love no longer being single rather more than we love the partner who spared us being so.

But unfortunately, after a certain age, society makes singlehood dangerously unpleasant. Communal life starts to wither; couples are too threatened by the independence of the single to invite them around very often; one starts to feel a leper when going to the cinema alone. Sex is hard to come by as well. For all the new gadgets and supposed freedoms of modernity, it continues to be maddeningly hard to get laid – and expecting to do so regularly with new people often ends in searing humiliation.

Far better to rearrange society so that it resembles a university or a kibbutz – with communal eating, shared facilities, constant parties and free sexual mingling... That way, anyone who did decide marriage was for them would be sure they were doing it for the positives of coupledom rather than as an escape from the negatives of singlehood.

When sex was only available within marriage, people recognised that this led people to marry for the wrong reasons: to obtain something that was artificially restricted in society as a whole. People are free to make much better choices about who they marry now they're not simply responding to a desperate desire for sex.

But we retain shortages in other areas. When company is only properly available in couples, people will pair up just to spare themselves loneliness. It's time to liberate 'companionship' from the shackles of coupledom and make it as widely and as easily available as sexual liberators wanted sex to be.

5
Instinct has too much prestige

Back in the olden days, marriage was a rational business, all to do with matching your bit of land with theirs. It was cold, ruthless and disconnected from the happiness of the protagonists. We are still traumatised by this.

What replaced the Marriage of Reason was the Marriage of Instinct, the Romantic marriage. It dictated that how one felt about someone should be the only guide to action. If one felt 'in love', that was enough. No more questions asked. Feeling was triumphant. Outsiders could only applaud the feeling's arrival, respecting it as one might the visitation of a divine spirit. Parents might be aghast, but they had to suppose that only a couple could ever really know what was good for themselves. We have for three hundred years been in collective reaction against many centuries of very unhelpful interference based on prejudice, snobbery and lack of imagination.

So pedantic and cautious was the old Marriage of Reason that one of the features of the Marriage of Feeling is the assumption that one shouldn't think too much about why one is marrying. To analyse the decision feels 'un-Romantic'. To write out charts of pros and cons seems absurd and cold. The most Romantic thing one can do is just to propose quickly and suddenly, perhaps after only a few weeks, in a rush of enthusiasm – without any chance to do the horrible 'reasoning' that guaranteed misery to people for thousands of years previously. The recklessness at play seems a sign that the marriage can work, precisely because the old kind of 'safety' was such a danger to one's happiness.

6
We don't go to schools of love

The time has come for a third kind of marriage: the Marriage of Psychology, where one doesn't marry either just for practical reasons (land, money, etc.), or for intuitive reasons ('strong feelings'), but where our aspirations are properly submitted to examination and soberly understood, over many months, in the light of the daunting complexities of our respective psyches.

Presently, we marry without any information. We almost never read books specifically on the subject, we never spend more than a short time with children, and we don't rigorously interrogate other married couples or speak with any sincerity to divorced ones. We go into it without any insightful reasons as to why marriages fail – beyond what we presume to be the idiocy or lack of imagination of their protagonists.

In the long-gone age of the Marriage of Reason, we might have considered the following criteria when marrying:

– *who are their parents?*
– *how much land do they have?*
– *how culturally similar are they?*

In the Romantic age, we might have looked out for the following signs to determine rightness:

- *an inability to stop thinking of the lover*
- *a sexual obsession*
- *a belief that they are an angel*
- *a longing for constant contact*

For the age of the Marriage of Psychology, we need a new set of criteria. We should wonder:

- *how are they mad?*
- *how can we raise children with them?*
- *how can we develop together?*
- *how can we remain friends?*
- *how can we accommodate our competing needs for extracurricular sex on the one hand and loyalty on the other?*

7
We want to freeze happiness

We have a desperate and fateful urge to try to make nice things permanent. We want to own the car we saw on the screen; we want to live in the country we enjoyed as a tourist. And we want to marry the person we are having a terrific time with at the moment.

We imagine that marriage is a guarantor of the happiness we're presently enjoying with someone. It will make permanent what might otherwise be fleeting. It will help us to bottle our joy – the joy we felt when the thought of proposing first came to us: we were in Venice, on the lagoon, in a motorboat, with the evening sun throwing golden flakes of light across the sea, the prospect of dinner in a little fish restaurant, our beloved in a cashmere jumper in our arms... We got married to make this feeling permanent.

Unfortunately, there is no causal or necessary connection between marriage and this sort of feeling. The feeling was produced by Venice, a time of day, a lack of work, an excitement at dinner, a two-month acquaintance with someone... none of which 'marriage' increases or guarantees.

Marriage doesn't freeze the moment at all. That moment was dependent on the fact that you had only known each other for a bit, that you weren't working, that you were staying in a beautiful hotel near the Grand Canal, that you'd had a pleasant afternoon in the Guggenheim Museum, that you'd just had a chocolate gelato...

Getting married has no power to keep a relationship at this beautiful stage. It is not in command of the ingredients of happiness that propelled us into it. In fact, marriage will decisively move the relationship to another, very different stage: to a suburban house, a long commute, two small children. The only ingredient in common is the partner. And that might have been the wrong ingredient to bottle.

The Impressionist painters of the 19th century had an implicit philosophy of transience that points us in a wise direction. They accepted the transience of happiness as an inherent feature of existence and they could in turn help us to grow more at peace with it. Alfred Sisley's painting of a winter scene in France focuses on a set of attractive but utterly fugitive things. Towards dusk, the sun nearly breaks through the landscape. For a little time, the glow of the sky makes the bare branches less severe. The snow and the grey walls have a quiet harmony; the cold seems manageable, almost exciting. In a few minutes, night will close in.

Impressionism is interested in the fact that the things we love most change, are only around a very short time and then disappear. It celebrates the

Alfred Sisley, *The Watering Place at Marly-le-Roi*, c. 1875

sort of happiness that lasts a few minutes, rather than years. In this painting, the snow looks lovely, but it will melt. The sky is beautiful at this moment, but it is about to go dark. This style of art cultivates a skill that extends far beyond art itself: a skill at accepting and attending to short-lived moments of satisfaction.

The peaks of life tend to be brief. Happiness doesn't come in year-long blocks. With the Impressionists to guide us, we should be ready to appreciate isolated moments of everyday paradise whenever they come our way, without making the mistake of thinking them permanent, without the need to turn them into a 'marriage'.

8
We believe we are special

The statistics are not encouraging. Everyone has before them plenty of examples of terrible marriages. They've seen their friends try it and come unstuck. They know perfectly well that – in general – marriages face immense challenges. And yet we do not easily apply this insight to our own case. Without specifically formulating it, we assume that misery is a rule that applies to other people.

That's because a raw statistical chance of one in two of failing at marriage seems wholly acceptable, given that – when we are in love – we feel we have already beaten far more extraordinary odds. The beloved feels like around one in a million. With such a winning streak, the gamble of marrying a person seems entirely containable.

We silently exclude ourselves from the general principle of marital unhappiness. We're not to be blamed for this. But we could benefit from being encouraged to see ourselves as invariably a little exposed to the general fate.

9
We want to stop thinking about love

Before we get married, we are likely to have had many years of turbulence in our love lives. We will have tried to get together with people who didn't like us; we will have started and broken up unions; we will have gone out to a succession of parties, in the hope of meeting someone; and known excitement and searing disappointment.

No wonder if, at a certain point, we have had enough. Part of the reason we feel like getting married is to interrupt the all-consuming grip that love has over our psyches. We are exhausted by the melodramas and thrills that go nowhere. We are restless for other challenges. We hope that marriage can conclusively end love's painful rule over our lives.

Marriage can't and won't do this: there is as much doubt, hope, fear, rejection and betrayal inside a marriage as there is outside of one. It's only from the perspective of singledom that a marriage can look peaceful, uneventful – and enviably boring.

–

Preparing us for marriage is, ideally, an educational task that falls on culture as a whole. We have stopped believing in dynastic marriages. We are starting to see the drawbacks of Romantic marriages. Now comes the time for psychological marriages.

II
When is One Ready to Get Married?

It used to be when you'd hit certain financial and social milestones: when you had a home to your name, a set of qualifications on the mantelpiece and a few cows and a parcel of land in your possession.

But when, under the influence of Romantic ideology, this grew to seem altogether too mercenary and calculating, the focus shifted to emotions. It came to be thought important to *feel* the right way. That was the true sign of a good union. And the right feelings included the sense that the other was 'the one', that you understood one another perfectly and that you'd both never want to sleep with anyone else again.

These ideas, though touching, have proved to be an almost sure recipe for the eventual dissolution of marriages – and have caused havoc in the emotional lives of millions of otherwise cautious and well-meaning couples.

As a corrective to them, what follows is a proposal for a very different set of principles, more Classical in temper, which indicate when two people should properly consider themselves ready for marriage.

We are ready for marriage...

1
When we give up on perfection

We should not only admit in a general way that the person we are marrying is very far from perfect. We should also grasp the specifics of their imperfections: how they will be irritating, difficult, sometimes irrational, and often unable to sympathise with or understand us. Vows should be rewritten to include the terse line: 'I agree to marry this person even though they will, on a regular basis, drive me to distraction.'

However, these flaws should never be interpreted as merely capturing a local problem. No one else would be better. Everyone is as bad. We are a flawed species. Whomever one got together with would be radically imperfect in a host of deeply serious ways. One must conclusively kill the idea that things would be ideal with any other creature in this galaxy. There can only ever be a 'good-enough' marriage.

For this realisation to sink in, it helps to have had a number of relationships before marrying; not in order to have the chance to locate 'the right person', but so that one can have ample opportunity to discover at first hand, in many different contexts, the truth that everyone (even the most initially exciting prospect) really is a bit wrong from close up.

2
When we despair of being understood

Love starts with the experience of being understood in a deeply and uncommonly supportive way. They understand the lonely parts of you; you don't have to explain why you find a particular joke so funny; you hate the same people; they too want to try out a particular sexual scenario.

This will not continue. Another vow should read: 'However much the other seems to understand me, there will always be large tracts of my psyche that will remain incomprehensible to them and anyone else.'

We shouldn't, therefore, blame our lovers for a dereliction of duty in failing to interpret and grasp our internal workings. They were not tragically inept. They simply couldn't understand who we were and what we needed – which is wholly normal. No one properly understands, and can therefore fully sympathise with, anyone else.

3
When we realise we are crazy

This is deeply counter-intuitive. We seem so normal and mostly so good. It's the others who are the crazy ones.

But maturity is founded on an active sense of one's own folly. One is out of control for long periods; one has failed to master one's past; one projects unhelpfully; one is permanently anxious. One is, to put it mildly, an idiot.

If we are not regularly and very deeply embarrassed by who we are, it can only be because we haven't begun to understand our own narrative.

4
When we are ready to love rather than be loved

Confusingly, we speak of 'love' as one thing, rather than discerning the two very different varieties that lie beneath the single word: *being loved* and *loving*. We should marry when we are ready to do the latter and are aware of our unnatural, immature fixation on the former.

We start out knowing only about 'being loved'. It comes to seem – very wrongly – like the norm. To the child, it feels as if the parent is simply spontaneously on hand to comfort, guide, entertain, feed, clear up and remain almost always warm and cheerful. Parents don't reveal how often they have bitten their tongue, fought back the tears and been too tired to take off their clothes after a day of childcare. The relationship is almost entirely non-reciprocal. The parent loves, but they do not expect the favour to be returned in any significant way. The parent does not get upset when the child has not noticed the new haircut, asked carefully calibrated questions about how the meeting at work went or suggested that they go upstairs to take a nap. Parent and child may both 'love', but each party is on a very different end of the axis, unbeknownst to the child.

In adulthood, when we first say we long for love, what we predominantly mean is that we want to *be* loved as we were once loved by a parent. We want a recreation in adulthood of what it felt like to be ministered to and indulged. In a secret part of our minds, we picture someone who will understand our needs, bring us what we want, be immensely patient and sympathetic with us, act selflessly and make it all better.

This is – naturally – a disaster. For a marriage to work, we need to move firmly out of the child – and into the parental position. We need to become someone who will be willing to subordinate their own demands and concerns to the needs of another.

There's a further lesson to be learned. When a child says to its parent 'I hate you', the parent does not automatically go numb with shock or threaten to leave the house and never come back, because the parent knows that the child is not giving the executive summary of a deeply thought-out and patient investigation into the state of the relationship. The cause of these words might be hunger, a lost but crucial piece of Lego, the fact that they went to a cocktail party last night, that they won't let them play a computer game, or that they have an earache...

Parents become very good at not hearing the explicit words and listening instead to what the child means but doesn't yet know how to say: 'I'm lonely, in pain, or frightened' – distress that then unfairly comes out as an attack on the safest, kindest, most reliable thing in the child's world: the parent.

We find it exceptionally hard to make this move with our partners: to hear what they truly mean, rather than responding (furiously) to what they are saying.

A third vow should state: 'Whenever I have the strength in me to do so, I will imitate those who once loved me and take care of my partner as these figures cared for me. The task isn't an unfair chore or a departure from the true nature of love. It is the only kind of love really worthy of that exalted word.'

5
When we are ready for administration

The Romantic person instinctively sees marriage in terms of emotions. But what a couple actually get up to together over a lifetime has much more in common with the workings of a small business. They must draw up work rosters, clean, chauffeur, cook, fix, throw away, hire, fire, reconcile and budget.

None of these activities have any glamour whatsoever within the current arrangement of society. Those obliged to do them are therefore highly likely to resent them and feel that something has gone wrong with their lives for having to involve themselves so closely with them. And yet these tasks are what is truly 'romantic' in the sense of 'conducive and sustaining of love'. They should be interpreted as the bedrock of a successful marriage and accorded all the honour currently given to other activities in society, like mountain climbing or motor sport.

A central vow should read: 'I accept the dignity of the ironing board.'

6
When we understand that sex and love do and don't belong together

The Romantic view expects that love and sex will be aligned. But in truth, they won't stay so beyond a few months or, at best, one or two years. This is not anyone's fault. Because marriage has other key concerns (companionship, administration, another generation), sex will suffer. We are ready to get married when we accept a large degree of sexual resignation and the task of sublimation.

Both parties must therefore scrupulously avoid making the marriage 'about sex'. They must also, from the outset, plan for the most challenging issue that will, statistically speaking, arise for them: that one or the other will have affairs. Someone is properly ready for marriage when they are ready to behave maturely around betraying and being betrayed.

The inexperienced, immature view of betrayal goes like this: sex doesn't have to be part of love. It can be quick and meaningless, just like playing tennis. Two people shouldn't try to own each other's bodies. It's just a bit of fun. So one's partner shouldn't mind so much.

But this is wilfully to ignore impregnable basics of human nature. No one can be the victim of adultery and not feel that they have been found fundamentally wanting and cut to the core of their being. They will never get over it. It makes no sense, of course, but that isn't the point. Many things about us make little sense – and yet have to be respected. The adulterer has to be ready to honour and forgive the partner's extreme capacity for jealousy, and so must, as far as is possible, resist the urge to have sex with other people, must take every possible measure to prevent it being known if they do and must respond with extraordinary kindness and patience if the truth does ever emerge. They should above all never try to persuade their partner that it isn't right to be jealous or that jealousy is unnatural, 'bad' or a bourgeois construct.

On the other side of the equation, one should ready oneself for betrayal. That is, one should make strenuous efforts to try to understand what might go through the partner's mind when they have sex with someone else. One is likely to think that there is no other option but that they are deliberately trying to humiliate one and that all their love has evaporated. The more likely truth – that one's partner just wants to have more, or different, sex – is as hard to master as Mandarin or the oboe and requires as much practice.

One is ready to get married when two very difficult things are in place: one is ready to believe in one's partner's genuine capacity to separate love and sex. And at the same time, one is ready to believe in one's partner's stubborn inability to keep love and sex apart.

Two people have to be able to master both feats, because they may – over a lifetime – be called upon to demonstrate both capacities. This – rather than a vow never to have sex with another human again – should be the relevant test for getting married.

7
When we are happy to be taught and calm about teaching

We are ready for marriage when we accept that, in certain very significant areas, our partners will be wiser, more reasonable and more mature than we are. We should want to learn from them. We should bear having things pointed out to us. We should, at key points, see them as the teacher and ourselves as pupils. At the same time, we should be ready to take on the task of teaching them certain things and, like good teachers, not shout, lose our tempers or expect them simply to know. Marriage should be recognised as a process of mutual education.

8
When we realise we're not that compatible

The Romantic view of marriage stresses that the 'right' person means some-one who shares our tastes, interests and general attitudes to life. This might be true in the short term. But, over an extended period of time, the relevance of this fades dramatically, because differences inevitably emerge. The person who is truly best suited to us is not the person who shares our tastes, but the person who can negotiate differences in taste intelligently and wisely.

Rather than some notional idea of perfect complementarity, it is the capacity to tolerate difference that is the true marker of the 'right' person. Compatibility is an achievement of love; it shouldn't be its precondition.

Conclusion

We have accepted that it is a truly good idea to attend some classes before having children. This is now the norm for all educated people in all developed nations.

Yet there is as yet no widespread acceptability for the idea of taking classes before getting married. The results are around for all to see.

The time has come to bury the Romantic intuition-based view of marriage and to learn to practise and rehearse marriage as one would ice skating or violin playing, activities no more complex and no more deserving of systematic periods of instruction.

For now, while the infrastructure of new vows and classes is put in place, we all deserve untold sympathy for our struggles. We are trying to do something enormously difficult without the bare minimum of support necessary. It is not surprising if – very often – we don't succeed.

III
How Love Stories Ruin Our Love Lives

It sounds strange to ask what a love story might be for. We tend not to wonder too much what role made-up stories should play in our lives. Generally, we suppose we just read them for 'entertainment'.

Yet that is to be unstrategic about a major cultural resource. A love novel is a machine for simulating experience, a 'life simulator' and – like its flight equivalent – it allows us safely to experience what it might – in real life – take us years and great danger to go through. Unaided, we are puny in our powers of empathy and comprehension, isolated from the inner lives of others, limited in our experiences, short of time and able to encounter only a tiny portion of the world first hand. Fiction extends our range – it takes us inside the intimate consciousness of strangers, and it lets us sit in on experiences that would be terrifying or reckless in reality; it lends us more lives than we have been given.

There are three ways in particular in which novels deliver their assistance:

1
As cautionary tales

Love stories give us early warnings. They alert us to dangers that we're not adept at recognising: where envy might lead us, what indifference can do to a relationship, where lust can drive us... They trace the links between apparently minor errors of personality and the monumental catastrophes they can unleash, in the hope that by showing us the pitfalls, our own tendencies to disaster and folly may be curbed.

2
As maps of progress

Fiction provides models of development, demonstrations of triumph over difficulties, case studies in maturation and the acquisition of wisdom. We are carefully taken through ways in which certain people have learned, perhaps over many years and with much pain, how to cope with problems that are, in some ways, also our own.

3
As exhortations

There are many good things that we may not have known close up but that we would benefit from experiencing – and that fiction can create for us. It can show us a couple who have understood how to resolve their difficulties with grace and humour, a father who can be at once authoritative and kind, and a mother who has an unhelpful desire for perfection. It's not simply that we need to know there are such people at large. It's that by spending time in their company, the painful lessons of human nature have an opportunity to rub off on us a little.

Unfortunately, there are too many bad love novels out there – by which one means novels that do not give us a correct map of love, that leave us unprepared to deal adequately with the difficulties of being in a couple. In moments of acute distress in relationships, our grief is too often complicated by a sense that things have become, for us alone, unusually and perversely difficult. Not only are we suffering, but it seems that our suffering has no equivalent in the lives of other more or less sane people.

Our attitudes to our own love lives are in large part formed by the tradition of the Romantic novel (which nowadays is advanced not only in literary fiction but in film, music and advertising). The narrative arts of the Romantic novel have unwittingly constructed a devilish template of expectations of what relationships are supposed to be like – in the light of which our own love lives often look grievously and deeply unsatisfying. We break up or feel ourselves cursed in significant part because we are exposed to the wrong works of literature.

If this 'wrong' kind is to be termed Romantic, then the right kind – of which there are so few – might be deemed Classical. Here are some of the differences:

The plot

Romantic novel: In the archetypal Romantic novel, the drama hinges entirely on how a couple get together: the 'love story' is no such thing; it is merely the account of how love begins. All sorts of obstacles are placed in the way of love's birth, and the interest lies in watching their steady overcoming: there might be misunderstandings, bad luck, prejudice, war, a rival, a fear of intimacy, or – most poignantly – shyness... But in the end, after tribulations, the right people eventually get into couples. Love begins – and the typical story ends.

Classical novel: This wiser, less immediately seductive genre knows that the real problem isn't finding a partner: it is tolerating them, and being tolerated, over a long time. It knows that the start of relationships is not the high point that Romantic culture assumes; it is merely the first step with a far longer, more ambivalent and yet quietly more heroic journey – on which it directs its intelligence and scrutiny.

Work

Romantic novel: The characters may have jobs, but on the whole they have little impact on their psyches. Work goes on somewhere else. What one does for a living is not thought relevant to an understanding of love.

Classical novel: Here we see that work is in fact a huge part of life, with an overwhelming role in shaping our relationships. Whatever our emotional dispositions, it is the stress of work that ends up generating a sizeable share of the trouble that lovers will have with each other.

Children

Romantic novel: Children are incidental, sweet symbols of mutual love, or naughty in an endearing way. They rarely cry, take up little time and are generally wise, exhibiting a native, unschooled intelligence.

Classical novel: In a wiser sort of story we would see that relationships are fundamentally oriented towards the having and raising of children – and at the same time, that children place the couple under unbearable strains. They kill the passion that made them possible. Life moves from the sublime to the quotidian. There are toys in the living room, pieces of chicken under the table, and no time to talk. Everyone is always tired. This too is love.

Practicalities

Romantic novel: In this genre, we have only a hazy idea of who does the housework. It is not seen as relevant to a relationship. Domesticity is a corrupting force and people who care a lot about it are likely to be unhappy in their relationships. We are unlikely to learn a great deal concerning a couple's thinking on homework or television for the under-fours.

Classical novel: Here, relationships are understood to be institutions, not just emotions. Part of their rationale is to enable two people to function as a joint economic unit for the education of the next generation. This is in no way banal. There are opportunities for genuine heroism. Especially around laundry.

Sex

Romantic novel: Sex and love are shown to belong together. The high point of love is intercourse. Adultery, in the Romantic view, is therefore fatal: if you were with the right person, you could never be unfaithful.

Classical novel: It knows that long-term love may not set up the best preconditions for sex. The Classical attitude sees love and sex as distinct and at times divergent themes in life. And therefore sexual problems do not in themselves indicate that a relationship is, overall, a disaster...

Compatibility

Romantic novel: The Romantic novel cares about the harmony (or lack of it) between the souls of the protagonists. It believes that the fundamental challenge of emotional life is to find someone who completely understands us and with whom there need never be any more secrets. It believes that love is finding your other half, your spiritual twin. Love is not about training or education; it is an instinct, a feeling – and is generally mysterious in its workings.

Classical novel: It accepts that no one ever fully understands anyone else; that there must be secrets, that there will be loneliness, that there must be compromise. It believes that we have to learn how to sustain good relationships, that there are learnable skills involved, and that love is not just a chance endowment of nature.

–

The Romantic novel is deeply unhelpful. We have learned to judge ourselves by the hopes and expectations fostered by a misleading medium. By its standards, our own relationships are almost all damaged and unsatisfactory. No wonder separation or divorce so often appear to be inevitable.

They shouldn't be; we merely need to change our reading matter: to tell ourselves more accurate stories about the progress of relationships, stories that normalise troubles and show us an intelligent, helpful path through them.

Why We Hate Cheap Things

I

Why We Hate Cheap Things

We don't think we hate cheap things, but we frequently behave as if we do. Consider the pineapple. Christopher Columbus (1451–1506) was the first European to be delighted by the physical grandeur and vibrant sweetness of the pineapple, which is native to South America but had reached the Caribbean by the time he arrived there. The first time Europeans encountered pineapples was in November 1493, in a Carib village on the island of Guadeloupe. Columbus's crew spotted the fruit next to a pot of stewing human limbs. The outside reminded them of a pine cone; the interior pulp of an apple.

However, pineapples proved difficult to transport and costly to cultivate. For a long time only royalty could afford to eat them. Russia's Catherine the Great was a huge fan, as was England's Charles II. A single fruit in the 17th century sold for today's equivalent of £5,000. The pineapple was such a status symbol that, if they could obtain one, people would keep it for display until it rotted and fell apart. In the mid-18th century, at the height of the pineapple craze, whole aristocratic evenings were structured around the ritual display of these fruits. Poems were written in their honour. Savouring a tiny sliver could be the high point of a year.

Christopher Wren had no hesitation in topping the South Towers of St Paul's with this evidently divine fruit. The pineapple was so exciting and so loved that John Murray, the 4th Earl of Dunmore, built a temple on his Scottish estate in its honour.

Then, at the end of the 19th century, two things changed. Large-scale commercial pineapple plantations were established in Hawaii, and there were huge advances in steamship technology. Consequently, production and

TOP The South Towers of St Paul's Cathedral by Christopher Wren, 1711, topped by a golden pineapple

BOTTOM The Dunmore Pineapple, a folly built in 1761 to honour this unusually high-status fruit

transport costs plummeted and, unwittingly, transformed the psychology of pineapple eating. Today, you can buy a pineapple for around £1.50. The fruit still tastes the same. But now the pineapple is one of the world's least glamorous fruits. It is rarely served at smart dinner parties and it would never be carved on the top of a major civic building.

The pineapple itself has not changed; only our attitude to it has. Contemplation of the history of the pineapple suggests a curious overlap between love and economics: when we have to pay a lot for something nice, we appreciate it to the full. Yet as its price in the market falls, passion has a habit of fading away. If the object has no merit to begin with, a high price won't do anything for it, but if it has real virtue and yet a low price, it is in danger of falling into grievous neglect.

It's a pattern that we see recurring in a range of areas: for example, with the sight of clouds from above. In 1927, a hitherto-unknown air-mail pilot called Charles Lindbergh (1902–1974) became the first man to complete a solo crossing of the Atlantic in his fragile plane, *The Spirit of St Louis*.

For hours, Lindbergh flew in the most arduous conditions, braving wind, rain and storms. He saw clouds passing below him and distant lightning bolts on the horizon. It was one of the profoundest moments of his life. He was awestruck and felt he was becoming, for a time, almost god-like. For much of the 20th century, his experience remained rare and extremely costly. There was never any danger that the human value of crossing an ocean by air would be overlooked.

This lasted until the arrival of the Boeing 747 and the cheap plane ticket in the summer of 1970. The jumbo fundamentally changed the economics of flying. The experience of gazing down at clouds and seeing the world spread out below stopped being (as it had been for Lindbergh) a life-changing encounter; it started to feel commonplace and even a little boring. It became peculiar to wax lyrical about taking the red-eye to JFK or to mention a

TOP Charles Lindbergh with the plane in which he made the first solo crossing of the Atlantic, 31 May 1927

BOTTOM Jean-Baptiste Joseph Pater, *The Bath*, 1730–1736
Before the advent of indoor plumbing, having a bath was a rare privilege even for the elite.

spectacular column of clouds that one had spotted shortly after the arrival of the chicken lunch. A trip that would have mesmerised Leonardo da Vinci or John Constable was now passed over in silence.

The view from the plane window underwent an economic miracle that led to a psychological catastrophe: its cost dropped and it ceased to matter, although its real value hadn't changed.

Consider also the bath. For centuries, having a hot bath all to yourself at home was a remarkable, highly prized experience, out of reach to all except a very few at the pinnacle of society. It required the assistance of several attendants to heat the water and fill the tub, fend off draughts, hold the towels, and proffer the soap. It was a special occasion – like a coronation or a victory in battle – worthy of being recorded in a grand work of art. It would be an experience to ponder and remember, to reflect upon and discuss with your friends. One would dwell for days on the wonder of immersing the body in a warm, buoyant liquid.

But improvements in plumbing and water supply, expansion in the size of the average dwelling space per inhabitant, and the introduction of less expensive tubs have made the bath an ordinary experience. It doesn't feel particularly special. In fact, it's often a bit too slow: it might be preferable to take a shower instead.

The pattern is the same: a reduction in our esteem for an experience follows a reduction in the cost of obtaining it. There is a similar parallel history for light in the evening (highly prized in the age of candles, boring in the age of the halogen bulb), or for freshly laundered clothes. This was an astonishing, unusual phenomenon for centuries, but now the clean cotton T-shirt (which would have deeply impressed Charlemagne or Louis XVI) is barely worth noticing.

Why, then, do we associate cheap prices with a lack of value? Our response is a hangover from our long pre-industrial past. For most of human history, there was a strong correlation between cost and value. The higher the price, the better things tended to be – because there was no way both for prices to be low and quality to be high. Everything had to be made by hand, by expensively trained artisans, with raw materials that were difficult to transport. The expensive sword, jacket, window or wheelbarrow was always the better one.

This relationship between price and value held true without interruption until the end of the 18th century. Then, thanks to the Industrial Revolution, something unusual happened: human beings discovered how to make high-quality goods cheaply, because of technology and new methods of organising the labour force.

If you live in a craft-based society, the quality of any object invariably depends upon how much skilled labour went into producing it. In the 15th century, swords and helmets made by the Missaglia family in Milan were especially pricey, because they were especially skilled, and produced armour that was stronger, lighter, better balanced and more cleverly designed than anyone else's. This was a general principle for goods at the time: a more expensive cloak would be more durable, warmer and more elegantly decorated than a cheaper version. A more expensive window would let in more light, keep out more draughts, open more easily, and last in good condition much longer than its less expensive rivals: it would be a more skilfully made product constructed from more durable materials.

On the back of this long experience, an entrenched cultural association has formed between the rare, the expensive and the good, with each coming to suggest the other. The converse also holds, so that items that are widely available and inexpensive are seen as unimpressive or unexciting.

In principle, industrialisation was supposed to undo these connections. The price would fall and widespread happiness would follow. High-quality objects would enter the mass market, and excellence would be democratised.

Antonio Missaglia, sallet and armour, c. 1450
The extremely skilled craftsmanship of these goods was reflected in their high price and high value.

This promised to be an exciting moment. Evangelists regularly proclaimed a new age in which universal political suffrage would be accompanied by material dignity and honour for every social class.

In 1911, Henry Ford started developing the car assembly line, which replaced the slower individual skilled worker. The price of cars came down quickly so that it became possible for ordinary workers to afford cars themselves. The modernist designers of the Bauhaus movement in 1920s Germany were similarly motivated by the idea of creating household items that would be both highly attractive and very cheap – available to anyone, even on the most modest of salaries. However, despite the good intention of these efforts, instead of making wonderful experiences universally available, industrialisation has inadvertently produced a different effect: it has robbed certain experiences of their loveliness, interest and worth.

It's not that we refuse to buy inexpensive or cheap things; it's that getting excited over cheap things has come to seem a little bizarre. One is allowed to get worked up over the eggs of a sturgeon (£100 for a small pot), but have to be circumspect about one's enthusiasm for the eggs of a chicken (£2 for 12). There is an intimidating hierarchy operating in the background, shaping what we are grateful for and feel that we lack and must have.

The tragedy for our relationship with money is that the hierarchy operates in favour of the expensive things. This means that we often end up feeling that we can't afford good things and that our lives are therefore sad and incomplete. The money hierarchy constantly makes us feel impoverished, while the truth is that there are more good things within our grasp than we believe (and tend to notice only when we are dying or recovering from a bad illness). We are rich enough to purchase the superlative egg of the chicken, but we don't experience our wealth here; we are left lamenting our inability to buy the hugely expensive (but not actually much nicer) eggs of the almost infertile and evasive Iranian sturgeon.

Director's room of Walter Gropius, Bauhaus, Dessau, 1926
The promise of modernity in the 1920s: attractive chairs, desks, lamps and rugs for everyone.

How do we reverse this? The answer lies in a slightly unexpected area: the mind of a 4-year-old. It started raining an hour ago and now the street is full of puddles, and there could be nothing better in the world. The riches of the Indies would be nothing compared to the pleasures of being able to see the rippling of the water created by a jump in one's wellingtons, the eddies and whirlpools, the minute waves, the oceans beneath one...

Children have two advantages: they don't know what they're supposed to like, and they don't understand money, so price is never a guide of value for them. They rely instead on their own delight in the intrinsic merits of the things they're presented with, and this can take them in astonishing (and sometimes maddening) directions. They'll spend an hour with one button. One buys them the £49 wooden toy made by Swedish artisans who hope to teach lessons in symmetry and finds that they prefer the cardboard box that it came in. They become mesmerised by the wonders of turning on the light and therefore think it sensible to try it a hundred times. They prefer the nail and screw section of a DIY shop to the fancy toy department or the prestigious national museum.

This attitude allows them to be entranced by objects that long ago ceased to hold our wonder. If asked to put a price on things, children tend to answer by the utility and charm of an object, not its manufacturing costs. This leads to unusual but, we might recognise, more rightful results. A child might guess that a stapler costs £100 and would be deeply surprised, even shocked, to learn that a USB stick can be bought for just over £1. Children would be right, if prices were determined by human worth and value, but they're not; they just reflect what things cost to make. The pity is that we treat cost as a guide to what matters, when financial price should never be used for this.

At a certain age (around 8), something very debilitating happens to children. They start to learn about 'expensive' and 'cheap' and absorb the view that the more expensive something is, the better it is. They are encouraged to think well of saving up pocket money and to see the 'big' toy they are given as much better than the 'cheaper' one.

We can't go backwards, so we can't forget what we know of prices. However, we can pay less attention to what things cost and more to our own responses. The people who have most to teach us here are artists. They are the experts at recording and communicating their enthusiasms, which, as with children, can take them in unexpected directions.

The French artist Paul Cézanne (1839–1906) spent a good deal of the late 19th century painting groups of apples in his studio in Provence. He was thrilled by their texture, shapes and colours. He loved the transitions between the yellowy golds and the deep reds across their skins. He was an expert at noticing how the generic word 'apple' covers infinite highly individual examples. Under his gaze, each apple becomes its own planet, a veritable universe of distinctive colour and aura – and hence a source of delight and solace.

The apple that has only a limited life, that will make a slow transition from sourness to sweetness, that grew patiently on a particular tree, that survived the curiosity of birds and spiders, that weathered the mistral and a particularly blustery May is honoured and given its proper due by the artist. Cézanne himself was extremely wealthy, the heir of an enormous banking fortune. It seems important to state this, as Cézanne wasn't just making a virtue of necessity and would have worshipped gold bullion if he'd had the chance. He did have the chance; and he didn't. Cézanne had all the awe, love and excitement before the apple that Catherine the Great and Charles II had before the pineapple, but Cézanne's wonderful discovery was that these elevated and powerful emotions are just as valid in relation to things that can be purchased for the small change in our pockets. Cézanne in his studio was generating his own revolution – not an Industrial Revolution that would make once costly objects available to everyone, but a Revolution in Appreciation, a far deeper process, that would get us to notice what we already have to hand. Instead of reducing prices, he is raising levels of appreciation. This is perhaps more precious to us economically, because it means that we can suddenly get many more great things for very little money.

Some of what we find 'moving' in an encounter with the apples is that we are restored to a familiar but forgotten attitude of appreciation, one that we knew in childhood when we loved the toggles on our rain jackets and found a paperclip fascinating and didn't know what anything cost. Since then, life has pushed us into the world of money where prices loom too large, we now acknowledge, in our relation to things. While we enjoy Cézanne's work, it might also make us unexpectedly sad: the sadness is a recognition of how many of our genuine enthusiasms and loves we've had to surrender in the name of the adult world. We've given up on too many of our native loves. The apple is one instance of a whole continent we've ceased to marvel at.

There is a commercial version of Cézanne's work, which we call advertising. Like Cézanne's work, advertising throws the best things about objects into relief and tells us in insistent and enthusiastic ways what is loveable about parts of the world. Advertising is skilled, for example, at pointing out the loveable things in the new top-of-the-range BMW: the cylinders, the leather seat surrounds, the moulding around the wheel arches (lithe and muscular), and the army of lights, skilfully massing their beams ready to attack the darkness on the road ahead.

The only problem with advertising is that it isn't done for enough things, or indeed the things that would be most helpful and convenient for us to appreciate. People who attack advertising get it slightly wrong: the problem is not that we love BMWs, but that so much of our love and awe has been syphoned in that direction and hasn't been properly excited in other, more realistic, areas.

Paul Cézanne, *Apples*,
1878–1879

We need advertising pursued with the same sense of drama and intensity and ambition but directed towards biros, puddles and olives. The reason this doesn't happen is not sinister or profound. It's just that we haven't yet found a way to pay the enormous sums required to glamorise objects through advertising in the case of lower-priced items.

Our reluctance to be excited by inexpensive things is not a fixed debility of human nature; it is just a current cultural misfortune. As children, we all used to know the solution. The ingredients of the solution are intrinsically familiar. We get hints of what should happen in the art gallery and in front of adverts. We need to rethink our relationship to prices. The price of something is principally determined by what it cost to make, not how much human value is potentially to be derived from it. We have been looking at prices in the wrong way: we have fetishised them as tokens of intrinsic value, and we have allowed them to set how much excitement we are allowed to have in given areas, how much joy is to be mined in particular places. But prices were never meant to be like this: we are breathing too much life into them, and therefore dulling too many of our responses to the inexpensive world.

There are two ways to get richer: one is to make more money; the second is to discover that more of the things we could love are already to hand (thanks to the miracles of the Industrial Revolution). We are, astonishingly, already a good deal richer than we are encouraged to think we are.

II

Why We Look Down on People Who Don't Earn Very Much

We're not necessarily involved in this kind of judgement ourselves, but we recognise the phenomenon in our society well enough: the more someone earns, the more they are likely to be admired by strangers, and perceived as interesting and exciting. Respect appears all too often to be awarded according to earnings. And, in a related move, if you don't have much economic endorsement, it can be hard for your character or views to be taken seriously by your society.

It is not a mystery how this relationship became established, because there are so many conspicuous cases where we find a genuine link between talent, effort, skill, contribution and income. The most impressive examples involve the brilliant surgeon, the authors of *Matilda* and *Harry Potter*, or the team behind the development of graphene. All these geniuses had a lot of talent, they made a lot of money, and their contributions are terrific. They make the connection between high income and virtue seem right and natural.

It's cases like this that lead us to suppose that income is an accurate and proper indicator of the value a person is making to the lives of others – and therefore that respect should closely track income. This is the view of modern capitalism, and is the spirit one breathes in the big cities of the world's rich countries.

Such an intuitive emotional response to wages operates with a background economic theory, which we may never describe to ourselves explicitly but that could be stated as follows: a person's wages are determined by the scale of their social contribution.

But turn to the pages of economics textbooks and a very different, far less emotive, account of wages emerges. Economics states that wages are a much simpler business. They are exclusively determined, not by social contribution per se, but by the number of people able and willing to do a given job that others want done. If there are lots of people able to complete the task, you won't need to offer very much money to obtain their labour; if there are very few people able to do the job, you will have to pay much more. But in all this, there is no room to judge the worth of the work being done; the determinant of wages is simply the strength of demand in relation to supply.

Taken in one direction, this explains the salary of a hitman. This person can – for the most exacting and difficult missions, where the target possesses private guards and is protected by triple glazed Bosch-security glass – extract an early seven-figure sum, because almost no one else can carry out such a complex manoeuvre. Taken in the other direction, the same theory of wages explains the salary of the modern hospice nurse, charged with accompanying people through their last days (a task as meaningful as one could imagine), yet whose yearly salary is a tiny fraction of the murderer's stipend. In neither case do the wages have any connection to the contributions being made; it simply has to do with how many people are capable of carrying out a task and how much demand there is for it.

It so happens that in our society, some wonderful qualities – consideration, sympathy and hard work – are fairly widespread. This is lovely, but also has a paradoxical consequence: that you can employ someone with astonishing qualities and get away with offering them very little.

The hitman may have made his money in appalling ways, but unless society asks very careful questions, the world will mostly just see his money and be impressed: they will admire his villa, his sports car, his attractive girlfriends. In time he may even emerge as a respected member of the community, who in his declining years wins hearts by funding a neonatal unit or new brain scanning department.

As for the nurse, however much we may pay lip service to the idea that she's very valuable, much of the time she will just be an anonymous figure in the bus queue; she will not be sought out, people visiting her tiny flat will be a touch sorry for her because the bathroom really needs some work, and her washing machine is held together by duct tape.

When these divergent fates are vivid in our minds – the fêted hitman and the downtrodden nurse – the whole economic system can seem unjust: our minds rebel against the gross violation of the principles of fairness. It's normal if we should then scan the horizon in the hope of finding some answers that can attenuate the pain.

In the history of the West, there have been two major intellectual attempts to resolve this impression of injustice.

The first is Christianity: a doctrine that has insisted that a person's worth has no relation to their financial standing. After death, a person's soul will be weighed by God, and his or her true merits perfectly rewarded for eternity. The kindness and devotion of the nurse would be celebrated by the angels. Wages can't change on earth, but the meaning of the wage will, in the eyes of Christianity, be altered, and the humiliation of poverty should hence lose its sting.

The other major attempt to introduce justice took place under the tranquil dome of the central reading room of the British Library in the mid-19th century, where a bearded man sat through long sultry summers and gelid winters penning a dense treatise on capital. Karl Marx (1818–1883) argued for a new world in which workers would for the first time be rewarded according to the worth of their contributions to society. Down would go the wages of the hitmen, casino owners and mining tycoons; up would go the wages of the nurse and the farmer. Communism would return justice to incomes.

In their own day, these seemed like very impressive solutions. Yet, for different reasons, they are not ideas we can put our hopes on now. The current economic order seems pretty firmly established and is not about to change any time soon. However, hopes remain for some way of dealing with the disjuncture between wages and contribution or wages and respect.

It may be an odd place to look, but the most immediately usable solution may lie in an unexpected place: the walls of an upper gallery in the Wallace Collection in London's Manchester Square, home to a small painting called *The Lace Maker* (1662), by the little-known German artist Caspar Netscher (1639–1684).

We've caught the lacemaker in what looks like a quiet mid-afternoon. She's concentrating on her difficult task, carefully threading her needle. It will take her around five hours to make just one square centimetre. Her eyes will tire. She will make something dazzling and moving, an externalisation of the best sides of her nature. And the reward for her exquisite craftsmanship was a few pennies at best.

Lacemaking was a major industry for women in the 17th and 18th centuries, but also one of the lowest paid, for a stubborn, unbudgeable reason we're now coming to understand: lots of people could do this work.

Interestingly, many artists were drawn to painting lacemakers at their task. These artists had no hopes of reforming how lacemakers were paid, but they had an ambition to change the lives of lacemakers nevertheless. They wanted to use art to alter the status of these craftswomen. By directing viewers to the intelligence and dignity of the craft of lacemaking, they hoped to redeem the social standing of this economically slighted class.

The artists painted lacemakers with all the tenderness and appreciation one might accord a wealthy patron. Through art, we were to stop seeing lacemakers as people who deserved to be ignored and whose low income was

TOP Caspar Netscher, *The Lace Maker*, 1662

BOTTOM Johannes Vermeer, *The Lacemaker*, 1669–1670

any kind of reflection of a lack of merit. Instead we would see them as people full of talent and humanity who were doing a low-wage job by the accident of the economic laws of supply and demand.

What the artists were doing with lacemakers reflects a general capacity of art: to redraw what we think of as prestigious and to return proper appreciation for what certain people, especially those deemed marginal by the dominant social hierarchy, are and do. Art offers us a sensitive reappraisal of a person's true merit – and a willingness to disregard wages as a guide to human value.

Sadly, for all the status we accord it, art is a small thing in the world. But the move that art has made needs to, and can, be redeployed on a much larger scale – not just for lacemakers, but for all those whose contribution is not properly reflected in their wages.

Art insists that we be suspicious of wages as an inviolable guide to the value of human beings. They are nothing of the sort, for they regularly leave out of the orbit of status people who eminently deserve our honour. We can live in hope of a fairer economy and must search for how to bring it about, but we should recognise that a realistic path to it is currently hard to chart. It is here that Netscher can offer us such powerful solace.

The way art operates promises an end to a sense of being randomly ignored and humiliated just on the basis of how much we earn. Art is a mechanism for appreciation, and is particularly adept at the close study of the ways in which an individual might deserve tenderness, sympathy and admiration – and yet neglected by the prestigious world.

Art suggests a remedy for at least a part of the problem of the gap between money and human value. The goal of art is to increase the amount of dense and accurate information about people's jobs, so we can stop using mere wages as our measuring rods. Once we get to know people well, in art or otherwise, the importance of the state of their bank balance will invariably decline, and what they are really bringing to the task starts to emerge, along with a fairer way of distributing honour.

III
On Being an Unemployed Arts Graduate

Arts graduates across the developed world complain bitterly about the difficulties they face in finding employment. They spend long and costly years studying such subjects as history, art, philosophy, poetry and drama; then they reach the jobs market and discover that no one has any use for their distinctive skills and interests. If they're extremely lucky, they may find some kind of job, but it will almost certainly have no connection with what they studied or pay very much. A great number end up making coffee while deeply resenting – against the backdrop of frothing milk and roasting beans – how their years studying Foucault or Herodotus seem to have gone nowhere.

It is tempting to dismiss such moans: if someone wants to spend their time finding out about post-colonial theory, reading South American novels or deconstructing vampire films, then that's very nice – as a hobby. But it's harder to see why anyone should expect to get paid for doing so. You don't get paid for going to the cinema or attending parties either.

But in truth, the extraordinary rate of unemployment – or misemployment – of graduates in the humanities is a sign of something grievously wrong with modern societies and their university systems. It's evidence that we have no real clue what the humanities, including culture and art, are really for. We pay them a certain amount of lip service; we like to declare them worthy and noble and fund a few professors to dig away in their archives; but basically, as societies, we don't know what the humanities could do for us and, therefore, how people trained in them should spend their days other than in preparing frappuccinos.

The problem lies squarely with universities. If you ask these universities why young people should bother to study history or literature, they can't give a straight answer. Fearing that they cannot compete effectively against practical departments like physics or computer science, humanities faculties take refuge in ambiguity and silence, having calculated that they retain just enough prestige to get away with leaving the reasons for their existence somewhat murky. Instead, they make their students perform a range of deeply arcane manoeuvres. For example, a BA in philosophy at the University of Oxford currently requires you to achieve familiarity with metaphysics (substance, individuation, universals) and to do a thesis on concepts of intentionality in Quine, Frege or Putnam. An equivalent degree in English literature is awarded to those who can successfully tackle *The Waste Land* on allegorical and anagogic levels and trace the influence of Seneca's dramatic theories on the development of Jacobean theatre.

This represents a gross neglect of what the humanities are really for: they are for helping us to live and to die. The humanities are the closest things we have to a replacement for religion. They are a storehouse of vitally important knowledge about how to lead our lives: novels teach us about relationships, works of art reframe our perspectives, drama provides us with cathartic experiences, history is a catalogue of case studies into any number of personal and political scenarios. Like the religions of old, culture is there to have a therapeutic effect on us, which is why it matters so much in a troubled world.

But in order to bring out this therapeutic effect, we need to reinvent universities. Departments like 'history' and 'literature' operate under superficial categories that don't throw the spotlight on the important aspects of the material they are dealing with. So in the redesigned universities of the future, there would be a Department for Relationships, an Institute of Dying and a Centre for Self-Knowledge. There would be centres of expertise on changing jobs and improving bonds with children, reconnecting with nature and facing illness.

One would still study novels, histories, plays, psychoanalysis and paintings, but one would do so for explicitly therapeutic ends. So *Anna Karenina* and *Madame Bovary* would be assigned in a course on 'How to manage the tensions of marriage' instead of belonging in a course on 'Trends in 19th-century fiction', just as the works of Epicurus and Seneca would appear in a course on 'How to die' rather than in one on 'Hellenistic philosophy'.

One would witness a surge in demand from the population at large for the services of people trained in culture in this new way – given that no one currently knows how to run a relationship, everyone is confused about bringing up kids, few of us have a clue how to manage our anxieties and death is universally terrifying.

The unemployment of arts graduates is shameful and unnecessary, because culture has answers and highly useful consolations to the urgent dilemmas of real people. We just need to get these insights out, package them properly, and commercialise them adequately, so that the armies of people currently serving coffee can put their minds to proper use.

We aren't creatures who need only practical things like food and drink, cement and running shoes. We also desperately crave nourishment for what we might as well, with no superficial associations, call our souls. This soul-related work should become a huge and legitimate part of the world economy, worth as many billions as the cement trade.

The sooner we clarify what culture is for, and learn how to use it as intended by its creators, the sooner we will start to view arts graduates as being no less useful than their colleagues in computer science or accountancy – and the sooner they'll have other options beyond the coffee counter.

IV
Good Materialism

It doesn't seem to make sense to suggest that there might be such a thing as 'good materialism': after all, surely materialism is just plain bad? When people want to pinpoint the root cause of corruption in our age, they generally only need to point the finger at our attachment to material things. We're apparently sick because we're so materialistic.

It can seem as if we're faced with a stark choice. *Either* you can be materialistic: obsessed with money and possessions, shallow and selfish. *Or*, you can reject materialism, be good and focus on more important matters of the spirit.

But most of us are, in our hearts, stuck somewhere between these two choices, which is uncomfortable. We are still enmeshed in the desire to possess – but we are encouraged to feel rather bad about it.

Yet, crucially, it's not actually materialism – the pure fact of buying things and getting excited by possessions – that's ever really the problem. We're failing to make a clear distinction between *good* and *bad* versions of materialism.

Let's try to understand good materialism through a slightly unusual route: religion. Because we see them as focused exclusively on spiritual things, it can be surprising to note how much use religions have made of material things. They have spent a lot of time making, and thinking about shrines, temples, monasteries, artworks, scrolls to hang in houses, clothes and ceremonies.

However, they have cared about these things for one reason only – because they have wanted material things to serve the highest and noblest purpose: the development of our souls. It is just that they have recognised that we are incarnate sensory bodily beings – and that the way to get through to our souls has to be, at least in part, through our bodies (rather than merely through the intellect).

The importance of material things was, for centuries, at the core of Christianity, which proposed that Jesus was both the highest spiritual being, *and* a flesh-and-blood person: he was the spirit incarnate, holiness em*bodied*.

In the Catholic Mass, great significance is accorded to bread and wine, which are believed to be transubstantiations of Christ: that is, material objects which simultaneously have a spiritual identity, just as Jesus himself combined the spiritual and the bodily while on earth.

This can sound like a very weird and arcane point entirely removed from the local shopping mall – but exactly the same concept actually applies outside of religions. Many good material possessions can be said to involve a kind of 'transubstantiation', whereby they are both practical and physical and also embody or allude to a positive personality or spirit.

One can imagine a handsome wooden chair that 'transubstantiates' a set of important values: straightforwardness, strength, honesty and elegance. By getting closer to the chair, we could become a little more like it, which is an important piece of inner evolution.

Material objects can therefore be said to play a positive psychological (or spiritual) role in our lives when higher more positive ideals are 'materialised' in them, and so when buying and using them daily gives us a chance to get closer to our better selves. When they are contained in physical things, valuable psychological qualities that are otherwise often intermittent in our thoughts and conduct can become more stable and resilient.

This is not to say that all consumerism just conveniently turns out to be great. It depends on what a given material object stands for. An object can transubstantiate the very worst sides of human nature – greed, callousness, the desire to triumph – as much as it can the best. So we must be careful not to decry or celebrate all material consumption: we have to ensure that the objects we invest in, and tire ourselves and the planet by making, are those that lend most encouragement to our higher, better natures.

V

Why We Are So Bad at Shopping

It sounds very strange to suggest that we might need to learn how to shop. We know we have to learn how to *make* money, but spending it is overwhelmingly understood to be the straightforward bit. The only conceivable problem is not having enough to spend.

Yet, when we're out to buy a present for someone else, we can often see that we don't quite know what would really please them. We wisely acknowledge that shopping for others is hugely tricky, but we don't extend the same generous – and ultimately productive – recognition to shopping for ourselves.

A host of obstacles frequently prevents us from deploying our capital as accurately and fruitfully as we should – a serious matter, given just how much of our lives we sacrifice in the name of making money in the first place.

For a start, far more than we normally recognise, we're guided by group instincts – which can tug us far from our own native inclinations. A major defence of capitalism has been the impressive notion that it provides us with unrivalled consumer choice and it can indeed seem as if the system actively caters to every possible nuance of taste. Yet, while seeming to provide for an apparently inexhaustible individuality, surprisingly standardised consumer patterns in fact dominate the economy.

Day-to-day, it feels like we are wholly in charge of our consumer decisions – but when we look back in history, we can see how strangely impersonal shopping choices really are. Our desires may feel intensely our own, yet they seem social creations first and foremost.

How else to explain why in the 1950s, so many people arrived – apparently by their own free will – at the feeling that orange was a properly appropriate colour for a sofa? Or why in the 1960s, many otherwise very sober people spontaneously (yet simultaneously) discovered they were keen on tail fins on their cars? Or why in the 1970s, almost everyone in the world was struck by the urge to buy shirts with very large collars?

The choices may well have suited many, but it is impossible not to believe that at least a few of those who shopped woke up from the age of wide shirt collars or orange sofas with a puzzled sense that they had been induced to want things which had precious little to do with who they were.

Yet at the same time, the fear of being thought strange prevents us from taking less socially endorsed desires more seriously. We might, in our hearts, love to wear a pair of Wallabee shoes.

And we might – if left entirely to our own devices – not want to follow every customary detail in the script of how to arrange a holiday, celebrate a child's birthday or prepare a dinner party, but we may be as shy here as we are with certain of our sexual desires. We are taught to think of ourselves as highly focused on our own pleasures, but most of our trouble stems from a quite opposite problem: just how tentative we are about taking our own feelings at all seriously.

It seems we are so much more distinctive than consumer society allows. It isn't – as certain political fantasies suppose – that our tastes are, in reality, truly simple, more that they are hugely varied and anomalous. We might be deep into middle age before we finally abandon the dominant story of what we're meant to wear, eat, admire or ignore.

Part of the problem is that we lack the ability to know, looking back over experiences, what truly brought us pleasure. Our brains aren't so keen on taking apart their satisfactions – and therefore plotting how to recreate them. If one asks a 7-year-old why they like a favourite TV programme, they will most likely find the question irritating. They just like it overall, they say. The idea of going into detail and realising that they find the relationship between the main character and their dog inspiring but the urban setting less appealing is alien. We're not natural critical dissectors of our own experience. It takes a long, arduous process of training before someone becomes an incisive literary critic or gets good at analysing their own reactions to a work of art. These moves force the mind to do an unnatural thing. And so, correspondingly, it feels strange and difficult to comb through the details of a holiday or a party or a relationship with a jacket or computer in a rigorous search for the pleasurable or painful elements which should ideally guide our expenditure going forward.

Our problems are compounded by the way that reviews are organised. A lot of cultural attention is paid to the business of choosing – with one curious and significant limitation. It's assumed we're accurate in wanting to invest in a particular class of product, we just need help in choosing its best example. Reviews don't question the overall aptness of looking to get a phone, a car or a hotel at the beach in southern Spain, they simply guide us to the best among these options. So the position of a single choice within an overall picture of a life falls outside their scope; the more complex trade-offs or opportunity costs aren't considered. Despite the plethora of reviews, we lack organised, prestigious support for the existential decisions that sit above any single consumer commitment. No wonder we get muddled.

Finally, though the things we buy might truly be lovely, our pleasure is hugely vulnerable to our inner emotional climate. All the advantages of a resort hotel can be destroyed by an argument. Loneliness destroys the charm of any of the clothes we might buy. And yet, somehow, the idea of our dependence on emotional factors that lie outside the purchase remains curiously elusive whenever we are at the till.

None of this means that we shouldn't shop, or expend so much energy on our consumption. Quite the opposite. It isn't that we are too focused on shopping, we are not thinking deeply enough about what we're doing. We haven't yet learnt to be doggedly precise enough about pinning down our own fun and making sure we get it.

VI
Using Sex to Sell

We're used to the idea of sex being used to sell stuff. It happens all the time, usually around cars, or perfumes. Or even less substantial things like ice creams. It's a sad state of affairs.

Making use of another human being's sexuality to generate an enthusiasm for consumer products seems a pretty depressing manoeuvre – demeaning as much to buyers as it is to producers. But before we despair of our shallowness, let's go back a few centuries to consider the educational theories of one of the greatest Renaissance Italian philosophers, Marsilio Ficino (1433–1499).

Ficino was unfazed by our tendencies to be interested in sex. This was, he thought, simply an inevitable consequence of our bodily nature, which dictates that our initial interest in things will almost invariably spring from our sexual and sensory faculties.

The reason Ficino was undisturbed by this is that this wasn't, in his eyes, the end of the story. Though our interest in things may well begin at the sexual level, this is merely the starting point: the destiny of our interests is to move on to a stage of higher engagement that Ficino called 'love'. And from there, we may ascend to a third stage: the longing and capacity to understand.

So our interests are naturally inclined, if well tended, to follow a path from sex to love to intellectual engagement – and this holds true for an interest in people, in virtues and even in abstract ideas.

Ficino was above all else an educator. That is, he thought profoundly about how people learn and how one can best teach people.

TOP Filippo Lippi, *Madonna and Child with Two Angels*, 1465

BOTTOM Titian, *Sacred and Profane Love*, 1514

He concluded that the best way to get an idea into someone's mind is not to try at once coldly to engage their reason – it is first to reach them via their senses and in particular via their interest in sex.

Ficino was employed by the great Renaissance patron and statesman Lorenzo de Medici (1449–1492): both were desperate to educate as many people as possible in Florence to be wise and good, using the lessons of antiquity and Christianity. And they wanted to use art to do this, launching what was in effect a giant ad campaign for the highest goals.

Ficino's ideas lent this educational programme a unique angle. Ficino proposed that the artists Lorenzo was employing should devote themselves to painting successions of beautiful, or plain sexy people.

We may have often been struck by how many attractive people there are in Renaissance art: this is no coincidence. It's a deliberate consequence of Ficino's educational theories. Artists – guided by the philosopher – were commissioned to use sex to sell: but sell the highest things, like piety, virtue and modesty, commitment to the intellect and devotion to scholarship.

It's a manoeuvre we've come to forget in our own times. We still use sex, but only ever to sell the lowest things, so when it comes to the highest things, we deem them above the grubby task of being sold – and therefore, they languish.

With Ficino's lessons in mind, we should be more strategic. We should recognise that there's nothing wrong with using sex to sell: so long as what we are selling happens to be noble. Indeed, selling higher things with sex is a generous act that graciously acknowledges how our minds really work. We cannot or should not be expected to learn without our senses first having been lit up.

We just have to make sure we're selling the right things, not cars or confectionery. But perhaps things like a book devoted to wisdom and philosophy. Ficino would have approved.

Sandro Botticelli, *Madonna del Magnificat (Madonna of the Magnificat)*, 1484–1485

How to Reform Capitalism

I
The *Nautilus* and Capitalism

Science fiction is one of the most popular but at the same time one of the least prestigious of the literary arts, frequently dismissed as a sub-genre consumed primarily by young males obsessed by the goriest or oddest possibilities for the future of our species.

Yet science fiction is a much-underestimated tool in business; in its utopian (as opposed to dystopian) versions, it invites us to explore imaginatively what we might want the future to be like – a little ahead of our practical abilities to mould it as we would wish.

Science fiction may not contain precise answers (how actually to make a jetpack or a robot that loves us) but it encourages us in something that is logically prior to, and in its own way as important as, technological mastery: the identification of issues we would like to see solved. Changes in society and business seldom begin with actual inventions; they begin with acts of the imagination, with a sharpened sense of a need for something new, be this for an engine, a piece of legislation or a social movement. The details of change may eventually get worked out in laboratories, committee rooms and parliaments, but the crystallisation of the wish for change takes place at a prior stage, in the imaginations of people who know how to envisage what doesn't yet exist.

In his novel *Twenty Thousand Leagues Under the Sea*, published in Paris in 1870, Jules Verne (1828–1905) narrated the adventures of the *Nautilus*, a large submarine that tours the world's oceans often at great depth (the 20,000 leagues – about 80,000 kilometres – refer to the distance travelled). When writing the story, Verne didn't worry too much about solving every technical

Alphonse de Neuville and Edouard Riou, illustrations for Jules Verne's *Twenty Thousand Leagues Under the Sea*, 1871
'Wouldn't glass shatter at that pressure?'
Keeping certain questions at bay for long enough to shape a vision.

issue involved with undersea exploration: he was intent on pinning down capacities he felt it would one day be important to have. He described the *Nautilus* as being equipped with a huge window even though he had no idea how to make glass that could withstand immense barometric pressures. He imagined the vessel having a machine that could make seawater potable, although the science behind desalination was extremely primitive at the time. And he described the *Nautilus* as being powered by batteries – even though this technology was in its infancy.

Jules Verne was not an enemy of technology. He was deeply fascinated by practical problems. But in writing his novels, he held off from worrying too much about the 'how' questions. He wanted to picture the way things could be, while warding off – for a time – the many practical objections that would one day have to be addressed. He was thereby able to bring the idea of the submarine into the minds of millions while the technology slowly emerged that would allow the reality to take hold.

The key mental move in science fiction – 'What would we want life to be like one day?' – has traditionally been focused on technology. However, there is no reason why we would not perform equally dramatic thought experiments in other fields, in relation to family life, relationships and, as we're about to do here, capitalism.

Asking oneself what a better version of something might be like, without direct tools for a fix to hand, can feel immature and naive. Yet it's by formulating visions of the future that we can more clearly start to define what might be wrong with what we have – and set the wheels of change in motion. Through science fiction experiments, we can get into the habit of counteracting detrimental tendencies to inhibit our thinking around wished-for scenarios that seem (in gloomy present moments at least) deeply unlikely. Such experiments are often hugely relevant, because when we look back in history we can see that so many machines, projects and ways of life

TOP Captain Kirk with communicator from *Star Trek*, 1967

BOTTOM Communicator from *Star Trek*, 1967
Sometimes ideas drafted in science fiction pave the way for real-life developments.

that once appeared simply utopian have come to pass. Not least Captain Kirk's phone.

We all have a science fiction side to our brains, which we are normally careful to disguise for fear of humiliation. Yet, as Verne showed us, our visions are what carve out the space in which later developments can occur.

What follows is an attempt to work out aspects of a wiser future for capitalism.

II
Artists and Supermarket Tycoons

The Shanghai-based artist Xu Zhen (b. 1977) is one of the most celebrated Chinese artists of our age. He operates in a variety of media, including video, sculpture and fine art. His work displays a deep interest in business; he appears at once charmed and horrified by commercial life. In recent years, he has become especially fascinated by supermarkets. He's interested, in part, in how lovely they can be.

Xu Zhen loves the alluring packaging, the abundance (the feel of lifting something off a shelf and seeing multiple versions of it waiting just behind) and the exquisite precision with which items are displayed. He particularly likes the claim of comprehensiveness that supermarkets implicitly make: the suggestion that they can, within their cavernous interiors, provide us with everything we could possibly need to thrive.

At the same time, Xu Zhen feels that there is something quite wrong with real supermarkets – and with commercial life in general. The products sold are rarely the things we genuinely need. Despite the enormous choice, what we require to thrive isn't on offer. Meanwhile, the backstories of the brightly coloured things on sale are often exploitative and dark. Everything has been carefully calculated to get us to spend more than we mean to. There's cynicism throughout the system.

In response, the Chinese artist mocks supermarkets repeatedly. His work involves recreating, at very large scale, entire supermarkets in galleries and museums. The products in these supermarkets look real; you're invited to pick them up, but then you find out they are empty, as physically empty as Xu Zhen feels they are spiritually incomplete. His checkouts are similarly

Xu Zhen, *ShanghArt Supermarket*
[Installation], 2007/2014

deceptive. They seem genuine: you scan your products at a high-tech counter, but you then get a receipt that turns out to be a fake; you've bought nothing of value.

The supermarket installation takes us on a journey. At first it gets us to share the artist's excitement around supermarkets, then it punctures the illusion: it's a giant, deliberate letdown. It's significant that Xu Zhen's critique of supermarkets is ironic. We tend to become ironic around things that we feel disappointed by but don't feel we'll ever be able to change. It's a manoeuvre of disappointment stoically handled.

A lot of art is ironic in its critiques of capitalism; we've come to expect this. It mocks all that is wrong but has no alternatives to put forward. A kind of hollow, sad laughter seems the only fitting response to the compromises of commercial life.

Xu Zhen is trapped in the paradigm of what an artist does. A real artist, we have come to suppose – and the current ideology of the art world insists – couldn't be enthusiastic about improving a supermarket. He or she could only mock from the sidelines. Nowadays, fortunately, we've loosened the restrictive definitions of what a 'real' man or a 'real' woman might be like, but there remain strict social taboos hemming in the idea of what a 'real' artist could be allowed to get up to. They can be as experimental and surprising as they like – unless they want to run a food shop or an airline or an energy corporation, at which point they cross a decisive boundary, fall from grace, lose their special status as artists and become the supposed polar opposites: mere business people.

We should take Xu Zhen seriously, perhaps more seriously than he takes himself. Beneath the irony, Xu Zhen has the ambition to discover what an ideal supermarket might be like, how it might be a successful business, and how capitalism could be reformed. Somewhere within his project, he carries a hope: that a corporation like a supermarket could be brought into line with the best values of art and assume psychological and spiritual importance inside the framework of commerce.

Thousands of miles away from Shanghai, in the flatlands of East Anglia in the northeastern tip of southern England, just outside of Norwich, lies an impressive modern building completed in 1978 by the architect Norman Foster. The Sainsbury Centre for Visual Arts is filled with some of the greatest works of contemporary art: here we find masterpieces by Henry Moore, Giacometti and Francis Bacon.

The collection is made possible thanks to the enormous wealth of the Sainsbury family, which owns and runs the large supermarket chain that bears its name. Discounted shoulders of lamb, white bread and 3-for-2 offers on tangerines have led to exquisite display cases containing Giacometti's elongated, haunting figures and Barbara Hepworth's hollowed-out ovaloids.

The gallery seems guided by values that are light years from any supermarket. It is intent on feeding the soul. The patrons and curators are deeply ambitious about the emotional and educational benefit of the experience: they want you to come out cleansed and improved.

From a very different direction, the Sainsbury family arrive at a strikingly similar conclusion to Xu Zhen. Art and supermarkets are essentially opposed. Like Xu Zhen, the Sainsburys are caught in an identity trap, although a very different one: that of the philanthropist. The philanthropist has been imagined as a person who makes a lot of money in the brutish world of commerce, with all the normal expectations of maximising returns, squeezing wages and focusing on obvious opportunities – and then makes a clean break. In their spare hours, they can devote their wealth to projects that are profoundly non-commercial: the patient collection of Roman coins, Islamic vases or modern sculptures. But the philanthropist knows that if they ever took an art-loving attitude to their businesses, they might suffer economic collapse. Instead of making big things happen in the real world, they would

The interior of the Sainsbury Centre for Visual Arts, Norwich.

become mere artists who make interesting little things in the sheltered, subsidised world of the gallery.

The situation is strangely tantalising. The artist finds a little that is loveable and much that's wrong around supermarkets, but can't imagine running or bringing the ideals of art into action in one. The supermarket owners love art, but can't imagine bringing their psychologically and aesthetically ambitious sides into focus in their business. These two parties are both like pioneers, at the edges of unexplored territory. There is a huge idea they are both circling round. The goal is a synthesis of business and art: a supermarket that was truly guided by the ideals of art, a capitalism that could be compatible with the higher values of humanity.

Up to now, we have collectively learned to admire the values of the arts (which can be summed up as a devotion to truth, beauty and goodness) in the special arena of galleries. But their more important application is in the general, daily fabric of our lives – the area that is currently dominated by an often-depleted vision of commerce. It is a tragic polarisation: we encounter the values we need, but only in a rarefied setting, while we regard these values as alien to the circumstances in which we most need to meet them. For most of history, artists have laboured to render a few square inches of canvas utterly perfect or to chisel a single block of stone into its most expressive form. Traditionally, the most common size for a work of art was between three and six feet across. And while artists have articulated their visions across such expanses, the large-scale projects have been given over wholesale to businesses and governments – who have generally operated with much lower ambitions. We're so familiar with this polarisation, we regard it as if it were an inevitable fact of nature, rather than what it really is – a cultural and commercial failing.

Ideally, artists should absorb the best qualities of business and vice versa. Rather than seeing such qualities as opposed to what they stand for as artists or business people, they should see these as great enabling capacities, which help them fulfil their missions to the world. Xu Zhen will probably never get to build an airport, a marina, an old people's home or a supermarket, but the ideal next version of him will. We should want to simultaneously raise and combine the ambitions of artists (to make the noblest concepts powerful in our lives) and of business (to serve us successfully).

III
The Birth of Consumer Society

For most of history, the overwhelming majority of the world's inhabitants have owned more or less nothing: the clothes they stood up in, some bowls, a pot and a pan, perhaps a broom and, if things were going well, a few farming implements. Nations and peoples remained consistently poor: global GDP did not grow at all from year to year. Most of the world was as hard up in 1800 as it had been at the beginning of time. But then, starting in the early 18th century, in the countries of north western Europe, a remarkable phenomenon occurred: economies began to expand and wages to rise. Families who had never before had any money beyond what they needed to survive found they could go shopping for small luxuries: a comb or a mirror, a spare set of underwear, a pillow, some thicker boots or a towel. Their expenditure created a virtuous economic circle: the more they spent, the more businesses grew, and the more wages rose.

By the mid-18th century, observers recognised that they were living through a period of epochal change that historians have since described as the world's first 'consumer revolution'. In Britain, where the changes were most marked, enormous new industries sprang up to cater for the widespread demand for goods that had once been the preserve of the very rich. In England's cities, you could buy furniture from Chippendale, Hepplewhite and Sheraton; pottery from Wedgwood and Derby; cutlery from the smitheries of Sheffield; and hats, shoes and dresses featured in bestselling magazines like *The Gallery of Fashion* and *The Lady's Magazine*. Styles for clothes and hair, which had formerly gone unchanged for decades, now altered every year – often in extremely theatrical and impractical directions. In the early 1770s, there was a craze for decorated wigs so tall their tops could only be accessed by standing on a chair. It was fun for the cartoonists. So vivid and numerous were the consumer novelties that the austere Samuel Johnson (1709–1784), often referred to as Dr Johnson, wryly wondered whether prisoners were also soon 'to be hanged in a new way'.

The Christian church looked on and did not approve. Up and down England, clergymen delivered bitter sermons against the new materialism. Sons and daughters were to be kept away from shops; God would not look kindly on those who paid more attention to household decoration than to the state of their souls.

Along with the consumer revolution, there also emerged an intellectual revolution that sharply altered the understanding of the role of 'vanities' in an economy. In 1723, a London physician called Bernard Mandeville (1670–1733) published an economic tract (unusually but charmingly written in verse) titled *The Fable of the Bees*. This proposed that – contrary to centuries of religious and moral thinking – what made countries rich (and therefore safe, honest, generous-spirited and strong) was a very minor, un-elevated and apparently undignified activity: shopping for pleasure. It was the consumption of what Mandeville called 'fripperies' – hats, bonnets, gloves, butter dishes, soup tureens, shoehorns and hairclips – that provided the engine for national prosperity and allowed the government to do in practice what the Church only knew how to sermonise about in theory: make a genuine difference to the lives of the weak and the poor. The only way to generate wealth, argued Mandeville, was to ensure high demand for absurd and unnecessary things. Of course, no one needed embroidered handbags, silk-lined slippers or ice creams, but it was a blessing that they could be prompted by fashion to want them, for on the back of demand for such trifles, workshops could be built, apprentices trained and hospitals funded.

Matthew Darly, *The Extravaganza, or, The Mountain Head Dress of 1776*, 1776
The motor of a sound economy: fripperies such as extraordinary wigs.

Rather than condemn recreational expenditures as Christian moralists had done, Mandeville celebrated them for their consequences. As Mandeville's subtitle put it, it was a case of: 'Private Vices, Public Benefits'. 'It is the sensual courtier who sets no limit to his luxury, the fickle strumpet who invents new fashions every week and the profuse rake and the lavish heir who most effectively help the poor,' he wrote. 'He that gives most trouble to thousands of his neighbours and invents the most operose manufactures is, right or wrong, the greatest friend to society. Mercers, upholsterers, tailors and many others would be starved in half a year's time if pride and luxury were at once to be banished from the nation'. Mandeville shocked his audience with the starkness of the choice he placed before them. A nation could either be very high-minded, spiritually elevated, intellectually refined and dirt poor, or a slave to luxury and idle consumption, and very rich.

Mandeville's dark thesis went on to convince almost all the great Anglophone economists and political thinkers of the 18th century. In his essay *Of Luxury* (1752), the philosopher David Hume (1711–1776) repeated Mandeville's defence of an economy built on making and selling unnecessary things: 'In a nation, where there is no demand for superfluities, men sink into indolence, lose all enjoyment of life, and are useless to the public, which cannot maintain or support its fleets and armies'. The 'superfluities' were clearly silly, Hume was in no doubt, but they paved the way for something very important and grand: military and welfare spending.

There were some departures from the new economic orthodoxy. One of the most spirited and impassioned voices was that of Switzerland's greatest philosopher, Jean-Jacques Rousseau (1712–1778). Shocked by the impact of the consumer revolution on the manners and atmosphere of his native Geneva, Rousseau called for a return to a simpler, older way of life of the sort he had experienced in Alpine villages or read about in travellers' accounts of the native tribes of North America. In the remote corners of Appenzell or the vast forests of Missouri, there was, blessedly, no concern for fashion and no one-upmanship around hair extensions.

Rousseau recommended closing Geneva's borders and imposing crippling taxes on luxury goods so that people's energies could be redirected towards non-material values. He looked back with fondness to the austere martial spirit of Sparta and complained, partly with Mandeville and Hume in mind: 'Ancient treatises of politics continually made mention of morals and virtue; ours speak of nothing but commerce and money.' However, even if Rousseau disagreed with Hume and Mandeville, he did not seek to deny the basic premise behind their analyses: it truly appeared to be a choice between decadent consumption and wealth on the one hand, and virtuous restraint and poverty on the other. It was simply that Rousseau, unusually, preferred virtue to wealth.

The parameters of this debate have continued to dominate economic thinking ever since. We re-encounter them in ideological arguments between capitalists and communists and free marketeers and environmentalists. But for most of us, the debate is no longer pertinent. We simply accept that we will live in consumer economies with some very unfortunate side effects (crass advertising, unhealthy foodstuffs, products that are disconnected from any reasonable assessment of our needs) in exchange for economic growth and high employment. We have chosen wealth over virtue.

An irony-laden acceptance of this dichotomy is what underpinned the approach of many Pop artists of mid-20th-century America. Claes Oldenburg (1929–2022) developed a reputation for taking modest consumer items, many of them food related, and reproducing them as large-scale soft vinyl forms. In galleries typically devoted to high art where one would have expected to find oil paintings and marble sculptures, one now came across an outsized hamburger, a giant slab of cake or a huge plate of fries decked with ketchup. In the mid-70s, Oldenburg began a long and productive

Claes Oldenburg and Coosje van Bruggen, *Dropped Cone*, 2001

partnership with Dutch/American writer and art historian Coosje van Bruggen (1942–2009). They too worked on a grand scale – installing huge steel-and-aluminium outdoor sculptures in university grounds, plazas and parks. One of their most famous collaborations continued the fascination with fast food – a twelve-metre-high stainless-steel ice cream cone, upturned on a shopping mall on the corner of the busy Neumarkt Square in Cologne, a city whose skyline is filled with conical church spires.

Oldenburg's vast versions of small things playfully direct our attention to the peculiar dependence of modern economies on the mass consumption of what are, in human terms, some deeply negligible products. Yet the scale of Oldenburg's works is only superficially absurd, for it rather precisely reflects their central importance in our collective economic destinies. Nevertheless, as Oldenburg seemed to concede, it was peculiar to be living in a civilization founded on the back of buns and sweetened tomato paste – a bathos hinted at by the deflated, detumescent appearance of the giant comestibles that feature throughout his work.

The one question that has rarely been asked is whether there might be a way to attenuate the dispiriting choice, to draw on the best aspects of consumerism on the one hand and high-mindedness on the other without suffering their worst sides – moral decadence and profound poverty. Might it be possible for a society to develop that allows for consumer spending (and therefore provides employment and welfare), yet of a kind directed at something other than 'vanities' and 'superfluities'? Might we shop for something other than nonsense? In other words, might we have wealth and (a degree of) virtue?

It is this possibility of which we find some intriguing hints in the work of Adam Smith (1723–1790), an economist too often read as a blunt apologist for all aspects of consumer society, but in fact one of its more subtle and visionary analysts. In his book *The Wealth of Nations* (1776), Smith

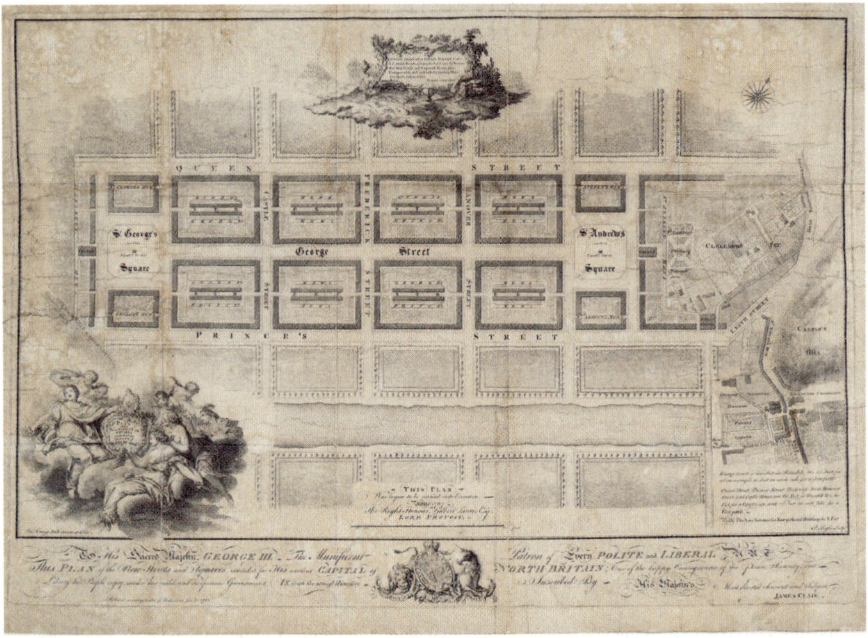

James Craig, *Plan for Edinburgh New Town*, 1768
A promise of noble consumption.

seems at points willing to concede to key aspects of Mandeville's argument: consumer societies do help the poor by providing employment based around satisfying what are often rather suboptimal purchases. Smith was as ready as other Anglophone economists to mock the triviality of some consumer choices, while admiring their consequences. All those embroidered lace handkerchiefs, jewelled snuff-boxes and miniature temples made of cream for dessert were flippant, he conceded, but they encouraged trade, created employment and generated immense wealth – and could be defended on this score.

However, Smith held out some fascinating hopes for the future. He pointed out that consumption did not invariably have to involve the trading of frivolous things. He had seen the expansion of the Edinburgh book trade and knew how large a market higher education might become. He understood how much wealth was being accumulated through the construction of Edinburgh's extremely handsome and noble New Town. He understood that humans have many 'higher' needs that require a lot of labour, intelligence and work to fulfil, but that lie outside of capitalist enterprise as conceived of by 'realists' such as Hume or Mandeville: among these, our need for education, for self-understanding, for beautiful cities and for rewarding social lives. The ultimate goal of capitalism was to tackle 'happiness' in all its complexities, psychological as opposed to merely material.

The capitalism of our times still has not entirely managed to resolve the awkward choices that Mandeville and Rousseau circled. But the crucial hope for the future is that we may not forever need to be making money off exploitative or vain consumer appetite; we may also learn to generate sizeable profits from helping people – as consumers and producers – in the truly important and ambitious aspects of their lives. The reform of capitalism hinges on an odd-sounding, but critical task: a conception of an economy focused around higher needs.

IV
Higher Needs, a Pyramid and Capitalism

The idea that capitalism can give us what we need has always been central to its defence. More efficiently than any other system, capitalism has, in theory, been able to identify what we're lacking and deliver it to us with unparalleled efficiency. Capitalism is the most skilled machine we have ever constructed for satiating human needs.

Because businesses have been so extraordinarily productive over the last 200 years, it has become easy to think – in the wealthier parts of the world, at least – that consumer capitalism must by now have reached a stage of exhausted stagnant maturity, which may explain both relatively high rates of unemployment and low levels of growth. The heroic period of development, driven in part by breakthroughs in technology, that equipped a mass public in the advanced nations with the basics of food, shelter, hygiene and entertainment, appears to have been brought up against some natural limits. We seem to be in the strange position of having too much of everything: shoes, dishcloths, televisions, chocolates, woollen hats... In the eyes of some, it is normal that we should have arrived at this end-point. The planet and its resources are limited, so we should not expect growth to be unlimited. Flat-lining reflects the attainment of an enviable degree of maturity. We are ceasing to buy quite so much for an understandable reason: we have all we need.

Yet, despite its evident successes, consumer capitalism cannot realistically be credited with having fulfilled a mission of accurately satiating our needs, because of one evident failing: we aren't happy. Indeed, most of us are, a good deal of the time, properly at sea: burdened by complaints, unfulfilled hopes, barely formulated longings, restlessness, anger and grief –

little of which our plethora of shops and services appear remotely equipped to address. Given the range of our outstanding needs and capitalism's theoretical commitment to fulfilling them, it would be profoundly paradoxical to count the economy as in any way mature and beyond expansion. Far from it; it is arguably a good deal too small and desperately undeveloped in relation to what we would truly want from it, once we reflect on the full extent of our sorrows and appetites. Despite all the factories, the concrete, the highways and the logistics chains, consumer capitalism has – arguably – not even properly started on its tasks. A good future may depend not on minimising consumer capitalism but on radically extending its reach and depth, via a slightly unfamiliar route: a close study of our unattended needs.

If a proverbial Martian were to attempt to guess what human beings required in order to be satisfied by scanning lists of the top corporations in the leading wealthy countries, they would guess that *Homo sapiens* had immense requirements for food, warmth, shelter, credit, insurance, missiles, packets of data, strips of cotton or wool to wrap around their limbs and, of course, a lot of ketchup. This, the world's bourses seem to tell us, is what human satisfaction is made up of.

But the reality is more complicated. The most concise yet penetrating picture of human needs ever drawn up was the work of the American psychologist Abraham Maslow (1908–1970). In a paper titled 'A Theory of Human Motivation' published in *Psychological Review* in 1943, Maslow arranged our longings and appetites on a pyramid-shaped continuum, ranging from what he called the lower needs, largely focused on the body, to the higher needs, largely focused on the psyche, and encompassing such elements as the need for status, recognition and friendship. At the apex stood the need for a complete development of our potential of a kind Maslow had seen in the lives of the cultural figures he most admired: Montaigne, Voltaire, Goethe, Tolstoy and Freud.

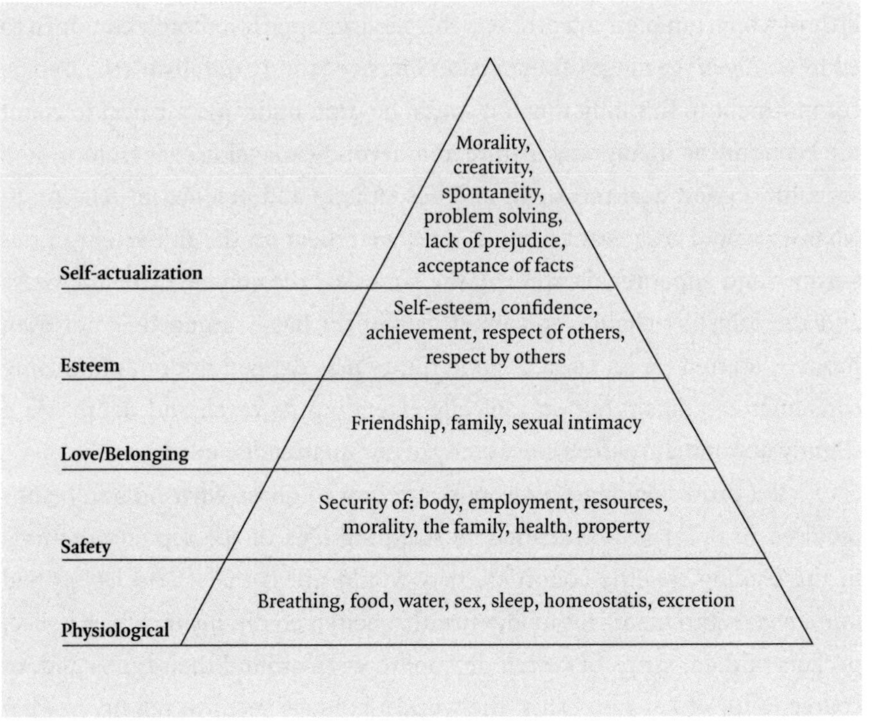

The pyramid of our needs according to American psychologist Abraham Maslow.

If we were to align the world's largest corporations with the pyramid, we would find that the needs to which they cater are overwhelmingly those at the bottom of the pyramid. Our most successful businesses are those that aim to satisfy our physical and simpler psychological selves: they operate in oil and gas, mining, construction, agriculture, pharmaceuticals, electronics, telecommunications, insurance, banking and light entertainment.

What is surprising is how unambitious consumer capitalism has, until now, been about many of the things that deliver higher sorts of satisfaction. Business has helped us to be warm, safe and distracted. It has been markedly indifferent to our flourishing.

This is the task ahead of us. The true destiny of, and millennial opportunity for, consumer capitalism, is to travel up the pyramid, to generate ever more of its profits from the satisfaction of the full range of 'higher needs' that currently lie outside the realm of industrialisation and commodification.

Capitalists and companies are seemingly – at least semi-consciously – aware of their failure to engage with many of the elements at the top of the pyramid, including friendship, belonging, meaningfulness and a sense of agency and autonomy. Evidence for this lies in one of the key institutions for driving the sales of capitalism's products: advertising.

V
The Promises of Advertising

When advertising began in a significant way in the early 19th century, it was a relatively straightforward business. It showed you a product, told you what it did, where you could get it and what it cost.

Then, in 1960s America, a remarkable new way of advertising emerged, led by Madison Avenue luminaries such as William Bernbach, David Ogilvy and Mary Wells Lawrence. In their work for brands like Esso, Avis and Life Cereal, adverts ceased to be in a narrow sense about the things they were selling. The focus of an ad might ostensibly be on a car, but our attention was also directed at the harmonious, handsome couple holding hands beside it. It might on the surface be an advert about soap, but the true emphasis was on the state of calm that accompanied the ablutions. It might be whisky one was being invited to drink, but it was the attitude of resoluteness and resilience on display that provided the compelling focal point. Madison Avenue had made an extraordinary discovery: however appealing a product might be, there were many other things that were likely to be even more appealing to customers; by entwining their products with these ingredients, sales could be transformed.

Patek Philippe is one of the giants of the global watchmaking industry. Since 1996, they have been running a distinctive series of adverts featuring parents and children. It is almost impossible not to have glimpsed one somewhere.

In one example, a father and son are together in a motorboat, a scene that tenderly evokes filial and paternal loyalty and love. The son is listening carefully while his kindly dad tells him about aspects of seafaring. We can

Patek Philippe advertise their watches with an appeal to our real longing: family happiness.

It is love we want; it is Calvin Klein we buy.

imagine the boy will grow up confident and independent – yet also respectful and warm. He'll be keen to follow in his father's footsteps and emulate his best sides. The father has put a lot of work into the relationship (one senses they've been out on the water a number of times) and now the love is being properly paid back. The advertisement understands our deepest hopes around our children. It is moving because what it depicts is so hard to find in real life. We are often brought to tears not so much by what we have as by what we long for but cannot reach.

Father–son relations tend to be highly ambivalent. Despite a lot of effort, there can be extensive feelings of neglect, rebellion and, on both sides, bitterness. Capitalism doesn't allow dads to be too present. There may not be too much chance to talk. But in the world of Patek Philippe, we glimpse a psychological paradise.

We turn to Calvin Klein. Here the parents and children have tumbled together in a happy heap. There is laughter; everyone can be silly together, there is no need to put up a front, because everyone is trusting and on the same side. No one understands you like these people do. In the anonymous airport lounge, in the lonely hotel room, you'll think back to this cosy group and ache. Alternatively, you might already long for those years, quite a way back, when it was so much easier than it's become. Now the kids are shadowy presences around the house. Your relationship with your spouse has suffered too. Calvin Klein knows this; it too has brilliantly latched on to our deepest and most elusive inner longings.

Adverts wouldn't work if they didn't operate with a very good understanding of what our real needs are, what we truly require to be happy. Their emotional pull is based on knowing us eerily well. As they recognise, we are creatures who hunger for good family relationships, connections with others, a sense of freedom and joy, a promise of self-development, dignity, calm and the feeling that we are respected.

Yet, armed with this knowledge, they – and the corporations who bankroll them – are unwittingly cruel to us. While they excite us with reminders of our buried longings, they cannot do anything wholehearted about quenching them. Adverts may want to sell us things, but these are incommensurate things in relation to the hopes that they have aroused. Calvin Klein makes lovely cologne. Patek Philippe's watches are reliable and beautiful agents of time-keeping. But these items cannot help us secure the goods our unconscious believed were on offer.

The real crisis of capitalism is that product development lags so far behind the best insights of advertising. Since the 1960s, advertising has worked out just how much we need help with the true challenges of life. It has fathomed how deeply we want to have better careers, stronger relationships and greater confidence. In most adverts, the pain and the hope of our lives have been superbly identified, but the products are almost comically at odds with the problems at hand. Advertisers are hardly to blame. They are, in fact, the victims of an extraordinary problem of modern capitalism. While we have so many complex needs, we have nothing better to offer ourselves than, perhaps, a slightly more accurate timepiece or more subtly blended perfume. Business needs to become more ambitious in the creation of new kinds of 'products', in their own way as strange sounding today as a wrist watch would have seemed to observers in 1500. We need the drive of commerce to get behind filling the world – and our lives – with goods that can really help us to thrive, flourish, find contentment and manage our relationships well.

To trace the future shape of capitalism, we only have to think of all the needs we have that currently lie outside of commerce. We need help in forming cohesive, interesting, benevolent communities. We need help in bringing up children. We need help in calming down at key moments (the cost of our high anxiety and rage is appalling in aggregate). We require immense assistance in discovering our real talents in the workplace and in understanding where we can best deploy them. We have aesthetic desires that we can't seem to get satisfied at scale, especially in relation to housing.

Our higher needs are not trivial or minor wants, insignificant things we could easily survive without. They are, in many ways, central to our lives. We have simply accepted, without adequate protest, that there is nothing business could do to address them, when being able to structure businesses around these needs would be the commercial equivalent of the discovery of steam power or the invention of the electric light bulb.

We don't know, today, quite what the businesses of the future will look like, just as half a century ago no one could describe the corporate essence of the current large technology companies. But we can know the direction we need to head to: one where the drive and inventiveness of capitalism tackle the higher, deeper problems of life. This will offer an exit from the failings that attend business today. In the ideal future for consumer capitalism, our materialism would be refined, our work would be rendered more meaningful and our profits more honourable.

Advertising has at least done us the great service of hinting at the future shape of the economy; it already trades on all the right ingredients. The challenge now is to narrow the gap between the fantasies being offered and what we spend our lives making and our money buying.

VI
The Depression of the Business Community

Throughout history, when business has been harshly judged, criticism has focused on the idea of greed; business is bad because it is an activity driven by greed.

However, this badly misses the point. If one were to accuse business of any single flaw, it should not be greed but *pessimism*. Business has been surprisingly pessimistic about how money can be made. Hard-headed managers have rarely been outright corrupt or unnaturally avaricious: but they have very often suffered from a curious kind of melancholy, a distinctive sadness about the world and its inhabitants. This sadness shows itself in six major assumptions that operate beneath the workings of modern business:

Customers will never care about workers

A great many businesses employ the very cheapest labour they are able to locate on the planet. They negotiate contracts that mean that millions of people have to work in dangerous or at least uncomfortable factories and warehouses until their premature deaths.

It is tempting to assume that pure nastiness drives these mean-minded decisions: employers must be screwing their workers because they are greedy. But the truth is far stranger: they are pessimistic and uncreative about the mindsets of their customers.

Capitalists have a primordial need to stay in business and must be ready to do whatever is compatible with this aim. If it turned out that paying staff extremely well was in line with this ambition, they would do so at once without rancour or qualm.

They don't, because they have made some dark assumptions about these customers. They are bleakly sure that few customers will ever care much about the well-being of workers; they won't give a damn how many 8-year-olds are making their trousers or how much suffering went into harvesting their tea leaves – and therefore, for businesses to start caring about such issues will simply lead to a decimation in profits.

It is not a personal longing on the part of businesses to have people work for as little as possible. The low salaries stem from the assumption that unless businesses stick to rock-bottom wages, customers will go elsewhere and their enterprises will fail.

Customers have low appetites that can't be improved

There is a deep belief in many areas of business that high-mindedness, sincerity and complexity are fatal to sales and that any attempt to 'raise' the aspirations of consumers in these directions is guaranteed to lose money.

There is, for example, rampant pessimism around what would happen if you used less salt in a restaurant, or made certain magazines a little more thoughtful or produced a car that was gentle on its surroundings. As the business community is fond of rehearsing: no one ever failed to make money underestimating the tastes of the public.

The only way to sell is through deception

There is a painful background belief that in order to thrive, a business must make enormous claims for its products, and ideally create semi-conscious associations between what is sold and success, fun, love and sex.

The people behind adverts don't themselves believe that buying a certain perfume, car or phone will be closely connected to physical intimacy or popularity. But they are confronted with some gloomy facts about human nature: that people do seem to buy such items if you skilfully make airy promises about them.

Few businesses can possibly believe that advertising in its current state is admirable. If they resort to it, it is just from a desolate conclusion seemingly drawn from experience. A company can of course choose to be above such things but sales will fall, profits will drop, salaries will be cut; they won't be able to raise capital and the whole venture will eventually fold. You can participate in a charade – or you can be poor.

You can only make big money from the bottom of the pyramid

As we have established, most of the big and most profitable corporations on the planet address needs grouped at the lower levels of Maslow's pyramid. These businesses efficiently target the basic needs: for shelter, security, communication and energy. They are engaged in real estate, mining, oil, insurance or transport. None of these industries are currently focused in any ambitious way on what happens around their products. The oil company doesn't care much what your journey is about, so long as you travel a lot; the real estate corporation isn't concerned with the kind of life you live in your apartment, so long as you pay the rent.

It's not that people in business don't care about meaning, creativity and the pursuit of self-knowledge. It's just that they have a pessimistic conviction that it is impossible to make money from concerns that will always remain elusive and private.

You can't afford to care about the psychology of your staff

This is no reflection of personal indifference to the inner lives of others; it's just (many in business will feel) a crucial fact about running an enterprise: if you start getting concerned about the people who work in an organisation, focus will be taken away from the harsh task of turning a profit. Then it won't matter how kindly you feel towards your people, as you won't be able to give them the one thing they actually want from you: a job. Business requires the softer or more generous aspects of one's nature to be held in check.

The only legitimate role for surplus wealth is philanthropic donation

Successful capitalists can be extremely generous. The arts have been noted beneficiaries of their largesse, and scientific organisations too. Yet the area that tends not to benefit so much is the core activity: the profitable business itself. This is generally run with extreme rigour and no eye towards the finer more meaningful element. The higher things are what you commune with on the weekend and give away money to on your retirement; they can't be part of your core activity. You squeeze margins, shave quality and bat away riskier projects for forty years, and only then help to fund the opera house.

It is these pessimistic ideas about commerce and work that lead many companies – and the people who run them – to make very poor decisions.

What is really at play is a pained vision of life in which any higher aspiration seems condemned to failure.

The big claim here is that this pessimism is not always warranted and that in order to overcome it, business should look to an unusual source for inspiration: culture. It is culture that possesses a welter of antidotes to much of the underlying despair about humanity evident in commerce.

If this antidote has never been explored, it's because business understandably has some deep suspicions of its own when it comes to culture. The whole field seems negligible. When you look at what really counts in the world, none of it seems to have much to do with culture. The big corporations are concerned about millions of things – drilling rights, exchange rates, employment laws, tax credits, regional instability, technological advances. Culture appears marginal to this. It is just an upmarket area of entertainment; a hobby. You might know of a CEO who paints watercolours to relax, or a wealthy family that subsidises a ballet company. This is delightful, but it shows where the arts fit in – you become involved in the arts once you have made money. The arts use up money; they don't make it. In essence, for business, culture looks like something you might become interested in once you have succeeded, but it can't help you to succeed.

But in this arena too, there has been excessive pessimism. There's a way of considering culture that brings out a hitherto unexplored and highly intriguing set of ideas for business. With the right mindset, we can go through the six pessimistic assumptions, one by one, and see alternative – and more optimistic – attitudes that might be available through the history and practice of culture:

We care about those we can imagine

Art is ambitious about the possibility of creating emotional connections between strangers. The basis of many artistic works has been the desire to generate sympathy where none initially existed. A central skill of art is to guide us to perceive a common humanity where at first there was anonymity and otherness. In her novel *Middlemarch*, Mary Ann Evans (1819–1880), who published as 'George Eliot', was concerned with teasing out the hidden dignity and honour of people living unglamorous lives: a small-scale builder, a modest farmer, a carpenter, a servant, a poor clergyman. She made large numbers of readers feel kindly and concerned about these characters; she added new regions to our maps of sympathy.

Her technique did not involve telling her readers they ought to care. She didn't scold. She described people's lives carefully, feeling that the more we know about others, the more we will feel for them. She was deeply against overt didacticism and lecturing about the plight of the poor. Eliot's style was 'psychological realism'; she gave her readers a sense of what it was to be other people, and then let readers come to their own conclusions – which they have been doing successfully for over a hundred years.

George Eliot may be one of the most famous writers in the world's most influential language, but she remains a very small deal in a noisy, distracted planet. Nevertheless, her example justifies a degree of confidence that wider sympathy can be engaged: a sympathy for bricklayers and surveyors, but also garment makers, tea leaf pickers, fast-food workers and (in case we were to forget) bankers and CEOs. The pessimistic view that customers are only selfish – and can never care about the workforce, and so will never bear the costs connected with care, is not true to the emotional mechanics of culture.

Taste can vary immensely

The idea that companies should give people what they currently want is a guiding principle of business. But the bigger facts of culture show just how flexible, surprising and fast-moving changes in taste can be.

In 18th-century Britain, members of the same species as we belong to today became interested on a large scale in poetry. Alexander Pope (1688–1744), the leading poet of the day, introduced the twelve-syllable hexameter (against the advice of many) and was convinced that consumers would be highly sensitive to its rhythms. He was right. People loved the slightly slower pace and the neater rhymes it made possible – and he was able to buy himself a magnificent villa, just outside London, on the proceeds.

The raking of gravel is not something that, at present, seems like a major human concern. But in Japan, over many centuries, people became interested in the patterns into which gravel could be arranged in even very small gardens. Getting it right was hugely important to them. They also became very aware of the different characteristics of moss and the best ways of grouping rocks together. It's evidence of how – with the right encouragement – enormous groups of people can become highly sensitive to features that, in other societies, go entirely unnoticed.

These cultural instances reveal a fundamental fact about how the whole basis of our excitement can shift. Taste is a variable factor. We're good at appreciating moves of taste in retrospect. It's in advance that we are much less alive to the phenomenon. Therefore, businesses routinely end up assuming that their customers can't care about anything that goes too strongly against what currently exists.

Culture should embolden business. Until around 1919, no one had really thought that you could like a painting that didn't try to represent anything. Then came Piet Mondrian (1872–1944), who avoided painting trees

Piet Mondrian, *Composition with Yellow, Blue and Red*, 1937–1942

or sunsets or mothers and babies so as to focus our attention more clearly on distinctive abstract qualities: harmony, balance and purity. Mondrian shook off a depressed sense that preferences are fixed. He approached public taste with a justified optimism that, in principle, and with a bit of time and support, many people can be brought to recognise the appeal of novel and interesting things. It worked. A modest Mondrian now costs the price of a medium-sized jet.

If the expansion of taste works in relation to lines on a canvas, it must work in other, far more important, areas than art: the immensely significant realms of food, cars, hydroelectric turbines, data storage and clothing.

Goodness can be advertised

Business is familiar with the idea of seduction, but it takes a limited view of where seduction can be usefully deployed. For its part, culture has also been interested in charm, but it has used it far more ambitiously: to try to 'sell' difficult and higher things.

The Ancient Greeks, for instance, often presented rationality (the potentially austere demand that we think carefully and logically) via the god Apollo. But they knew that in order to get their ideas across, they would have to make Apollo attractive. So in a lot of their art, he looks like a cross between a model and a football player, his hair always a tumble of locks, his forearms strong.

The optimistic assumption was that we can be enticed towards elevated, noble or serious tasks with the help of the right sensory associations, if they are introduced in a sufficiently alluring way. The very techniques that could be used to sell bullshit can also be deployed to sell wisdom and self-understanding.

Important sensations can be commodified

Culture addresses the top level of Maslow's pyramid of needs: it is concerned with the pursuit of meaning and the exploration of individuality and freedom. At certain important moments, it has also succeeded in commodifying experiences in these areas and turning them into very profitable commercial operations.

Impressionism – one of the most commercially successful ventures of all time (if it was a stock, it would be near the very top of most exchanges) – began when a group of painters living and working around Paris in the 1860s became entranced by the play of light on the top of clouds, the delicate tones of shadows in city streets, and the shimmering reflection of sunshine on water. They had had really lovely experiences walking by rivers, strolling through gardens and picnicking in woodland.

The largely deserted, rugged coast of Normandy was visited by Claude Monet (1840–1926). He was particularly attracted to the cliffs near the village of Etretat. Many local people and one or two rare visitors must occasionally have had the fleeting thought that it was a charming place as they drew up a fishing boat on the sand or collected the iodine-rich kelp.

The difference with Monet is that he took the pleasure of looking at the cliffs very seriously. He painted a series of works closely examining how beautiful the light could be at different times of day and studied the pattern of shadows on the rocks.

His paintings kick-started Normandy's tourism business, now one of the most important in France. The pessimistic idea that big profits cluster around lower needs isn't justified. Billions of dollars of value can be created out of people's interest in how a cliff can look after a heavy spring shower.

TOP François Girardon, *Apollo Attended by the Nymphs of Thetis* (copy of Greek original), c. 1666–1673
A classical advert – for wisdom

BOTTOM Claude Monet, *The Cliffs at Étretat*, 1885

People will do more or less anything for you, if the purpose feels high enough

The pessimistic idea is that people only work for money. Yet across history, we see people – often celebrated in art – touched by other significant motivating ambitions to make the highest sacrifices.

The medieval monks who designed and constructed the buildings on the Scottish island of Iona did not have competitive salary packages. They worked because they were motivated by an idea that had been compellingly presented to them: that their labour would be pleasing to God.

Revolutionaries have regularly sacrificed their lives not because they were going to be paid to liberate a building, but because they were drawn to the idea of serving their country, even if this were to come at a terrible personal price.

Churches and revolutions don't have a natural monopoly on the optimistic idea that people can be driven by things other than merely money; these are just a couple of areas in which proponents happened to have been particularly ambitious. Many corporations in fact serve the public good in important, if less overtly dramatic, ways. They too can benefit from our striking disinterest in money when meaning is on offer.

The true destination of art is outside the museum

We see how often surplus wealth goes into art, and art is surely a deserving recipient. But even more valuable are the sorts of things that works of art celebrate: kindness, empathy, goodness, beauty and meaning.

In the utopia, the qualities found in art would not remain in art. They would have more of a place in our daily lives, and especially in our offices and factories. The true desire of artists has never been just to make art; it has been to transform the world in line with the ideas housed (temporarily) in art. It is surely closer to the true spirit of art to run a business that properly enhances our lives – even at the cost of reducing rates of profit – than to over-promote, make false promises or cut corners for decades and then give a Renoir to the National Gallery. The world's museums would certainly be less well endowed if the world's entrepreneurs had not accumulated vast fortunes. The world's houses and shops would probably look a lot more beautiful and therefore more loyal to the aspirations of culture if entrepreneurs accepted a more modest rate of return on their investments in exchange for decent-looking, noble products.

What we've been seeing via culture is a set of reasons to be less pessimistic about business. An incidental skill of culture emerges: to correct the more melancholy accounts of how money can be made. It can do this by identifying a range of skills and ideas around inner life, communication, how to change people's minds and the role of higher needs that have real impact on business itself. Because we meet with certain ideas in culture, it is a ready assumption to think that they belong in culture alone. But culture is only a modest outlet for big capacities that deserve to exist far more widely and in a far more important arena: that of business.

VII
The Future of Brands

High-minded people are often instinctively suspicious of the idea of brands. Brands can seem hateful on many grounds: their maddening ubiquity (they surprise us on a mountain walk or on arrival in a new country where we'd gone specifically to experience a different culture); they squeeze out smaller independent alternatives to which they are often inferior; or they radiate values that appear to us fake, exaggerated or plain daft. It is natural to suppose that we would, ideally, live in an unbranded world.

It is not surprising we feel this way. There are, after all, a lot of bad brands around. Nevertheless, something important remains submerged within the essential concept of a brand. A good economy should not be one devoid of brands; it would be one with better brands.

In a narrow sense, a brand is a visual cue that declares the origins of a product or service. More broadly, it alludes to the underlying character or personality of a company. Brands present, in highly condensed forms, encompassing visions of what life might be about. So beguiling might these be that our desire to make a purchase can originate not so much in a desire for a particular product or service as in a wish to tie ourselves more closely to the philosophies that hover over them. Furthermore, brands usher in expectations of coherence and consistency. We expect that – under the umbrella of a brand – very similar things will happen across countries, employees and products. Brands allow qualities and ideas to multiply powerfully across the world.

This is the problem, for brands threaten to repeat idiocy on an industrial scale. However, with perspective, we can see that the true culprit is never the pure fact of repetition. The objection is to what is being repeated.

In the 16th century, the Italian architect Andrea Palladio (1508–1580) worked out a set of basic designs for villas, churches and public buildings, based on a set of ideas assembled from Roman and, to a lesser extent, Greek architecture. He built his first versions in the little town of Vicenza. But his views spread rapidly, first across the Veneto, then more broadly through northern Italy, France, England, Germany, Russia and – especially – the United States. With a few concessions to local materials and colours, more or less identical buildings appeared in St Petersburg and Edinburgh, Boston and Berlin. Libraries, palaces, schools and homes acquired an astonishing basic consistency of appearance. Palladio's highly readable architectural manual, *I Quattro Libri dell' Architettura* ('The Four Books of Architecture', Venice, 1570) detailed how to lay out rooms, organise façades and treat window decorations, and became an indispensable part of every architect's library in the West. In America, Thomas Jefferson (1743–1826) was the great defender of this Palladian brand. His own house at Monticello and the campus of the University of Virginia were key examples of a franchise architecture that became no less widespread or well known than that of roadside McDonald's restaurants two centuries later.

That we might not lament the ubiquity of Palladianism as much as the omnipresence of fast-food restaurants suggests that the issue with brands isn't really about repetition, but about the repetition of mediocrity. In fact, the potential of brands to repeat good things is central to what we should respect about them. Although our societies may be highly primed to respect individual genius, progress in many areas is dependent on an ability to institutionalise the insights of geniuses, codifying their moves and distilling and teaching their methods.

A good brand performs a critical function in this regard: it can compensate society for the rarity of talent. It may enable the ideas of one especially clever person to influence how half the world will look. As a

Thomas Jefferson, Monticello, Virginia, built 1772
Jefferson's aesthetic borrowed heavily from the 'brand' of architecture developed by Palladio.

result of brands, geniuses will not always be directly needed to bring about something of genius – which is important, given how few geniuses tend to be around. Brands move the focus away from individuals towards the collective, attempting to insulate quality from the chance feelings or attitudes of a lone creator. Brands ensure that the good need not always be unique.

To date, the idea of collecting great talent under a brand has found its most developed form in art. Titian (c. 1490–1576) was one of the most prolific artists in 16th-century Venice, but he also understood early on in his career that he would never be able to deliver personally all the many commissions he received. He therefore set up a large studio in which he employed a troop of highly talented artists – among them his nephew Marco and his brother Francesco – whose style became almost indistinguishable from his. The master's name would guarantee the quality of the object – but it would not necessarily have hovered too much over any one particular canvas. Lute players, landscapes and Madonnas that would otherwise have struggled to come into being emerged from the studio for the churches and palaces of Europe under a coherent Titian brand.

Brands almost invariably have logos. These too have a bad name. We accuse them of spoiling views, degrading the skyline and getting in the way. However, the issue is once again less with logos in their essence than with particular logos – and they might make up a majority – that come with unfortunate associations. Yet at a theoretical level, a logo simply possesses an important power to focus our minds almost instantaneously on qualities we can expect of a location or object that carries it. So attuned are our eyes to drawing out the meaning of shapes and colours that talented graphic artists can hope to inscribe highly nuanced philosophies of life fairly accurately into the smallest visual cues. The Christian lamb, or *Agnus Dei*, is one of the most successful of all logos, appearing on stained-glass windows, pulpits, tunics or weather vanes, condensing the spirit of the Gospels into a single redolent image.

William Warrington, *Agnus Dei* stained glass window,
Field Dalling, Norfolk, 1856
This 'logo' has been used to transmit the spirit of the Gospels in one condensed image.

We should not aim to eliminate brands and their logos, but to grow more ambitious about what a global brand might be capable of. For example, it is a pity that the British child psychoanalyst Donald Winnicott (1896–1971) remains just one individual who produced a few immensely wise books and lectures that colour the education of some present-day analysts rather than, as should have happened, a brand that kept certain of Winnicott's lessons permanently in our minds, through the use of buildings, education programmes, films, a clear ideology – and a good logo.

Winnicott stood for close bonds between parents and children, a gracious acceptance of our psychological eccentricities, a wise accommodation with what is 'good enough' in life, work and love, and a recognition of the importance of games and toys (especially teddy bears) in the emotional development of children. These values could, in the hands of a talented graphic designer, find themselves distilled into a logo that would, when glimpsed on the city skyline or the side of a domestic object, trigger a rehearsal of a crucial set of ideas and embed these more securely in our fragile and forgetful minds.

A morally neutral approach to business defines a 'good brand' as one that is popular and well known. It is impressed by how many people recognise a logo. But we should be raising a different set of criteria for the value of a brand. A good brand is one built round a set of genuine virtues: of qualities properly anchored in a capacity to help us develop flourishing lives.

Brands invite the recognition that great things are not usually done by individuals acting in heroic isolation. The hallmark of a thriving culture is not, in fact, the dominance of the lone celebrity; it's the dominance of brands. Brands rescue good things from the cult of individualism, which, though flattering, creates a collective problem, for it denies the good the chance to be active in a widespread way. At some point, every decent idea and important insight should go through the process of becoming a brand and thereby gain from a huge extension of its reach. The world is in need of better brands.

VIII
The Future of Selling

New York's Times Square pays mesmerising tribute to the power of selling. Seeing it at night on foot, one can't fail to be awed by the quantity of effort and ambition focused here. The entire square and (it feels) the sky glow with the longing to persuade and seduce – in the name of a watch or a hamburger. It is easy to feel scornful.

Chartres Cathedral was built between 1194 and 1250. It too was a giant exercise in light and colour dedicated to selling. We may think that selling is at the root of modern problems, but it's the selling of low ambitions that is the true cause. The north transept rose window of Chartres Cathedral is ten metres in diameter and is one of the crowning glories of Western culture. In a central oculus shine Mary and Jesus, surrounded by twelve diamond-shaped windows containing the kings of Judah. In five lancet windows beneath, morality tales from the Old Testament are illuminated in vivid purples, yellows and blues: in one, Aaron triumphs over Pharaoh, warning us of the need to live godly, observant lives.

Chartres is selling as well: just at a more profound level. Its sponsoring organisation was trading in ideas concerning forgiveness, love and kindness. It wasn't doing this to make money; these were its foundational convictions.

The difference between Times Square and Chartres Cathedral isn't to do with selling; it's to do with ambition. We remain at the dawn of capitalism. We can imagine a Times Square of the future dedicated to the promotion of cures for loneliness, aids to forgiveness and those psychological ingredients that will help us be wise and kind. We don't have to stop selling: we need to learn to engage commercially with our highest needs.

Northern rose window of Chartres cathedral, France, c. 1235
This stunning artistic accomplishment 'sells' the highest Christian values.

We can imagine a Times Square of the future dedicated to the promotion of cures for loneliness, aids to forgiveness and those psychological ingredients that will help us be wise and kind.

The Sorrows of Work

I
Introduction

There is no more common emotion to feel around work than that we have failed. We have failed because we have made less money than we had hoped; because we have been sidelined in our organisation; because many of our acquaintances have triumphed; because our schemes have remained on the drawing board; because we have been constantly anxious and, for long stretches, tired and bored.

We tend to meet our sorrows personally. We believe that our failures are tightly bound up with our own character and choices. But the suggestion here is that the single greatest cause of our professional failure lies in an area that self-aware, moderate and modest people are instinctively loath to blame: the system we live within. Whatever our natural hesitancy, it seems we deserve to recast at least some of the explanations for our woes away from intimate experience and towards large-scale historical and economic forces. Although on a daily basis we are enmeshed in problems (inadequacies, desires and panics) that feel as if they must be our responsibility alone, the real causes may lie far beyond ourselves, in the greater, grander currents of history: in the way our industries are structured, our values are determined, and our assumptions generated. For a long time now, capitalism has been a confirmedly tricky system in which to retain equilibrium, make peace with ourselves, find fulfilment in our work – and cope. It's not quite our fault if, rather too often, we feel like losers.

This isn't to make a particular dig at capitalism, or to suggest that there may be easier alternatives at hand. Every economy that has ever existed has been bound up with multiple sorrows. Organising an equitable system of incentives, goads and rewards is as yet beyond us. We should be allowed to level criticisms, not in the name of arguing for an alternative utopia, but in order to depersonalise our sense of failure.

Work disappoints us, not by coincidence but by necessity, for at least eight central reasons:

1. The demand for specialisation limits our potential.
2. The concentration of capital squeezes out personal initiative.
3. The extent of consumer choice forces us to commercialise our work beyond what feels tolerable.
4. The scale of industry robs us of a sense of meaning.
5. Competition generates a state of perpetual anxiety.
6. The requirement for collaboration maddens us.
7. Our high aspirations embitter us.
8. The notion that the world is meritocratic imposes a crushing burden of responsibility on us for our defeats.

Understanding the sorrows of work will not magically remove them, but it at least spares us the burden of feeling that we must be uniquely stupid and clumsy for suffering them.

II
Specialisation

One of the greatest sorrows of work stems from a sense that only a small portion of our talents has been taken up and engaged by the job we have signed up to do every day. We are likely to be so much more than our labour allows us to be. The title on our business card is only one of thousands of titles we theoretically possess.

In his 'Song of Myself', published in 1855, the American poet Walt Whitman (1819–1892) gave our multiplicity memorable expression: 'I am large, I contain multitudes' – by which he meant that there are many interesting, attractive and viable versions of oneself, many good ways one could potentially live and work, and yet very few of these are ever properly played out in the course of the single life we have. No wonder that we are quietly and painfully conscious of our unfulfilled destinies, and at times recognise, with a legitimate sense of agony, that we could have been something and someone else.

The major economic reason why we cannot explore our potential as we might is that it is much more productive for us not to do so. In *The Wealth of Nations*, published in 1776, the Scottish economist and philosopher Adam Smith (1723–1790) first explained how what he termed the 'division of labour' was at the heart of the increased productivity of capitalism. Smith zeroed in on the dazzling efficiency that could be achieved in pin manufacturing, if everyone focused on one narrow task (and stopped, as it were, exploring their Whitman-esque 'multitudes'):

The title on our business card is only one of thousands of titles we theoretically possess.

One man draws out the wire, another straights it, a third cuts it, a fourth points it, a fifth grinds it at the top for receiving the head; to make the head requires two or three distinct operations; to put it on is a peculiar business, to whiten the pins is another; it is even a trade by itself to put them into the paper; and the important business of making a pin is, in this manner, divided into about eighteen distinct operations, all performed by distinct hands. I have seen a small manufactory where they could make upwards of forty-eight thousand pins in a day. But if they had all wrought separately and independently, and without any of them having been educated to this peculiar business, they could have made perhaps not one pin in a day.

– Adam Smith, *The Wealth of Nations*, Book 1, Chapter 1, *Of the Division of Labour* (1776)

Adam Smith was astonishingly prescient. Doing one job, preferably for most of one's life, makes perfect economic sense. It is a tribute to the world that Smith foresaw – and helped to bring into being – that we have ended up doing such specific jobs, and carry titles like Senior Packaging & Branding Designer, Intake and Triage Clinician, Research Centre Manager, Risk and Internal Audit Controller, and Transport Policy Consultant. We have become tiny, relatively wealthy cogs in giant, efficient machines. And yet, in our quiet moments, we reverberate with private longings to give our multitudinous selves expression.

One of Adam Smith's most intelligent and penetrating readers was the German economist Karl Marx (1818–1883). Marx agreed entirely with Smith's analysis; specialisation had indeed transformed the world and possessed a revolutionary power to enrich individuals and nations. But where he differed from Smith was in his assessment of how desirable this development might be. We would certainly make ourselves wealthier by specialising, but – as Marx pointed out with passion – we would also dull our lives and cauterise our talents. In describing his utopian communist society, Marx placed enormous emphasis on the idea of everyone having many different jobs. There were to be no specialists here. In a pointed dig at Smith, Marx wrote:

> *In communist society . . . nobody has one exclusive sphere of activity but each can become accomplished in any branch he wishes . . . thus it is possible for me to do one thing today and another tomorrow, to hunt in the morning, to fish in the afternoon, rear cattle in the evening, criticize after dinner . . . without ever becoming a hunter, fisherman, shepherd or critic.*
>
> – Karl Marx, *The German Ideology* (1846)

One reason why the job we do (and the jobs we don't get to do) matters so much is that our occupations decisively shape who we are. How our characters are marked by work is often hard for us to notice, as our outlooks just feel natural to us, but we can observe the identity-defining nature of work well enough in the presence of practitioners from different fields. The primary school teacher treats even the middle-aged a little as if they were in need of careful shepherding; the psychoanalyst has a studied way of listening and seeming not to judge while exuding a pensive, reflexive air; the politician lapses into speeches at intimate dinner parties.

Every occupation weakens or reinforces aspects of our nature. There are jobs that keep us constantly tethered to the immediate moment (A&E nurse, news editor), others that train our attention on the outlying fringes of the time horizon (futurist, urban planner, reforester). Certain jobs daily sharpen our suspicions of our fellow humans, suggesting that the real agenda must always be far from what is being said overtly (journalist, antique dealer); other sorts intersect with people at candid, intimate moments of their lives (anaesthetist, hairdresser, funeral director). In some jobs, it is clear what you have to do to move forward and how promotion occurs (civil servant, lawyer, surgeon), a dynamic that lends calm and steadiness to the soul, and diminishes tendencies to plot and manoeuvre. In other jobs (television producer, politician), the rules are muddied and seem bound up with accidents of friendship and fortuitous alliances, inspiring tendencies to anxiety, distrust and shiftiness.

The psychology inculcated by work doesn't neatly stay at work; it colours the whole of who we end up being. We start to behave across our whole lives like the people work has required us to be. This tends to narrow character. When certain ways of thinking become called for daily, others start to feel peculiar or threatening. By giving a large part of one's life over to a specific occupation, one necessarily has to perform an injustice to other areas of latent potential. Whatever enlargements it offers our personalities, work also possesses a powerful capacity to trammel our spirits.

We can offer ourselves the poignant autobiographical question of what sort of people we might have been had we had the opportunity to do something else. There will be parts of us we have had to kill (perhaps rather brutally) or that lie in shadow, twitching occasionally on Sunday afternoons. Contained within other career paths are other plausible versions of ourselves – which, when we dare to contemplate them, reveal important, but undeveloped or sacrificed, elements of our characters.

We are meant to be monogamous about our work, and yet truly have talents for many more jobs than we will ever have the opportunity to explore. We can understand the origins of our restlessness when we look back at our childhoods. As children, in a single Saturday morning, we might put on an extra jumper and imagine being an Arctic explorer, then have brief stints as an architect making a Lego house, a rock star making up an anthem about cornflakes and an inventor working out how to speed up colouring in by gluing four felt-tip pens together. We'd put in a few minutes as a member of an emergency rescue team, then we'd try out being a pilot, brilliantly landing a cargo plane on the rug in the corridor. We would perform a life-saving operation on a knitted rabbit, and then we'd find employment as a sous-chef helping make a ham-and-cheese sandwich for lunch. Each one of these 'games' might have been the beginning of a career. And yet we have to settle on only a single option, done repeatedly over the next fifty years.

Compared to the play of childhood, we are leading fatally restricted lives. There is no easy cure. As Adam Smith argued, the causes don't lie in some personal error; it is a limitation forced upon us by the greater logic of a productive, competitive market economy. However, we can allow ourselves to mourn that there will always be large aspects of our character that won't be satisfied. We are not being silly or ungrateful; we are simply registering the clash between the demands of the employment market and the free, wide-ranging potential of every human life. There is a touch of sadness to this insight. But it is also a reminder that this lack of fulfilment will accompany us in whatever job we choose: we shouldn't attempt to overcome it by switching jobs. No one job can ever be enough.

There is a parallel here between our experience around work and what happens in relationships. There is no doubt that we could (without any blame attaching to a current partner) have great relationships with dozens, maybe hundreds, of different people. They would bring to the fore different sides of our personality, please us (and upset us) in different ways, and introduce us to new excitements. Yet, as with work, specialisation brings advantages: it means we can focus, bring up children in stable environments, and learn the disciplines of compromise. In love and work, life requires us to be specialists even though we are by nature equally suited for wide-ranging exploration.

We carry about within us, in embryonic form, many alluring versions of ourselves that will never be given the proper chance to live. This is a sombre thought, but also a consoling one. Our suffering is painful, but has a curious dignity, because it does not uniquely affect us as individuals. It applies as much to the CEO as to the intern, to the artist as much as to the accountant. Everyone could have found so many versions of happiness that will elude them. In suffering in this way, we are participating in the common human lot. We may with a certain melancholic pride remove the job search engine from our bookmarks and cancel our subscription to a dating site in due recognition of the fact that, whatever we do, parts of our potential will have to go undeveloped and die without ever having had the chance to come to full maturity – for the sake of the benefits of focus and specialisation.

III
Standardisation

The sorrows of work are not limited to the likelihood that we will be somewhat unwillingly tied to a single field throughout our careers; even worse, our chosen field may turn out to be boring. We are liable to think that this fall into a tedious role must be our fault, a sign of our exceptional ineptitude. However, looked at dispassionately, boring jobs are an inherent and often unavoidable part of the modern economy.

When we speak of the opposite sort of job – an interesting job – we tend to refer to work that allows for a high degree of autonomy, personal initiative and (without anything artistic being meant by the word) creativity. In an interesting job, we won't simply be following orders; we will have latitude about what path we select to meet an objective or what we think the right solution to a problem might be. A good job, defined like this, is one that allows for a good measure of personalisation: we have an opportunity to directly imprint who we are in the work we produce. We end up seeing the best parts of our personalities in the objects or services we generate.

A lot of the writing about the nature of work produced in Europe and the United States in the 19th century can be read as an attempt to understand how personalisation disappeared from the labour market, even as wages rose. The English art critic and social reformer John Ruskin (1819–1900) proposed that the medieval building industry had been marked by a high degree of personalisation, evident in the way that craftsmen carved gargoyles (grotesque animal or human faces) in distinctive shapes high up on cathedral roofs. The stonemasons might have had to work to a fixed overall design, and their toil was not always easy, but the gargoyles symbolised a fundamental freedom to place their own stamp on their work. Ruskin added more ruefully that the new housing developments of the industrial age were allowing no such freedom or individualism to flourish in the workforce.

Ruskin's most devoted disciple, the poet and designer William Morris (1834–1896), extended the range of this idea of personalisation to a discussion of the making of furniture – his own area of expertise. Morris argued that the traditional way of making chairs and tables allowed artisans to see parts of themselves reflected in the character of the things they made. Every chair made by hand was as distinctive as its creator. In the pre-industrial age, thousands of people had been actively engaged in designing chairs, and every worker had been able to develop their own nuanced ideas about what a nice chair should be like.

However, an inevitable part of capitalism is a process of concentration and standardisation. There is a tendency for money, expertise, marketing clout and sophisticated distribution systems to be pooled together by a few big players, who outcompete and crush rivals and so achieve a daunting position in the marketplace. Barriers to entry rise exponentially. A well-financed operation can cut costs, assiduously research the preferences of consumers, marshal the best technology, and provide goods that can be of huge appeal to consumers at the best possible price. As a result, the artisanal mode of production cannot possibly compete – as Morris himself discovered when the traditional workshop that he established to make chairs for the Victorian middle classes was forced into receivership in the wake of a price war.

Today, there are, of course, still a few furniture designers around – some of them very well known – but this cannot disguise that what we call 'design' is quite a niche field employing a minuscule number of actors. The majority of those involved in the making and selling of furniture will have no opportunity to put their own character into the objects they are dealing

TOP Gargoyle, Salisbury Cathedral
Art critic John Ruskin celebrated the latitude that medieval craftsmen had to create work imbued with their own unique style.

BOTTOM Morris & Co., Sussex armchair, c. 1860–1940
William Morris believed that the process of making artefacts by hand imbued the piece with the unique character of the maker.

with. They belong instead to a highly efficient army of labour that aims for rigorously anonymous execution.

Without intending to be mean-spirited or inherently hostile to the pleasures of work, capitalism has radically reduced the number of jobs that retain any component of personalisation.

For example, the Eames Aluminum Group chair was designed by American husband-and-wife team Charles (1907–1978) and Ray Eames (1912–1988) in 1958. It is a highly distinctive creation that reflects the ideals and outlook of the couple who designed it. If they had been artisans, operating their own small workshop, they might have sold a few dozen such chairs to their local customers in their lifetime. Instead, because they worked under capitalism for Herman Miller – a huge commercial office and home furniture manufacturing corporation – many hundreds of thousands of units have been, and continue to be, sold. A side effect of this triumph has been that the demand for well-designed, interesting chairs has been substantially cornered. Anyone wanting to make an office chair nowadays has to face the fact that it is already possible to buy a nice example, designed by two geniuses and available for rapid delivery by a global company at a competitive price from a highly efficient network of local branches.

We are familiar with the idea that the wealth of the world is being ever more tightly concentrated in the hands of a relatively small number of people – the infamous 1%. But capitalism doesn't only concentrate money. There's a more poignant, less familiar fact that only a small number of people – a sometimes overlapping, but often different 1% – have interesting, as in 'personalised', work.

It is telling that we are, at the same time, obsessed with the romance of individual genius. Our society has developed a near-fetishistic interest in the exploits of brilliant startups, colourful fashion gurus, and idiosyncratic film-makers and artists – characters who flamboyantly mould parts of the world

Charles and Ray Eames,
Aluminium Chair EA 103, 1958

in their own image and put their individual stamp on the things they do and make. We might like to think that we turn to them for inspiration, but it may be more the case that we use them to compensate ourselves for a painful gap in our own lives. The stories of successful personalisation have come to the fore just when the practical opportunities for personalised work have diminished. In a similar way, it was in the 19th century, during mass migration to cities, that novels about rural life achieved unprecedented popularity among newly urban audiences. We may, through our addiction to stories of lone creative geniuses, be trying to draw sustenance from qualities that are in woefully short supply in our own day-to-day working lives.

The prevalence of stories of individual creativity feed the illusion that personalised work is more normal than it really is. The many interviews and profiles mask the fact that, for almost all of us, it will prove nearly impossible to compete against the great forces of standardisation. For this reason, far more than because of anything we have done ourselves, many of us are likely to find a considerable portion of our work awkwardly tedious and dispiritingly free of any opportunities to carve our own gargoyles.

IV
Commercialisation

A complaint regularly aired around many careers is that, in order to succeed at them, there is no option but to 'sell out'. It appears that we will inevitably face a choice between authenticity and penury on the one hand, and idiocy and wealth on the other. We are familiar with this complaint in the arts, of course. But the same dilemma shows up when an interesting restaurant seems unable to make a profit; when a specialist bread company goes into receivership; when a garden supply firm focusing on rare native plants can't get a foothold in the market; when a sincere news site can't turn a profit; or when an ethically based investment firm is doomed to operate on a tiny scale in comparison with its less high-minded competitors.

Behind the complaint lies a very understandable but ambitious yearning: that our most passionately held beliefs and enthusiasms should, relatively painlessly, and by virtue of their merits, become high priorities for others. Our instincts lead us to suppose that what we are convinced of should prove equally compelling to strangers.

Young children are particularly prone to this assumption. On meeting a new adult, they may enthusiastically suggest that they join them in playing a favourite game, perhaps brew something on the miniature kitchen stove, or impersonate one of their dolls, which shows how hard it is for a child to grasp how alien his or her pleasures might be to another person. Children aren't silly; they are just highly attuned to their own natures and are convinced that others will share their tastes. In a naive but representative way, they illustrate an instinct that stays with us all of our lives: the supposition that others will and must be moved by what moves us; that their value systems are, or should be, like ours; and that what we love can automatically be what the world loves.

The reality is often humiliatingly and enragingly different. A novel that is filled with subtle character analyses and that takes inventive risks with plot structure might sell only modestly, while one that pits good against evil in a predictable way, relies on well-tried narrative tricks and arrives at an implausibly happy ending will dominate the bestseller lists. A high-street chain might do a fabulous trade in cut-price dark grey polyester-cotton socks, while a thoughtful, original brand involving striking colour combinations and materials ethically sourced from Peru will fail to find a market.

It is tempting to arrive at a despairing conclusion: that the economy is inherently devoted to delivering a personal affront to the better aspects of human nature. The truth is much less vindictive, but the tendency for the market to overlook or at least remain cool in relation to our more sincere and earnest efforts is nevertheless real – and founded on a raft of identifiable and stubborn forces in economic and psychological life.

One of the most basic of these forces is choice. It is in the nature of a growing, successful economy always to expand the range of choices offered to a consumer, and thereby, always to minimise the a priori claims of any one product or service. We can track the characteristic features of this development in relation to media. In 1952, a BBC radio broadcast of Beethoven's Fifth Symphony attracted an audience of five million listeners – approximately 16% of the UK's adult population. Today, such a broadcast would claim a fraction of these numbers. What explains the difference is not – as some cultural pessimists might claim – that the UK population has over a few generations become less sensitive to the emotive force of German Romantic music; the fundamental difference is that today's audience has many more options. In 1952, there were very few competing sources of entertainment. People listened en masse to the classical end of BBC radio because there was nothing much else to do. A producer who worked in the corporation had a great deal more authority than today's equivalent, not on the basis of superior genius, but because his listeners had few viable alternatives. This, rather nicely, gave certain high-brow things more opportunity to be attended to; but it also meant that many substandard services and products could enjoy a far larger role than their intrinsic merit warranted.

We know from the study of certain natural habitats that in situations of abundant choice (the warm seas around the Seychelles, for example), attention goes towards members of the species that appear colourful, variegated and theatrical. Much the same holds true for companies amid the din and buzz of the human marketplace. What is brusquely called 'selling out' typically refers to a series of moves no more and no less sinister than the elaborate signalling to which all living things must submit in their efforts to be noticed. Amid plenty, products and services must throw their qualities into dramatic relief, puff out their virtues, sound more confident than they perhaps are, and lodge themselves in the minds of their distracted audiences with unabashed insistence. It is understandable if those who are committed to higher values may balk at such demands, resentfully condemning the pitilessness of an unfeasibly vulgar system.

There is another reason why modern audiences are likely to sidestep opportunities for high-minded consumption: because they are exhausted. Modern work demands a punishing amount from its participants. We typically return from our jobs in a state of depletion: frazzled, tired, bored, enervated, sad. In such a state, the products and services for which we will be in the mood have to be of a very particular cast. We may be too brutalised to care much about the suffering of others, or to think empathetically of unfortunates in faraway tea plantations or cotton fields. We may have endured too much tedium to stay patient with arguments that are intelligently reticent and studiously subtle. We may be too anxious to have the strength to explore the more sincere sections of our own minds. We may hate ourselves a bit too much to want to eat and drink only what is good for us. Our lives may be too lacking in meaning to concentrate only on what is meaningful. To counterbalance what has happened at work, we may instinctively gravitate towards what is excessively sweet, salty, distracting, easy, colourful, explosive, sexual and sentimental.

This collectively creates a vicious circle. What we consume ends up determining what we produce – and, in turn, the quality of jobs that are on offer. So long as we only have the emotional resources to consume at the more narcotic and compromised end of the market, we will only generate employment that is itself challenged in meaning and compromised in dignity – which will further increase our demand for lower-order goods and services. We seem hampered by our existing conditions of employment from properly developing the sort of temperaments that could strengthen the sincerity and seriousness of our appetites and so expand the range of meaningful and non-depleting jobs we could have access to.

The price we pay for a marketplace that refuses to support high-minded efforts is not just practical and economic; it is also at some level emotional. One of our greatest cravings is to be recognised and accepted for who we are. We long for careful, insightful appreciation of our characters and interests. This was, if things went tolerably well, a little like what happened to us in earliest childhood, when a kindly adult, through the quality of their love, spared us any requirement to impress or, as we might put it, to market ourselves. In those early years, we did not need assiduously to 'sell' who we were; we did not have to smile in exaggerated ways, sound happier than we were, put on seductive accents or compress what we had to say into memorable jingles. We could take our time, hesitate, whisper, be a little elusive and complex and as serious as we needed to be – sure that another would be there to find, decode and accept us. Everything we learnt of love ran counter to the mechanisms of commercialisation.

It is no wonder if we harbour within us a degree of instinctive revulsion against commercial strictures. The need not to sell ourselves aggressively was not just part of an earlier, simpler point in the history of the world (as scholars rightly point out); it was, more poignantly, also a moment in each of our personal histories, to which we may always long to return.

V
Scale

One of the strangest aspects of work is that we don't do it solely, or sometimes even principally, for money. This makes us vulnerable not just to poverty, but also to crises of a more psychological kind. We harbour a demanding ambition to find work that can provide us with something that can best be captured by the word 'meaning'. We hunger for this meaning quite as much as we crave status or enrichment. Meaningful work comprises any activity that impacts positively on another's life, either by reducing suffering or increasing pleasure – a definition that can encompass everything from the life-saving interventions of the cardiac surgeon to the seductive efforts of a pastry chef or Anatolian rug weaver.

In truth, the vast majority of jobs contribute in some way to the welfare of others. Only a very few are properly devoid of meaning; for example, a career devoted to making fake remedies for hair loss or cancer, or one encouraging those on low incomes to gamble more. However, crucially, a great many jobs are in the odd position of being meaningful while not in any way feeling meaningful.

This problem is rife in the modern age for a very particular reason: the changes in the scale and tempo of work ushered in by industrialisation. Most work now takes place within gigantic organisations that are engaged in a variety of large, complicated and slow-moving projects – and where it can therefore be hard to derive, on a daily basis, any tangible sense of having improved anyone else's life in any way. The customer and the end product are, in the gigantic structures of modernity, simply too far-flung in space and too distant in time. It can be hard to reassure ourselves of our worth and purpose when we are only a single unit among a 20,000-strong team on four continents pushing forward a project that might be ready in five years.

There are sound reasons why the work practices of large organisations proceed at a glacial pace. Product development in sectors such as aeronautics and banking, oil and pharmaceuticals cannot happen overnight. The time frames are logical, but in terms of individual experience, they go directly against our natural, deeply embedded preference for a rapidly unfolding story.

The ancient Greek philosopher Aristotle (384–322 BCE) observed that a key requirement for a satisfying piece of theatre was that it should be over relatively quickly. There might be tensions and complications and unexpected changes of direction, but in a few hours and three acts, there should be a feeling of genuine completion.

It's not just in theatre that speed is attractive. The concentration of action also helps to explain the appeal of sport. In ninety minutes, a football match can take us from a perfect, neutral start to a precise result. However, if football were like modern work in terms of scale and pace, one can imagine it unfolding on eighteen pitches with twenty-two balls and 10,800 players kicking around for thousands of days without any overview of the progress of the game. By the standards of our innate longings, our work unfolds in a disordered, overextended and confusing way.

Our labour feels meaningful not only when it is fast, but also when we get to witness the ways we are helping others: when we can leave the office, factory or shop with an impression of having fixed a problem in someone else's life. This pleasure too is threatened by scale. In the massive organisations of modernity, we may be so distant from the end users of our products and services as to be unable to derive any real benefit from our constructive role in their lives. Spending days improving terms on contracts in the logistics industry truly will lead to a moment when a couple can contentedly enjoy some ginger biscuits together in front of the TV; optimising data management

Our labour
feels meaningful
not only when
it is fast,
but also when
we get to
witness the ways
we are helping
others.

across different parts of an aerospace firm – along with thousands of other coordinated efforts – truly will contribute to the moment when a young family can bond together on a beach holiday. The connections are genuine, but they may be so extended and convoluted as to feel dispiritingly flimsy and unreal in our minds.

It's a tantalising paradox, and a kind of tragedy, that because of the unavoidable scale of modern work, we may pass our lives helping other people – and yet, day to day, be burdened by a harrowing feeling of having made no difference whatsoever.

VI
Competition

At the heart of how all individuals function, there is a dream of security: security from humiliation, penury, dependence, arbitrary dismissal and uncertainty.

At the heart of how a modern capitalist economy functions, there is a dream of competitive advantage: one based on the intelligent exploitation of invested capital, on the effective deployment of technology, raw material and labour to reduce costs and improve quality and the triumph over competitors so as to maximise shareholder return.

At certain points, these two longings – those of individuals and those of capitalism – seem inherently aligned. At other points, it can seem as if our own well-being has grown entirely irrelevant to the economic machine in which we are enmeshed. We generally don't kick the machine; we are far more inclined to blame ourselves. There is, after all, always enough evidence of people who thrive and succeed to suggest to us that the fault must lie with something we have done. But in our more politically engaged moments, we may dare to complain that the system is not working 'as it should'.

Ironically, at precisely such moments, it is probably working very well; it's just that it was never intended to work in the way we would like – for our own well-being. Capitalism does not place the longings and aspirations of the labour force at the heart of its operations (the clue to its essential concerns lies in its name). It was not made to ensure that we have secure, good lives, plenty of time off and pleasant relationships with our families; it was made to maximise shareholder return. Labour has exactly the same status within capitalism as other production inputs, neither more nor less. Alongside rent, the price of fuel, plant, technology and taxes, labour (people) is just another cost. That it happens to be a 'cost' that cries, needs time off, has fragile nerves, sometimes catches the flu and in extremis commits suicide is – at most – a puzzling inconvenience. We should not believe that there is anything faulty about capitalism simply because we have minimal security of employment, little time to see our families, a lot of stress and an uncertain future. These belong to the very conditions that help the system to work well. Our mistake, which has imposed a heavy internal burden on us, has been to confuse our own ambitions for happiness with the goals of the overall economy.

We have innocently viewed a range of anxieties and fears as incidental and solvable, when they are in fact basic necessities for the correct functioning of enterprise. The first and largest of these is the fear of dismissal. A capitalist economy could not work well without it. It is a precondition of efficient business both that existing labour can be removed swiftly and cheaply and that there should be a ready supply of cooperative replacements. Unemployment is not a tragedy for business; it contributes to a willing pool of talent with low bargaining power.

Even the collapse and shuttering of whole firms is not to be lamented overall. Inefficient players who have failed to read market signals have to close, and their capital has to be deployed elsewhere. There is nothing less healthy for capitalism than an economy in which venerable firms, some perhaps very long established and with thousands of loyal workers within them, can't regularly and cleanly go bust.

The relationship we form with a company may last as long as a marriage, and we may give it as much time and devotion as we would give to a partner. But this is a relationship that should, for capitalism to flourish, be close to abusive, because our 'spouse' must at any point be allowed, on the grounds that they could save themselves 3% a year, fire us and take up with a more cooperative and flexible rival in Vietnam or Bolivia.

We have taken care to construct a world where, in many areas, there is an extreme sensitivity to upset and distress. We have rigorous health and safety requirements to ensure that people don't fall off ladders or strain their backs when moving heavy boxes. We make sure that words aren't used to demean or prejudice minorities. Kindergartens present a moving picture of our care for the next generation. Yet in the core area of our work, we operate in a system that is – from an emotional point of view – nothing short of inhuman. But through more sober economic lenses, it isn't anything as alarming: it is merely admirably competitive.

A second fear that prevails is that of not having done enough. We lie awake at night worrying about certain tasks we failed to perform. We cannot stop thinking about what certain competitors may be up to. We panic about the upcoming financial results. We don't sleep very well any more.

This too makes sense. It used to be far tougher on capitalists. Regular breaks used to be mandated. Religion was responsible for many of them; it told people that they should down tools and honour something far more important than their work, like the majesty of the creator of the whole world. This glance upwards to the heavens relativised and calmed the workforce; it put things in perspective and lent a relieving sense that those packages in the warehouse could probably be sent next week after all. On a bad day, there might even be a sermon reminding people to treat workers like God's children and to respect the holiness of every individual, however lowly.

In certain countries, labour organised itself and demanded that everyone in the company had to be given decent conditions and the odd holiday, or else the staff would walk out on strike. There were angry marches and some insane demands to restrict who could be fired and when.

There were some very frustrating limits to technology as well. There was the post, but it took an age. You might have to wait two weeks for a letter and there might be little to do in that time other than check up on the garden, go for long walks, read three Russian novels and talk to the children. Travel for work took an equal eternity. You might be sent to Hamburg by the firm, which could take four whole days, three of them at sea, some of them spent slowly eating kartoffelsalat and schnitzel, chatting to fellow passengers and staring out from the ship's window at the wheat fields near Neuharlingersiel.

It has been a miracle and an unbounded relief for capitalism that this painful age has at last passed. Religion now seldom gets in the way. Its irritating, calming pieties have been replaced by far more robust and motivating narratives drawn from social Darwinism. The labour movement has been effectively pulverised by flattering ambitious workers into believing that they would gain far more by ditching their fellow Indians and aiming to become chiefs themselves. Technology has at last made it possible for the line between leisure and work to be erased. We've been able to give people phones to make sure they are findable at all times and incentivised them to regard these devices as toys for their benefit rather than glorified tracking bracelets for their firms. Travel has been hugely speeded up too, so it is now possible to squeeze in meetings on a couple of continents in just a single day. There is blessedly little time left that a worker can call their own.

The consequence is that we now have almost no energy left to invest in our personal lives. We constantly search for that elusive holy grail quaintly described by magazines as 'work/life balance'. But anyone who sincerely believes that such an equilibrium might be possible has not begun to understand the logic of capitalism.

Work and love are our two greatest idols. But they are also locked in mortal combat. Work tends to win. The complaints against work from within love are notorious: we are never around, we are always tired, we never give our partner our wholehearted attention, we are obsessive about the office. It is helpful to recognise that modern ideas of love were invented in the late 18th century by artistic people who didn't have real jobs and therefore made great play of the importance of spending time with a lover explaining and sharing feelings and recounting the movements of one's heart. Unfortunately, combining Romanticism and modern capitalism, as we are expected to do, is a near-impossible task. The impressive philosophy of Romantic love – with its emphasis on intimacy and openness – sits very badly alongside the requirements of working routines that fill our heads with complex demands, keep us away from home for long stretches and render us insecure about our positions in a competitive environment.

According to the Romantic ideal, a lover can be kind and good only when they readily communicate their feelings. But the level of openness this assumes is wholly at odds with the realities of work. After a tricky day (or week), our minds are likely to be numb with worries and duties. We may not feel like doing much besides sitting in silence, staring at the kitchen appliances, running through a series of dramas and crises. Such preoccupation is not pleasant to witness: it risks expressing itself in a range of not very endearing symptoms: grunting, sighing, brooding silence and a short-fused temper. The most innocuous-sounding question about how the day might have gone can elicit a growl – then, if it is repeated, an explosion.

If there is consolation to be found, it lies in knowing enough history to realise that failure isn't personal. It isn't one's own incompetence or lack of drive that has set one's work and private life at loggerheads. We just happen to be living at a point in time when two big, opposed themes are at war, when we have demanding ideas about the needs of families and relationships and equally demanding ideas about work, efficiency, profit and competition. Both are founded on crucial insights; both aim to monopolise our lives. We deserve a high dose of sympathy for the situation we find ourselves in.

VII
Collaboration

One of the most frightening aspects of working life is that we will, unless we are the beneficiaries of extreme good fortune, be required to have colleagues. The colleague is a creature who, endured over any length of time in situations of high stress and procedural complexity, presents one of the greatest threats to calm, composure and soundness of mind.

It is noteworthy that, in the 19th century, one specific working environment developed into a hugely popular subject for painters: the artist's studio. Archetypal paintings of studios showed high-ceilinged rooms with large windows, views over neighbouring rooftops, sparse furniture, messy tables covered in tubes of paint, and half-finished masterpieces propped up against the walls. There was one additional factor that particularly enticed the collective imagination: there was no one in the studio apart from the artist. At exactly the time when more and more people were being gathered into ever-larger offices and experiencing for the first time all the attendant compromises and constrictions, there grew a craving for paintings of an alternative utopia: a place of work consolingly free of the damnable presence of the colleague.

We have ended up in offices not by bad luck, but by the unavoidable fact that the mighty tasks of modern capitalism simply cannot be undertaken on one's own. It remains (sadly) impossible to run an airline or to manage a bank solo.

The problem with colleagues begins with the fundamental challenge associated with trying to communicate the contents of one's mind to another person. When we are doing things by ourselves, the flow of information is immediate and friction-free. If we could listen in to our inner monologues, they would be made up of a speedy and baffling series of assertions and jumbled words: 'Narr, yes. Come on! Do it till then, after no more. Ah, nearly, no, no, no, no, back . . . OK, got it, got it . . . No! Yes. That's fine. So.'

But when we collaborate, we must laboriously turn the stream of consciousness that only we can follow into unwieldy, externally comprehensible messages. We have to translate feelings into language, temper our wilder impulses and affix paragraphs to intuitions in order to generate prompts and suggestions that have a chance of being effective in the minds of other people.

By a painful quirk of psychology, others can't by instinct alone understand what we need and want – although it can seem as though they surely must. The realisation that other people are not like us and can't guess what we want takes a long time to sink in – and the idea perhaps always remains a bit foreign and unjust. In their earliest days, babies simply don't realise that their mothers are separate beings, and so get frustrated when these reluctant appendages don't by magic obey their unstated wishes. Only after a long and difficult process of development (if ever) can a child realise that their parent is truly a distinct individual, and that, in order to make themselves understood by them, they will have to do more than grunt and imagine solutions in their heads. It can be the work of a lifetime, in which the office occupies a particularly painful passage, to gradually accept the impossibility of mutual mind reading.

If this were not bad enough, many colleagues are at risk of not sharing our underlying vision of what should be done. They have contrary opinions, their own quirks, pet peeves and obsessive interests. To get our point across and assuage their resistance requires us to deploy a battery of diplomatic skills. At the very moment when, agitated and overwhelmed, we would like simply to shout or bark, we have no option but to charm. This is because the colleague is, on top of it all, extremely sensitive. Unless they are spoken to correctly, they will become offended, develop grudges, start to cry or report us to a superior.

The imperative to be pleasant at work is a novel one that we are still getting used to. In the olden days, brusqueness used to be the norm: it was a good way to get people to turn a boat swiftly starboard, push coal trolleys faster, or increase the rate of production at the blast furnace in a steel mill. When most work was physical, management could be abrupt; workers could feel underappreciated or bullied and nevertheless perform their required tasks to perfection. Emotional distress didn't hold things up. You could still operate the brick-making machine at maximum speed, even if you hated the manager, or clean out the stables thoroughly even if you felt the foreman hadn't enquired deeply enough into the nature of your weekend.

But nowadays, most jobs require a high degree of psychological well-being in order to be performed adequately. A wounding comment can destroy a person's productivity for a whole day. Without ample respect, recognition and encouragement, huge sums of money will be wasted in silently resentful moods. If we have any concern for the bottom line, we have no alternative but to try to be a little bit nice.

At the same time, the inability to speak frankly has its own enormous cost. A huge amount of valuable information that should make its way around a company is held back by the imperative not to cause offence. We hold our tongues because we are scared to upset juniors, to alienate colleagues and to ruin our relationships with superiors – and, in the process, insights that might help an organisation to thrive stay locked in individual hearts.

Work relationships are no less tricky than romantic ones, but at least in the latter we have a basic sense of security that enables us to speak our minds and make the necessary cathartic moves – to call the other person a fuckwit and compress a range of ideas into the occasional expletive-loaded outburst. The office environment misses out on the cleansing frankness seemingly possible only when two people know they will have the option of having sex together after a bust-up.

At the heart of our office agonies is the complaint that we seldom like our colleagues as people. In a better world, we would be unlikely ever to want to spend any time with such disturbing, and often unlikely, figures. We shouldn't be surprised by our daily discomfort, given that these people were never picked out on the basis of psychological compatibility. We were formed into a unit because they had a range of technical and commercial competences necessary for a task, not because they were fun lunch companions or were graced with a pleasing manner. We are like the unfortunate bride in a power marriage in the Middle Ages. A princess would be obliged to marry a certain prince because he owned an important lead mine or because the archers in his country were especially proficient. It would have been nice if the two liked each other as well, but the stakes were generally too high for this to be a relevant factor. The success of the realm depended on such matters as access to raw materials and military strength, not on whether one partner had a maddening giggle or a daunting overbite.

There is yet another challenge posed by colleagues. Corporations and businesses are fundamentally hierarchical, with an ever-smaller number of desirable, better-rewarded places at the pinnacle. A naive outsider might imagine that career progression would be determined by clear, precise and public determinants of merit, probably of a technical or financial sort, akin to the straightforward nature of the examination results we all grew up with. But the reality is that, in many occupations, no verifiable measure of performance is available. Factors of success are numerous, opaque and shifting. What decides who is promoted is not talent per se, but success at a range of dark psychological arts best summed up by the term 'politics'.

Political skill has woefully little in common with the reasons we were trained and hired to do our jobs in the first place. We may, as part of a good business education, have spent years studying how to navigate a balance sheet, analyse competitors, negotiate contracts and administer a logistics chain. But when we reach the office, we will be confronted by other, less familiar, kinds of challenges: the person at the desk opposite us with the charming manner who enthusiastically agrees with whomever they're speaking to, yet harbours a range of toxic reservations and privately pursues their own undeclared agenda; the person who responds to polite criticism or well-meaning feedback with hurt and fury; the person who pretends to be our friend, but takes the credit for our best efforts.

In such situations, the most unlovely qualities may turn out to be the most necessary ones: the capacity to quietly accept glory for things that were not truly our doing; to distance ourselves from errors in which we were heavily implicated; to subtly foreground the failings of otherwise quite able colleagues; to turn cold at key moments towards emotionally vulnerable superiors; to flatter while not appearing to do so; to mould our views to suit the currently ascendant attitudes.

Such grey, underhand strategies are not easy to pick up, and they may feel impossible for us to practise if we pride ourselves on being straightforward, direct or even just somewhat ethical. Yet we can be certain that every high-minded refusal of duplicity will carry a heavy, perhaps career-damaging, cost.

Our problems with the collegial nature of work are compounded by the implication that matters should be straightforward. Our inevitable difficulties are aggravated by notions that offices are at heart giant families, that colleagues can be friends, that honesty is rewarded and that talent will win out. Kindly sentimentality is, in the end, just a disguised version of cruelty. It might be simpler if, in dark moments, we could simply admit to what we know in our hearts: that it would obviously be better if we could be shot of the whole business of colleagues and spend our days, as we used to so well, sitting comfortably on the floor in our room assembling cargo planes, city car parks and bear picnics on our own.

VIII
Equal Opportunity

The modern world was founded upon, and continues to be enthused by, the promise of equal opportunity – and infinite possibility – for all. Each of us grows up with a sense that a great deal could be possible. Adults listen respectfully when small children suggest they might travel to the Space Station, run the country or play for a winning team. Such feats aren't wholly fanciful, particularly when considered through parental eyes. Similarly transformative journeys are everywhere to behold. It would be churlish to ignore that extraordinary destinies are a regular feature of modern life.

The idea of equal opportunity springs from the most generous side of our nature and has been responsible for inspiring the most indispensable achievements. But it has also, unwittingly and far more quietly, been the source of unending sorrow. American psychologist William James (1842–1910) recognised the anxiety created by societies that promise their inhabitants infinite opportunities for social transformation and career success – and then can't always deliver. For James, satisfaction with ourselves does not require us to succeed in every area. We are not always humiliated by failing at things; we are humiliated only if we first invested our pride and sense of worth in a given achievement and then did not reach it. Our ambitions determine what we will interpret as a triumph and what must count as a failure. 'With no attempt there can be no failure; with no failure no humiliation. So our self-esteem in this world depends entirely on what we back ourselves to be and do', wrote James. 'It is determined by the ratio of our actualities to our supposed potentialities'. Thus:

$$\text{Self-esteem} = \frac{\text{Success}}{\text{Pretensions}}$$

The problem with the modern world is that it does not stop lending us extremely high expectations and inviting us to dream, and then leaving us with a bitter sense of failure.

A firm belief in the limitations of life was once one of humankind's most important assets, a bulwark against bitterness and envy, a wisdom cruelly undermined by the ideology of infinite expectation proclaimed by the modern worldview. Feeling 'successful' might not be so much about having many things, as a matter of having what we long for. Success is not an absolute. It is relative to desire; every time we seek something we cannot afford, we grow poorer, whatever our resources.

Insofar as advanced societies provide us with many options for success, they appear to be helping us. But in truth, the net effect may be to humiliate us: through a language of unlimited opportunity, these societies keep open a permanent gap between who we want to be and what we have achieved. There are two ways to make people feel more successful: to give them more success, or to narrow their ambitions. Modern capitalism has in certain areas succeeded spectacularly at the first option, but, by stretching our aspirations, it has left a painful gap between our hopes and our reality – a gap we are left to fill with shame and rage.

IX
Meritocracy

Modern politicians across the political spectrum show remarkable agreement on one goal: that of creating a fully meritocratic society, a society in which all those who make it to the top do so because of their own talents and abilities, rather than due to unfair privilege, upper-class parents or connections. The stated aim is to create a hierarchy based on ability, replacing chinless halfwits with the meritorious, wherever they may be found and whatever age, colour or gender they might be.

This meritocratic ideal has brought opportunity to millions. Gifted and intelligent individuals who for centuries were held down within immobile, caste-like hierarchies are now free to express their talents on a more or less level playing field. We have largely turned the page on a world that was filled with rulers who were too sick or stupid to govern; lords who couldn't manage their estates; commanders who didn't understand the principles of battle; peasants who were brighter than their masters; and maids who knew more than their mistresses. No longer is background an impassable obstacle to advancement. An element of justice has finally entered the distribution of rewards.

But there is a darker side to the idea of meritocracy: if we truly believe that we have created (or could one day create) a world where the successful truly merited all their success, it follows that we have to hold the 'failures' exclusively responsible for their failures. In a meritocratic age, an element of justice enters into the distribution of wealth, but also of poverty. Low status comes to seem not merely regrettable, but also deserved.

Succeeding financially (without inheritance or contacts) in an economic meritocracy endows individuals with an element of personal validation that the nobleman of old, who had been given his money and his castle by his father, had never been able to feel. But, at the same time, financial failure has become associated with a sense of shame that the peasant of old, denied all chances in life, had also been spared. The question of why, if one is good, clever or able, one is still poor becomes infinitely more acute and painful for the unsuccessful to have to answer (to themselves and others) in a new meritocratic age.

There has turned out to be no shortage of people willing to answer the question on behalf of the 'failed'. For a certain constituency, it is clear that the failures owe their position to their own stupidity and degeneracy. With the rise of an economic meritocracy, in certain quarters, the failures have moved from being described as 'unfortunates', the target of the charity and guilt of the paternally minded rich, to being described as 'losers', fair targets of contempt in the eyes of robust self-made individuals, who are disinclined to feel ashamed about their mansions or shed crocodile tears for those whose company they have escaped. In the harsher climate of opinion that can gestate in meritocratic societies, it has become possible to argue that social hierarchy rigorously reflects the qualities of the members on every rung of the ladder so that conditions are already in place for the good people to succeed and the dummies to flounder – attenuating the need for charity, welfare, redistributive measures or simple compassion. To the injury of poverty, a meritocratic system has added the insult of humiliation.

It is a symptom of our faith in meritocracy that it has largely become impossible to explain away professional failure as the result of 'bad luck'. Although it is granted that luck maintains a theoretical role in shaping our careers, the evaluation of people proceeds, in practical terms, as if they could fairly be held responsible for their biographies. It would seem unduly (and even suspiciously) modest to ascribe a victory to 'good luck' and, more importantly in this context, pitiable to blame defeat on the opposite. Winners make their own luck, insists the modern mantra, which would have puzzled the ancient Roman worshippers of the Goddess of Fortune.

We are paying a heavy price for our faith in a fairer world: that of having to take full responsibility for what we achieve and, more poignantly, fail to achieve, in the course of our lives.

X
Conclusion

We need an extraordinary run of good fortune to make a success of our careers: an early understanding of our talents and interests; the right educational opportunities; the best kind of inferiority complex; a benign political environment; physical and mental health; confidence, stamina, friends; a lack of scandals; a propitious number of lucky breaks; clumsy enemies; supportive relationships; an untragic sexuality; an upbeat temperament... And all this needs to be in place not for one or two years, but – so that we'll be more than mere flashes-in-the-pan – for four decades at least.

We should not be surprised if we don't quite get there. We were not uncommonly stupid. We were tricked into misunderstanding the statistics of success, in mistaking the unique for the possible. We longed for glorious destinies, of which there are always far fewer than there are numbers of the aspiring and the ardent. The game is close to rigged so as to cause heartbreak on a mass scale, although the sadness rarely recognises itself as collective, and is experienced in each individual soul as a uniquely personal defeat.

Our minds are partly to blame. We are hardwired for ambitious plans. It isn't our nature to rest with what is already to hand or easy to reach. We are inherently ungrateful, and feel alive only when we have taken on a struggle that has a good chance of crushing us. Even those we think of as successes will secretly nurse dreams they have had to forego. There is always a gap between achievement and desire. Feeling like a failure is the inevitable price for harbouring any sort of ambition.

We would be mad not to strive for success, but we will end up demented if we don't also, over time, develop capacities for making peace with defeat.

The task begins with forewarning, with a secure, calm, dark knowledge that we will inevitably be tripped up along the way.

We need to be free of a sense of persecution in this regard. It truly was not personal. Our dreams are like a fragile house of twigs exposed to a hurricane. We should stop fixating on what life has done to us, and check in with what it is doing to others every day – the ones who never make it into the magazines; the legions of the quietly despairing and dying. It is no loser's counsel to work with a vivid sense of how much worse it might, and will still, get.

We should make ourselves at home with mediocrity. 'Failure' sounds like too extreme a word for something that is so normal. We should be more alive to its ubiquity and wear it with greater ease, as something – like death – that is coming for us all. We might laugh defiantly at its embrace, refuse to be cowed by it and mock our pretensions without remorse or self-importance.

It isn't easy, of course, that we are typically surrounded by people trapped in a toxic ideology of ambition. The first question we will be asked when meeting almost any new person is: 'What do you do?' If our answer is insufficiently elevated, we will at once notice the loss of interest and our total dispensability to most members of the race.

These things continue to matter more than they should. We should try to be gentle on ourselves. We could reduce how often we'll be exposed to this sort of judgement. We might attempt to develop an identity not so exclusively connected to achievement, so that who we are becomes bound up not just with salary and rank, but also our character, our relationships, our interests and our unmonetised and unpublished skills.

We should learn the wisdom of a degree of melancholy in relation to our work, founded on an understanding that the sorrow isn't just about us, that our suffering belongs to humanity in general. This should not make us desperate, but rather more forgiving of our failure, kinder to that of others and better able to focus on what really matters, while there is still time.

What is
Culture For?

I
Introduction

Our societies frequently proclaim their enormous esteem for culture and the arts. Music, film, literature, painting, photography and sculpture enjoy superlative prestige and are viewed by many as close to the meaning of life.

But our societies also have a strict sense of what properly appreciating the arts should involve. Sensible homage is associated with acquiring technical knowledge, with taking advanced qualifications in the humanities, with knowing historical details and with respecting, at least in substantial part, the canon as it is now defined.

Strangely, what we are not generally encouraged to do – and indeed what we might be actively dissuaded from attempting – is to connect works of culture with the agonies and aspirations of our own lives. It is quickly deemed vulgar, even repugnant, to seek personal solace, encouragement, enlightenment or hope from high culture. We are not, especially if we are serious, meant to view cultural encounters as opportunities for didactic instruction.

In Ben Lerner's 2011 novel *Leaving the Atocha Station*, an American PhD student, used to considering art as material for academic analyses and scholarly seminars, visits Madrid's Prado museum. In one of the quieter rooms he spots a fellow visitor who moves slowly, looking intently at a range of key works, including Rogier van der Weyden's *Descent from the Cross* (c. 1435), Paolo de San Leocadio's *Christ the Saviour* (1482–1484) and Hieronymus Bosch's *The Garden of Earthly Delights* (1490–1500).

What astonishes the graduate student and eventually the guards of the museum is that in front of each of these masterpieces, the visitor doesn't

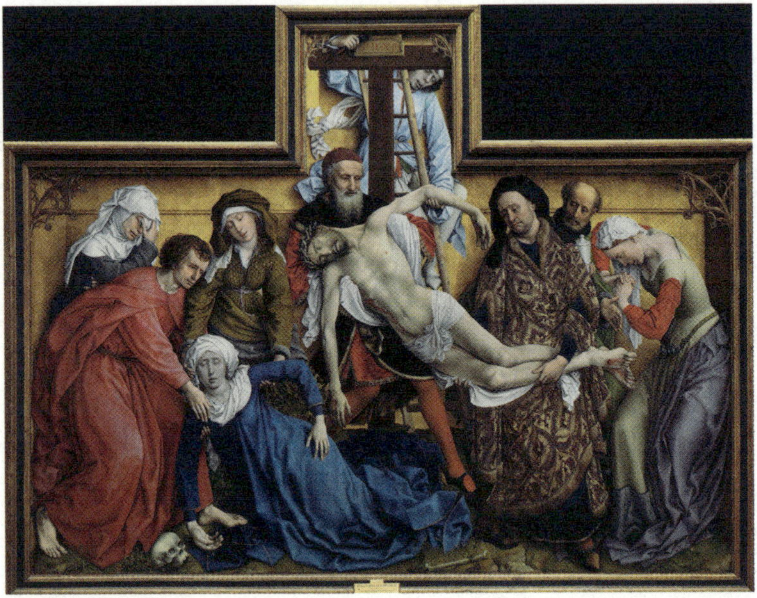

Rogier van der Weyden,
Descent from the Cross, c. 1435
What might it be right to do in front of this?

merely politely look at the caption or the guidebook; he doesn't just note the fine brushstrokes and the azure of the skies. He bursts into tears and cries openly at the sorrow and beauty on display, at the contrast between the difficulties of his own life and the spirit of dignity and nobility of the works on the wall. Such an outburst of intense emotion is deeply unusual in a museum (museums may routinely be referred to as our secular cathedrals, but they are not – as cathedrals once were – intended to be places to reveal our grief and gratitude). Listening to the man's sobs, the guards at the Prado grow understandably confused and nervous. As the author puts it, they cannot decide whether the man was

> perhaps the kind of man who would damage a painting, spit on it or tear it from the wall or scratch it with a key – or if the man was having a profound experience of art... What is a museum guard to do...? On the one hand, you are a member of a security force charged with protecting priceless materials from the crazed... on the other hand... if your position has any prestige it derives precisely from the belief that [great art] could legitimately move a man to tears... Should [the guards] ask the man to step into the hall and attempt to ascertain his mental state... or should they risk letting this potential lunatic loose among the treasures of their culture...?

The dilemma points with dry humour to the paradox of our contemporary engagement with culture: on the one hand, we insist on culture's importance. On the other, we limit what we are meant to do with culture to a relatively polite, restrained and principally academic relationship, at points frowning on those who might treat it more viscerally and emotionally, as if it might be a sophisticated branch of the notorious category 'self-help'.

This resistance, however well meant, nevertheless fails to notice that the great works of culture were almost invariably created to redeem, console

Great works of culture were almost invariably created to redeem, console and save the souls of their audiences.

and save the souls of their audiences. They were made, in one way or another, with the idea of changing lives. It is a particular quirk of modern aesthetics to sideline or ignore this powerful underlying ambition, to the point where to shed tears in front of a painting depicting the death of the son of God may put us at risk of ejection from a national museum.

Yet the power of culture arguably best emerges not when we conceive of it as an object of critical study or historical curiosity, but when we rely on it as a therapeutic tool that can be used in a quest to grow somewhat less isolated, frightened, shamed, restricted or skittish. Rather than focus on what a work of art might tell us about the time and place it was made or about the person who created it, we should develop the confidence to do exactly that which we might feel discouraged to do: relate cultural masterpieces to our own dilemmas and pains, using them as a resource with which to address a range of our most debilitating and pernicious agonies.

II
Companionship

The greatest share of art that humans have ever made for one another has had one thing in common: it has dealt, in one form or another, with sorrow. Unhappy love, poverty, discrimination, anxiety, sexual humiliation, rivalry, regret, shame, isolation and longing: these have been the chief constituents of art down the ages.

However, we are, in public discussion, often unhelpfully coy about the extent of our grief. The chat tends to be upbeat or glib; we are under awesome pressure to keep smiling in order not to shock, provide ammunition for enemies or sap the energy of the vulnerable.

We thereby end up not only sad, but sad that we are sad – without much public confirmation of the essential normality of our melancholy. We grow harmfully stoic or convinced of the desperate uniqueness of our fate.

All this, culture can correct – standing as a record of the tears of humanity, lending legitimacy to despair and replaying our miseries back to us with dignity, shorn of many of their haphazard or trivial particulars. 'A book [though the same could be said of any art form] must be the axe for the frozen sea within us,' proposed Kafka in a 1904 letter to his friend Oskar Pollak. In other words, a tool that can help release us from our numbness and provide catharsis in areas where we have for too long been wrong-headedly brave.

There is relief from our submerged sorrows to be found in all of history's great pessimists. For example, in the words of Seneca from his *On Consolation to Marcia* (c. 40 CE):

> What need is there to weep over parts of life?
> The whole of it calls for tears.

Or the ironic maxims of Schopenhauer in *The World as Will and Representation* (1818):

> There is only one inborn erroneous notion… that we exist in order to be happy…
> The wise know it would have been better never to have been born.

Such pessimism tempers prevailing sentimentality. It provides an acknowledgement that we are inherently flawed creatures: incapable of lasting happiness, beset by troubling sexual desires, obsessed by status, vulnerable to appalling accidents and always – slowly – dying.

The vast painting *Alkahest* (2011) – nearly four metres across – by Anselm Kiefer (b. 1945) could allude to the essentially sorrowful character of the human condition. Everything we love and care about will come to ruin, all that we put our hope in will fail. In a note to the painting, Kiefer writes: Even 'rock that looks as though it will last for ever is dissolved, crushed to sand and mud'. The dramatic scale is not accidental: it's a way of trying to make obvious something that is often repressed and ignored: dejection, sadness and disappointment are major parts of being human. The work's icy, grey, harsh character summons up equally grim thoughts about our own lives.

It's not an intimate picture because the fact Kiefer is asserting isn't a personal one: it's not so much we who are unduly down, it is life itself which demands a melancholy response. He's not attempting to delve into the unique painful details of our individual sorrows. The painting isn't about a relationship that didn't work out, a friendship that went wrong, a dead parent we never fully made peace with, a career choice that led to wasted years. Instead it sums up a feeling and an attitude: lonely, lost, cold, worried,

TOP Anselm Kiefer, *Alkahest*, 2011

BOTTOM Jean-Baptiste-Camille Corot, *The Leaning Tree Trunk*, c. 1855–1860

frightened. And instead of denying these feelings as worthy only of losers, the work proclaims them as important, serious and worthy. It is as if the picture is beaming out a collective message: 'I understand, I know, I feel the same as you do, you are not alone.' Our own private failings and woes – which may strike us as sordid or shameful or very much our own fault – are transformed; they are the personal way in which a tragic theme of existence happens to play out in our own lives. They are, in fact, ennobled, by their kinship to this grand work. It is like the way a national anthem works – by singing it the individual feels themselves part of a great community, they are strengthened, given confidence, they can see themselves as strangely heroic, irrespective of their circumstances. Kiefer's work is like a visual anthem for sorrow, one that invites us to see ourselves as part of the nation of sufferers, which includes, in fact, everyone who has ever lived.

Jean-Baptiste Corot (1796–1875) described his painting *The Leaning Tree Trunk* (c. 1855–1860) as a souvenir or memory. It is filled with the idea of farewell. The moment will pass, light will fade, night will fall. The years will disappear, we will wonder what we did with them. Corot was in his late 60s when he painted this work: the mood is elegiac, mourning what has gone and will never come back. Ultimately, it is a farewell to life but it is not a bitter or a desperate one. The mood is resigned, dignified and, although sad, accepting. Our own personal grief at the passing of our lives (if not soon, then someday – but always too soon) is set within a much wider context. A tree grows, it is bent and twisted by fate and eventually will dry up and wither, like that on the left-hand side of the painting. The sunlight illuminates the sky for a while and then is hidden behind the clouds and night descends. We are part of nature. Corot isn't glad that the day is over, that the years have gone and that the tree is dying, but his painting seeks to instil a mood of sad yet tranquil acceptance of our own share in the fate of all living things.

This is a move we encounter repeatedly in the arts: other people have had the same sorrows and troubles that we have, and it isn't that they don't matter, or that we shouldn't have them, or that they aren't worth bothering about. What counts is how we perceive them. By interacting with art, we encounter the spirit or voice of someone who profoundly sympathises with suffering, but who allows us to sense that through it, we're connecting with something universal and unashamed. We are not robbed of our dignity: we are discovering the deepest truths about being human – and therefore we are not degraded by sorrow but, strangely, elevated.

We can feel this elevation through sorrow especially in the presence of 'sad' music. One of the most calming things that societies have ever devised is the lullaby. In almost every culture there has ever been, parents have sung their babies to sleep. A humbling point that a lullaby reveals is that it's not necessarily the words of a song that make us feel more tranquil. The baby doesn't understand what's being said but the sound has its effect all the same. The baby shows that we are all tonal creatures long before we are creatures of understanding. As adults, we grasp the significance of words of course, but there remains a sensory level that cuts through and affects us far more than an argument or an idea ever could. The musician can, at points, trump anything the philosopher might tell us.

Ancient Greeks were fascinated by the story of the legendary musician Orpheus. At one point he had to rescue his wife from the underworld. To get there he needed to make his way past Cerberus, the ferocious three-headed dog that guarded the entrance to the land of the dead. Orpheus was said to have played such sweet, enchanting music that the wild beast calmed down and became – for a while – mild and docile. With this myth, the Greeks were reminding themselves of the psychological power of music. Orpheus didn't reason with Cerberus, he didn't try to explain how important it was that he should be allowed to pass, he didn't speak about how much he loved his wife and how much he wanted her back. Cerberus was – as we ourselves are at times of distress – pretty much immune to reason. But he was still open to influence. It was a matter of finding the right channel to reach him.

When we feel anxious or upset, kindly people sometimes try to comfort us by pointing to facts and ideas: they try to influence our thinking and – via careful arguments – to quieten our distress. But, as with Cerberus, the most effective way to deal with sorrow may simply be to play us music.

For instance, in Schubert's 'Ave Maria' (composed in 1825) we feel enfolded in a generous, tender embrace, encountering no criticism or rebuke, but endless depths of understanding and compassion for our troubles. The music lifts us up and gently distracts us from any immediate cause of agitation, as a parent might try to distract an upset child. Peter Gabriel's 'Don't Give Up' (1986) is designed as a similar kind of musical therapy. It's intended for those times when we do feel like giving up, when we've lost all confidence and feel crushed by the demands of the world. The strategy is to be as sympathetic as an imagined mother: first to acknowledge the horribly painful sense of failure and then to offer a kindly reassurance. The message is not that our plans will inevitably work out, but that our human worth is not on the line if they don't. The music offers us what at such points we can't offer ourselves: compassion and faith.

Between 1733 and 1749, J. S. Bach produced his *Mass in B minor*, perhaps the greatest musical axe ever to be brought to bear on that frozen sea within us. Near the beginning there is the 'Kyrie': a call to the congregation to recognise the ways they've hurt and wronged others, and a plea that God will forgive their unkindness. A five-voice fugue theme (soprano I, II, alto, tenor, bass) and a step-wise ascending melody, interrupted by a lower sighing motive, encourage us to feel repentance about our own failings while hinting at the eventual certainty of redemption.

Not only are we sad, we are also, most of us, lonely with what saddens us. We can imagine ourselves as a series of concentric circles. On the outside lie all the more obvious things about us: what we do for a living, our age, education, tastes in food and broad social background. We can usually find plenty of people who recognise us at this level. But deeper in are the circles that contain our more intimate selves, involving feelings about parents, secret fears, daydreams, ambitions that might never be realised, the stranger recesses of our sexual imagination and all that we find beautiful and moving.

Though we may long to share the inner circles, too often we seem able only to hover with others around the outer ones, returning home from yet another social gathering with the most sincere parts of us aching for recognition and companionship. Traditionally, religion provided an ideal explanation for, and solution to, this painful loneliness. The human soul – religious people would say – is made by God and so only God can know its deepest secrets. We are never truly alone, because God is always with us. In their touching way, religions had identified an important problem: they recognised the powerful need to be intimately known and appreciated and admitted frankly that this need could not realistically ever be met by other people.

Religion has been replaced in our imaginations by the cult of human-to-human love we now know as Romanticism, which bequeathed to us a beautiful, reckless idea that loneliness might be capable of being vanquished, if we were fortunate and determined enough to meet the one exalted being known as our soulmate, someone who could understand everything deep and strange about us, who would see us completely and be enchanted by our totality. But the legacy of Romanticism has been an epidemic of loneliness, as we are repeatedly brought up against the truth: the radical inability of any one other person to wholly grasp who we truly are. Yet there remains, besides the promises of love and religion, one other – and more solid – resource with which to address our loneliness: culture.

Henri Matisse,
Reader, 1918

Henri Matisse (1869–1954) began painting people reading in his early 20s and continued to do so throughout his life; at least thirty of his canvases tackle the theme. What gives these images their poignancy is that we recognise them as records of a loneliness that has been at least in part redeemed through culture. The figures may be on their own, their gaze often distant and melancholy, but they have to hand perhaps the best possible replacement when the immediate community has let us down: books.

The English psychoanalyst Donald Winnicott (1896–1971) – working in the middle years of the 20th century – was fascinated by how certain children cope with the absence of their parents. He identified the use of what he called 'transitional objects' to keep the memory of parental love strong even when the parents weren't there. So a teddy bear or a blanket, he realised, could be a mechanism for activating the memory of being cared for, a mechanism that is usefully mobile and portable and is always accessible when the parents are at bay.

Winnicott proposed that works of art can, for adults, function as more sophisticated versions of transitional objects. What we are at heart looking for in friendship is not necessarily someone we can touch and see in front of us, but a person who shares, and can help us develop, our sensibility and our values, someone to whom we can turn to and look for a sign that they too feel what we have felt, that they are attracted, amused and repulsed by similar things. Strangely, it appears that certain imaginary friends drawn from culture can end up feeling more real and in that sense more present to us than any of our real-life acquaintances, even if they have been dead a few centuries and lived on another continent. We can feel honoured to count them as among our best friends.

Christen Købke (1810–1848) lived in and around Copenhagen in the first half of the 19th century – he died of pneumonia in his late 30s in 1848 – but we might consider him as among our closest friends because of his sensitivity

Christen Købke,
A View of Østerbro from Dosseringen,
1838

to just the sort of everyday beauty that we may be deeply fond of, but that gets very little mention in the social circles around us. From a great distance, Købke acts like an ideal companion who gently works his way into the quiet, hidden parts of us and helps them grow in strength and self-awareness.

The arts provide a miraculous mechanism whereby a stranger is able to do the things that we properly identify as lying at the core of friendship. And when we find these 'art-friends', we are unpicking the experience of loneliness. We're finding intimacy at a distance. The arts allow us to become the soulmates of people who – despite having been born in 1630 or 1808 – are in limited, but crucial, ways our proper companions. The friendship may even be deeper than that which we could have enjoyed in person, for it is spared all the normal compromises that attend social interactions. Our cultural friends can't converse fully of course and we can't reply (except in our imagination). And yet, they travel into the same psychological space, at least in some key respects, as we are in at our most vulnerable and intimate points. They may not know of our latest technology, they have no idea of our families or jobs, and yet, in areas that really matter to us, they understand us to a degree that is at once a little shocking and deeply thrilling.

Confronted by the many failings of our real life communities, culture gives us the option of assembling a tribe for ourselves, drawing its members from across the widest ranges of time and space, blending some living friends with some dead authors, architects, musicians and composers, painters and poets.

The 15th-century Italian painter Verrocchio (1435–1488) – one of whose apprentices was Leonardo da Vinci – was deeply attracted to the biblical story of Tobias and the Angel. It tells of a young man, Tobias, who has to go on a long and dangerous journey. But he has two companions: one a little dog, another an angel who comes to walk by his side, advise him, encourage him and guard him.

Andrea del Verrocchio,
Tobias and the Angel, 1470–1480

The old religious idea was that we are never fully alone; there are always special beings around whose aid we can call on. Verrocchio's picture is touching not because it shows a real solution we can in fact count on, but because it points to the kind of companionship we would love to have and yet normally don't feel we can find.

Yet, there is an available version. Not, of course, in the form of winged creatures with golden halos round their heads. But, rather, imaginary friends that we can call on from the arts. You might feel physically isolated in the car, hanging around at the airport, going into a difficult meeting, having supper alone yet again or going through a tricky phase in a relationship – but you are not psychologically alone; key figures from your imaginary tribe (the modern version of angels and saints) are with you: their perspective, their habits of mind, their ways of looking at things are in your mind, just as if they were really by your side. And so we can confront the difficult stretches of existence not simply on the basis of our own small resources, but accompanied by the accumulated wisdom of the kindest, most intelligent voices of all ages gone by.

Given the enormous role of sadness in our lives, it is one of the greatest emotional skills to know how to arrange around us those cultural works that can best help to turn our panic or sense of persecution into consolation and nurture.

III
Hope

Much to the consternation of sophisticated people, a great deal of popular enthusiasm is directed at works of culture that are distinctly cheerful (songs about hope, films about couples that work through their problems), and in the visual arts, cheerful, pleasant scenes (meadows in spring, the shade of trees on hot summer days, pastoral landscapes, smiling children). The best-selling postcard of art in France turns out to be a reproduction of *Poppies, nearby Argenteuil* (1873) by Claude Monet.

Sophisticated people tend to scorn. They are afraid that such enthusiasms might be evidence of a failure to acknowledge or understand the awful dimensions of the world. But there is another way to interpret this taste: that it doesn't arise from an unfamiliarity with suffering, but from an all too close and pervasive involvement with it – from which we are impelled occasionally to seek relief if we are not to fall into despair and self-disgust. Far from naivety, it is precisely the background of suffering that lends an intensity and dignity to our engagement with hopeful cultural works.

In reality we rarely have the problem of being naively contented with our lives, or with the world in general. On the contrary, we are remorselessly confronted by our own failings and by the radical imperfections of society. Rather than needing a stern dose of disenchantment, we're more likely to require art tools that can feed and sustain our beleaguered optimism.

Pierre-Auguste Renoir's idyllic picture of friends having a picnic together in the shade on a sunny day isn't imagining a fantasy world in which people magically never have troubles or sorrows. They may have boring jobs or tricky partners; they may have long hours of loneliness. It's just that, all the

TOP Claude Monet, *Poppies, nearby Argenteuil*, 1873

BOTTOM Pierre-Auguste Renoir, *Picnic (Le Déjeuner sur l'herbe)*, c. 1893
Hope made visible

same, they can truly enjoy this opportunity of pleasant friendship in a lovely place. Renoir (1841–1919) isn't being sentimental. He's not implying that life as a whole is a picnic. He's portraying a much truer and more helpful idea of which we often need reminding: that despite the manifest failings of life and the world, it is still possible for us to experience true pleasure. Which leads to the odd conclusion: if (by some strange chance) normal life were to become consistently delightful, we would no longer need sweetly charming, hope-inducing works of art.

One of the less discussed powers of art is that, from time to time, it can bring tears to our eyes. It's normal to think that what makes people cry are sad things; that's certainly the way it works when you're a child. But the older we get, the more we start to notice an odd phenomenon: we start crying not when things are horrible (we toughen up a little), but when they are suddenly and unexpectedly precisely the opposite: when they are unusually sweet, tender, joyful, innocent or kind. This, far more than grimness, is what can increasingly prompt tears.

We can notice this in films. In Richard Linklater's *Before Midnight* (2013), most of the action comprises a bitter series of arguments between a 40-something couple, played by Julie Delpy and Ethan Hawke. They have been together for years, they are on holiday in Greece, and the film homes in on one day when the pair decide to spend time alone in a smart hotel. They arrive in their room with the possibility of sex somewhere in both of their minds but instead find themselves having a blazing argument. They rake up all the hurt from past years; they blame each other for every disappointment, and swear at and insult one another with abandon. Eventually, the wife storms out, leaving her room key and her husband behind. It feels agonisingly real. But, after a few hours of sulking, Hawke goes out in search of Delpy and finds her alone in a nearby restaurant terrace. They are both a little sheepish around each other, as one often is after a row, and he sits down opposite her with poignant formality. In a beautiful closing sequence, they start to talk with unusual honesty. It's difficult, but we can see that, despite everything (kids, too many sacrifices, exhaustion, not enough sex, perhaps a one-night stand or two), they do still love and desire one another very much. Their rage is an explosion of the frustration inherent within all long-term relationships. They get so deeply upset because they know that, day-to-day, they need so much from one another and they don't always get it. They're not magically going to stop bickering in the future, but this moment of kindness and sympathy, playfulness and gentleness, after such a bruising confrontation, comes as a huge relief and is deeply tender to behold. Their admission of shared love is moving because it reminds us at once of the struggles in our own lives and of what at heart we really want: reconciliation, forgiveness, tenderness, an end to the fighting, a chance to say sorry...

We start to cry at the brief vision of a state of grace from which we're exiled most of the time.

Something similar may happen around a much older work, with a very different theme – such as this 16th-century painting of the Virgin Mary with her child, Jesus. Its emotional force is independent of its religious meaning. We're seeing in her face the face of true love that we desperately wish might sometimes be turned on us – filled with delight in our existence, warm, forgiving, generous and sad for every trouble that will come our way. When we look upon the picture with these thoughts in mind, we glimpse the love we wish we could bestow on others, but never quite manage to convey; and we see the love we need but may never find. We would love someone to rest their head delicately upon ours, to close their eyes and think with every power of their imagination and understanding how deeply they long for our happiness, how readily they would stand in harm's way if only it were possible to save us from distress, how precious we are to them. And we cry because life is so seldom like this but so deeply should be. We are weeping at the loss of

Bernard van Orley
(workshop of), *Virgin and Child*,
c. 1520–1530

an idea, which means so much to us, and which we may catch sight of just for a moment when we look at a painting or read a passage in a children's story book, or catch the echoes of every lost love in the final notes of a song: the idea of true, redemptive love.

The more difficult our lives, the less it might take to make us cry; even a flower might start to move us. The tears – if they come – are in response not to how sad the flower is, but how its prettiness exists within such a very pitiless and mean world.

Across his life, Van Gogh (1853–1890) produced exquisite paintings of flowers. Yet, self-evidently, he was overwhelmingly conscious of the darker sides of the human condition. His deep love of flowers wasn't a denial of life's grimness – or a naive failure even to acknowledge it. It was his radical recognition of sorrow that made him extremely sensitive to, and appreciative of, the transient grace of delicately tinted roses in bloom.

There's a strange contrast we sometimes catch sight of around parents and children. The child might be joyfully singing and dancing along to a favourite song. As they watch, the parent's delight has a different quality: they are deeply conscious of how fragile and fleeting such moments of intense happiness are; they see this lovely, innocent moment against the backdrop of life's sorrows and troubles – adding a layer of poignancy and tenderness which the child can't as yet imagine. And this is what makes the sight so moving to the parent.

It's not fair to condemn all art that is joyful or sweet as 'sentimental' and therefore unworthy of the attention of an intelligent adult who has a realistic view of existence. The pleasure we take in pretty, charming or very gracious art doesn't at all mean we are naively denying the darker aspects of the world or of our own nature. We're not pretending that the pretty work is an accurate portrait of existence – in fact, we're agonisingly conscious that it isn't. It's because we're burdened with frustrations, disappointments,

The more difficult our lives, the less it might take to make us cry; even a flower might start to move us.

failings, errors, regrets and compromises that the sight of grace, innocence, lightness and carefree joy is so moving; and if we cry, it is because we're glimpsing something we love and need and yet cannot now hold on to.

For many of us, instead of being complacent and unwilling to confront awkward truths, we're liable to have the reverse problem: we're so aware of what's wrong that we're despondent and paralysed. The Beatles' warm, supportive song 'Hey Jude' (1968), with its key line, 'don't be afraid', sees the reasons for potential despair as obvious: we get withdrawn and lonely, we give up, our problems feel too big. The song's optimism isn't denying this. Instead, it sees hope and cheerfulness as important ingredients in facing difficult situations. Similarly, one of Mozart's most beautiful arias – 'Sleep Softly' from *Zaide* (1780) – captures a beautiful moment of love: you see your partner sleeping and you feel incredibly tender towards them. It's not a denial that couples often squabble, disappoint and frustrate one another. It's not pretending that this is how we always feel. Rather it's taking a rare, and very lovely, experience and preserving it, so that we can strategically reconnect with it when things have grown dark. It is because we are so aware of how hard relationships can be that we need an artificial way of reminding ourselves of the very positive and kindly feelings we also really do have towards our partners – but which tend to get lost amongst the normal conflicts and stand-offs of being together.

We're leaky creatures. Hope drains away, not because the situation is genuinely hopeless but because we are so attuned to seeing what's wrong. It's precisely because we so readily lose hope that the optimistic reminders provided by culture – hope in amber – are so important to us.

TOP
Vincent van Gogh,
Still Life: Vase with Pink Roses,
1890

BOTTOM
Vincent van Gogh,
Self-Portrait with Bandaged Ear,
1889

IV

Balance

Few of us are entirely well 'balanced'. Our psychological histories, relationships and working routines mean that many of our emotions incline a little too much in one direction or another. We may, for example, have a tendency to be too complacent. Or else too insecure or too trusting. Or too suspicious, too serious. Or too lighthearted, too calm or too excited.

The particular imbalances we suffer from may be specific to us, but the phenomenon of being unbalanced is general – and, surprisingly, it is an issue that culture is particularly placed to help us with, for works can put us powerfully in touch with concentrated doses of our missing dispositions, and thereby restore a measure of equilibrium to our listing inner selves.

It is an emotional skill to be ready to sense an inner imbalance and then to take the steps necessary to rectify it with the help of culture. We might register that we are suffering from a mood of longing and disenchantment with what strike us as our rather humdrum and ordinary lives. The realisation isn't complex in itself; what counts is the confidence to see that culture might have a solution to our mood – as well as the imagination to seek it out. We might find our way to a film about an ordinary schoolteacher who we, the audience, realise is delightful even though they lack any of the external markers of status. Through the film, we may be taught how to see the very real dignity and grace of ordinary life, and recognise that a little of this, fairly, belongs to us as well.

In another mood, we may discern that it is a different sort of film we need. We often go so far down the track of teaching ourselves about the importance of gentleness and compromise that sometimes we unwittingly

It is an emotional skill to be ready to sense an inner imbalance and then to take the steps necessary to rectify it with the help of culture.

develop a problem with self-assertion and resistance to the demands of others. We might have learned too well to suppress our own appetite for a fight, our own desire for victory. In a world where conflict is unavoidable, good people sometimes need to strengthen their willingness to face down opposition – not always to compromise and play it safe, but to take risks instead, to get out and fight, to relish victory and to be a bit more ruthless in the service of noble and deeply important ends. Sometimes it is not enough to be right: you also need to win.

So, some of us might well benefit from watching films that tell tales of heroism: that follow someone who has to navigate the world, kill a dragon, outwit some baddies, or penetrate a corrupt organisation. Ideally, the film shouldn't simply leave us in awe at the daring of another. It should do that far more valuable thing: educate us by example, so that we too become just a little more heroic and brave where we need to be.

The notion that art plays a crucial role in rebalancing us emotionally can answer the vexed question of why people differ so much in their aesthetic tastes. Why are some people drawn to minimalist architecture and others to the baroque? Why are some people excited by bare concrete walls and others by floral patterns? Why do some like quiet films about relationships and others war epics? Our tastes will depend on what spectrum of our emotional makeup lies in shadow and is hence in need of stimulation and emphasis. Every work of art is imbued with a particular psychological and moral atmosphere – serene or restless, courageous or careful, modest or confident, masculine or feminine, bourgeois or aristocratic – and our preferences for one kind over another reflects our varied psychological gaps. We hunger for artworks that will compensate for our inner fragilities and help to return us to a viable mean.

Life might be a frantic whirl of demands, deadlines, appointments and meetings; by the end of every day we're worn out and on edge; we've been on constant high alert for what feels like forever; there's scarcely a moment to

Mel Gibson,
Braveheart, 1995

think, to define our own priorities or to take stock of where we are in our lives. It wouldn't be at all surprising if, in such a state, we looked with longing at a serene, emphatically quiet interior as the much-needed ideal home to which we need to find our way for a period of respite.

Of course, the character of our individual lives varies enormously. So the balancing agents that instinctively appeal to us will be equally diverse. We might have a life too heavily impressed by routine: the tasks of one day are essentially the same as all the rest; we can predict from week to week what time we'll get home; perhaps a relationship has settled into an over-familiar groove; without maybe fully acknowledging it to ourselves, we feel that life has become a bit stale. In that case, we're not at all likely to feel the allure of Pawson's deeply calm and minimalist architecture. Instead we will perhaps feel strangely but powerfully attracted to the drama of a façade by the Roman Baroque architect Francesco Borromini (1599–1667) – a work with the power to rouse our slumbering souls.

Whole nations can manifest longings for balance and will use art to help them achieve it. After too much aristocratic decadence, many in late-18th-century France felt the need to get back in touch with martial solemnity and spartan simplicity and so found refuge in the pared-down works of Jacques-Louis David (1748–1825).

By the later part of the 19th century in England, the materialism, scientific obsession and capitalist rationality of the age drove many to long for more faithful, mystical days, and so to locate 'beauty' in images such as Edmund Leighton's *The End of the Song* (1902), inspired by the literature and history of the Middle Ages.

What we call 'beautiful' is any work of art that supplies a missing dose of a much-needed psychological component, while what we dismiss as 'ugly' is that which forces on us moods or motifs that we feel threatened or overwhelmed by. Our contact with art holds the promise of inner wholeness.

TOP John Pawson,
The Life House, 2011–2016
Art to counter our agitation

BOTTOM Francesco Borromini:
San Carlo alle Quattro Fontane,
Rome, 1638–1641
Art to rouse our sluggish passions

TOP Jacques-Louis David, *The Oath of the Horatii*, 1784

BOTTOM Edmund Blair Leighton, *The End of the Song*, 1902

V
Compassion

One of the things that makes us fear failure the most is the way we imagine we'd be seen by others. We'd not merely fail, we'd be called losers, burdened by the additional – and in some ways more ghastly – prospect of being figures of ridicule and contempt in the eyes of most people.

Our fear isn't unfounded. Generally, failure and personal disaster are treated very severely in social life. We can imagine how a mean-spirited group of people after work or at a party would make fun of the world's most august failures – the central characters of tragic novels and plays: Oedipus, Hamlet, Raskolnikov or Jay Gatsby. The media would be even crueller, coming up with lurid summations like a classic headline version of the ancient Greek story: SEX WITH MUM WAS BLINDING. They might state the fate of Hamlet as: BOOZY FOREIGN ARISTO DIES IN FIGHT AFTER KILLING SPREE; *Crime and Punishment* would be: CALL-GIRL MAKES PSYCHO KILLER CONFESS and *The Great Gatsby* would be reduced to: FAKE GENT SHOT IN DELUX POOL BY WRONG LOVE RIVAL.

These headlines come across as cheap and mean only because the stories behind them have been so powerfully elaborated by novelists and dramatists. Without Sophocles, Shakespeare, Dostoyevsky or Scott Fitzgerald, we'd never think of the complex, moving personal histories of the individuals that lie behind these harsh summaries. Figures like these strike us as fascinating and worthy of sympathy only because we've been taught by the best teachers to see them through the prism of artistic sympathy and compassion.

The idea of rescuing failure from unjust contempt lies behind one of the world's oldest and most impressive theories of art. The idea of Tragedy was developed by the ancient Greek philosopher Aristotle (384–322 BCE) in his *Poetics* (c. 330 BCE). In the book, Aristotle wasn't at all pretending that individual responsibility doesn't matter. His goal was to show that even perfectly decent people can end up in horrific situations and that therefore they deserve to be regarded with tender pity rather than disgust. It's not that it isn't in some way their fault. These people are not merely unlucky. But the thing in their nature that leads to their downfall isn't in itself all that different from our own failings. To capture this crucial point, Aristotle defined their failings as *harmatia* or 'flaws' – someone is a bit impetuous, they sometimes lose their temper; they let ambition get in the way of caution; they don't properly listen to what another person is saying. These are imperfections, but they are very common. And sometimes these flaws have terrible consequences. We might lose our temper at the worst possible moment and shout at someone who turns out to have the power to wreck our lives; a hasty decision might lead to financial ruin; or we might brush aside someone who is trying to tell us something that turns out to be really important. These are the staple moves of Greek Tragedy as analysed by Aristotle. And his point is this: those who end up in horrendous trouble haven't necessarily got any deeper flaws in their characters than we do in our own.

It's the polar opposite of an attitude that suggests that failure is always the sign of something being very wrong with someone (the attitude implied by media headlines). These headlines hint that their victims, caught up in grotesque events, are not at all like us; we don't have to feel for them because they belong almost to a different species. It could never happen to us. The whole thrust of Aristotle's *Poetics* is that tragedy is a vehicle of education. It teaches us to feel pity, rather than contempt, for those whose lives turn out very badly.

To drive this point home Aristotle makes a particular recommendation to people writing plays: make sure, he says, that the person to whom the bad things happen is 'like us, or only slightly better than us'. When we first meet the character, says Aristotle, they have to be likeable, even a touch impressive. We have to be invited to warmly identify with them or admire them. And then, he continues, their disasters have to unfold in a short span of time, so that our original liking for this person is still fresh in our minds. In life we often have weeks or months in which to forget that someone to whom disaster comes is really rather nice. We have time to detach emotionally from them before we start to see them simply as losers. By speeding up the process, Aristotle's hope is that we don't have time to forget; we can see that these awful things are happening to someone as nice as or slightly nicer than us and only for faults that are similar to or no worse than our own.

An attitude of mockery and contempt is driven by the background thesis that the 'loser' is fundamentally unlike us. This is what gives our severe attitudes free rein. We simply refuse to imagine that this kind of misfortune might come our way. We'd never end up there, we imagine. We'd never be on the receiving end of fate, so we have no motive to moderate our condemnations. We're prone to mocking a politician who freezes in an interview; a married father of three children who gets caught with his mistress; someone who puts their life savings into a business venture that doesn't work out... And the reason is that we don't have in mind the small steps which could take a perfectly ordinary person to these places. And this is where Aristotle comes up with a crucial idea. In a great tragic story, it is necessary to make the plot 'probable' – that is, we need to feel that what went wrong for this person happened little by little; they couldn't see at the time that it was all heading for disaster. Gradually, they got in deeper. Being able to imagine this kind of story is crucial to sympathy because it is the account of how we too might, without quite realising it, get caught up in a dreadful situation. We're often tempted to say 'I can't imagine how a sensible person could have done that.' Aristotle is proposing art as a way of making us more accurately imaginative.

In January 1872, a 35-year-old woman called Anna Pirogova committed suicide by throwing herself under a train at the recently opened railway station at Yasenki, a modest provincial town about 200 kilometres south of Moscow. It turned out she was the housekeeper of a local landowner whose wife had died some time before; they'd been having an affair and she'd been expecting to marry him. But he'd just told her that he was instead planning to marry the more alluring German governess who looked after his son. The inquest would have been a routine affair had it not been for the presence of Russia's most distinguished novelist, Leo Tolstoy (1828–1910), who had recently achieved huge success with the publication of *War and Peace*. It was his local station, his family estate lay just beyond the town and his wife was in fact distantly related to Anna Pirogova. The event made a deep impression on Tolstoy. It was obvious to him that many people would have limited sympathy for this woman. He could imagine how her suicide would be chatted about in the social circles of Moscow and St Petersburg. She'd already lost all right to pity when she had an affair; she had been angling to catch her boss; she was ditched for a more attractive rival – what did she expect? She was stupid, unprincipled and hysterical; it was all her own fault. The tabloid headline might read: STATION SUICIDE OF SOCIAL CLIMBING ADULTERESS.

Tolstoy's reaction was entirely different. He used the grim death of Anna Pirogova as a model for the climax of his next great novel, *Anna Karenina*, of which the first instalment was published the following year. At the end of the long novel, the heroine (also called Anna) commits suicide by throwing herself under a train, after being rejected by the man with whom she was having an illicit affair. But this only happens in the closing pages. Much of the rest of the long novel can be seen as an attempt to understand, as sympathetically as possible, how someone could end up doing this. In his novel, he ups the stakes. The Anna of the book is, when we first meet her, a deeply engaging person: she has a warm, generous nature, she's elegant and charming, she's cultivated and clever and she's married, with a child, to a leading official in the government.

Tolstoy then traces the unfortunate factors, the slight mistakes, the little steps that gradually bring this obviously lovely person to a horrific end. Anna Karenina has an awkward marriage, but it's not her fault. She was married off at a young age by her family, and she's tried very hard to be loyal to her husband. Quite by chance she meets a deeply fascinating man; she dances with him at a ball and then decides never to see him again. But he happens to be immensely persistent. He trails after her around the country, he gets himself invited to parties that she has to attend with her husband. Eventually, slowly, he seduces her. It's not a meaningless fling, he's genuinely in love with her, totally sincere, talented and sophisticated. Anna pleads for a divorce. But her husband rejects the idea for purely tactical reasons; he doesn't care about Anna personally but it would be inconvenient to go through divorce proceedings when he's so busy with work.

Eventually Anna elopes with her lover – but the price is that she can never again see her son. Her husband coldly refuses access, and this breaks her heart. They have to live in the country, because they would be rejected in the city; her lover has to give up his career, he grows restless. Increasingly desperate, Anna turns to drugs to calm herself. Her lover becomes more and more frustrated and brusque, frequently spending time away from Anna. They row constantly and Anna becomes convinced that he no longer loves her. She has destroyed everything she had for him and now she feels that it's been all for nothing. She takes a carriage to the station and throws herself under the wheels of an oncoming train.

Anna Karenina's story is not precisely the same as that of Anna Pirogova – the housekeeper whose suicide was an inspiration for the novel. Yet the difference between the novel and the gossip lies primarily in the way the story is told. Tolstoy's narrative is an unflinching but deeply generous account of how a life can be utterly ruined and how a person who is (at the start) immensely charming, kind and intelligent can end up, by their own action, a mangled corpse on a railway track. It is, in essence, the story as seen through the eyes of love, the opposite of the critical, dismissive, cold voice of gossip.

The point of being repeatedly exposed to this loving, understanding voice is that ultimately, it becomes the voice in which we can start to tell our own story. We too are inept, flawed, messy creatures heading – at some point – for a fall. So it matters immensely that lodged in our minds we have a voice that isn't just the punitive one of the public square, but one that can make some of the same moves as we witness in Sophocles, Shakespeare or Flaubert. It isn't a case of writing up our lives as they would have done. It's seeing that, in our failures, we deserve no less sympathy than the unfortunate victims of the world's greatest tragedies. A world in which people properly imbibed the lessons implicit within tragic art would be one in which the consequences of failure would cease to weigh upon us so heavily, a world in which we had learnt how to extend a loving perspective upon ourselves, and on our fellow wretched humans.

VI
Knowledge

One of the more frustrating, yet fundamental, things about being human is that we can't understand ourselves very well. Either side of the mind frequently has no clear picture of what the other happens to be upset about, anxious of or looking forward to. We make a lot of mistakes due to a pervasive self-ignorance.

Here too culture can help, because in many cases, it knows us better than we know ourselves and can provide us with an account (more accurate than any we might be capable of) of what is likely to be going on in our minds.

Marcel Proust's lengthy 1913 novel, *In Search of Lost Time*, is seemingly the story of a collection of aristocratic and high bourgeois characters living in early 20th-century France. However, towards the end of the book, Proust (1871–1922) makes a remarkable claim. His novel wasn't really about these distinctly remote-sounding people, it was about someone closer to home, you:

> In reality, every reader is, while he is reading, the reader of his own self. The writer's work is merely a kind of optical instrument which he offers to the reader to enable him to discern what, without this book, he would perhaps never have experienced in himself. And the recognition by the reader in his own self of what the book says is the proof of its veracity.

In the great works of culture, we have an impression of coming across orphaned pieces of ourselves, evoked with rare crispness and tenacity. We might wonder how on earth the author could have known certain deeply personal things about us, ideas that normally fracture in our clumsy fingers, but that are here perfectly preserved and illuminated. Take, for example, the self-knowledge offered by one of Proust's favourite writers, François VI, Duc de La Rochefoucauld (1613–1680), author of a slim volume of aphorisms known as the *Maxims* (1665–1678):

> We all have strength enough to bear the misfortunes of others.

It's an idea closely followed by the equally penetrating:

> There are some people who would never have fallen in love, if they had not heard there was such a thing.

And the no less accomplished:

> To say that one never flirts is in itself a form of flirtation.

We are likely to smile in recognition. We have been here ourselves. We just never knew how to condense our mental mulch into something this elegant.

When Proust compares literature to 'a kind of optical instrument', what he means is that it performs the function of a high-tech machine, helping us to focus on what is really unfolding within ourselves and within others around us. Great authors turn vagueness into clarity. For example, if we have read Proust, and are then later abandoned by a lover who very kindly professes their need to spend 'a little more time on their own', we will benefit from having seen the dynamic clearly captured in Proust's line from his 1923 work *The Prisoner*: 'When two people part, it is the one who is not in love who makes the tender speeches.' The clarity won't make the lover return; but it will do the next best thing: help us to feel less confused by, and alone with, the misery of having been left.

The more writers we read, the better our understanding of our own mind stands to be. Every great writer can be hailed as an explorer – no less extraordinary than Magellan or Cook – of new, hitherto mysterious, corners of the self. Some explorers discover continents, others spend their lives perfectly mapping one or two small islands, or just a single river valley or cove. All deserve to be feted for correcting the ignorance in which we otherwise meander through our internal world. The Japanese poet Matsuo Basho clarifies our feelings of loneliness, Tolstoy explains our ambition to us, Kafka makes us conscious of our dread of authority, Camus guides us to our alienated and numb selves, and under Philip Roth's guidance we become conscious of what happens to our sexuality in the shadow of mortality.

The 20th-century English writer Virginia Woolf (1882–1941) did not enjoy good health. In an essay titled '*On Being Ill*' (1930), she lamented how little we tend to clearly grasp what illness really feels like. We casually say we're not well, or have a headache, but we lack a focused vocabulary for our ailments. There is one large reason for this: because of how little illness has been written about by talented authors. As Woolf remarks:

> English, which can express the thoughts of Hamlet and the tragedy of Lear, has no words for the shiver and the headache. It has all grown one way. The merest schoolgirl, when she falls in love, has Shakespeare or Keats to speak her mind for her; but let a sufferer try to describe a pain in his head to a doctor and language at once runs dry. There is nothing ready made for him.

This turned out to be one of Woolf's great tasks as a literary explorer. She brought into focus what it's like to be tired, close to tears, too weak to open a drawer, irritated by a pressure in one's ears or beset by strange tremors in one's chest. Woolf became the Columbus of illness.

One effect of reading a book that has devoted attention to noticing such faint yet vital tremors is that once we've put the volume down and resumed our own lives, we find ourselves responding to precisely the things that the author would have noted, had he or she been in our place. With our new optical instrument, we're ready to pick up and see clearly all kinds of new objects floating through our consciousness. Our attention might be drawn to the shades of the sky, to the changeability of a face, to the hypocrisy of a friend, or to a submerged sadness about a situation that we had previously not even known we could feel sad about. A book will have sensitised us, stimulated our dormant antennae by evidence of its own developed sensitivity. Which is why Proust proposed, in words he would modestly never have extended to his own novel, that:

> If we read the new masterpiece of a man of genius, we are delighted to find in it those reflections of ours that we despised, joys and sorrows which we had repressed, a whole world of feeling we had scorned, and whose value the book in which we discover them suddenly teaches us.

These lines connect up with an equally prescient quote from Ralph Waldo Emerson's 1888 essay 'Self Reliance':

> In every work of genius we recognize our own rejected thoughts.

It isn't just ourselves we learn about through culture. It is also, of course, the minds of strangers, especially those we would not ordinarily have ever learnt much about. With our optical instruments in hand, we are able to learn about family life in Trinidad, about being a teenager in Iran, about school in Syria, love in Moldova and guilt in Korea. We get taken past the

The more writers we read, the better our understanding of our own mind stands to be.

guards right into the king's bedroom (we hear him whispering to his mistress or doubting his attendants) and the pauper's hovel, the upper middle-class family's holiday villa and the lower middle-class family's caravan.

Thanks to all this, we have a rare opportunity to spare ourselves time and error. Literature speeds up the years: it can take us through a whole life in an afternoon, and so lets us study the long-term consequences of decisions that, in our own cases, would work themselves out dangerously slowly. We have a chance to see in accelerated form what can happen when you worry only about art and not so much about money, or only about ambition and not so much about your own children; what happens when you despise ordinary people or are disturbingly concerned with what others think. Literature helps us avert mistakes. All those heroes who commit suicide, those unfortunate demented souls who murder their way out of trouble and those victims who die of loneliness in unfurnished rooms are able to teach us things. Literature is the very best reality simulator we have – a machine that, like its flight equivalent, allows us to safely experience the most appalling scenarios that would, in reality, take many years and great danger to go through, in the hope that we'll be ever so slightly less inclined to misunderstand ourselves, swerve blindly into danger or succumb before time.

VII
Encouragement

In England in the 1880s, a group of art lovers – most of them young, forward-looking and metropolitan – began a movement known as aestheticism. Their core belief was that in a rapidly secularising world, culture could provide us with a new moral framework; it could, as religion had once done, guide, inspire and console us. In particular, it could play a vital role in encouraging us to be good, because beautiful objects and environments were not, in the eyes of aestheticists, merely meaninglessly pretty. They were goads to virtue. The aestheticists believed – as the Ancient Greeks had done before them – that beauty was synonymous with goodness, while ugliness was an incarnation of corruption.

This analysis transformed badly designed objects and environments from unfortunate eyesores to political priorities; after all, they weren't just ugly, they might make us bad. Cities, houses, chairs, plates and teapots needed to be attractively made, in order to generate the right sort of atmosphere around which good lives could unfold.

The aestheticists were easy to mock. Many of them had somewhat earnest and precious airs. The satirical magazine *Punch* took regular aim at them. In one cartoon, an ardent young couple examine a teapot they have received as a wedding gift: 'It is quite consummate, is it not!' exclaims the bridegroom. 'It is indeed!' replies his bride, 'Oh, Algernon, let us live up to it!'

The idea of 'living up to' a teapot sounds daft, but it contains a not-at-all inane background thesis: that the quality of designed environments matters because we are hugely vulnerable to the suggestions emanating from them about how we might behave, and more broadly, who we might be. In degraded, battered, run-down streets (and in a lesser way, around ugly teapots), it is easier for hope to escape and for the worst sides of our nature to come to the fore, whereas on dignified thoroughfares (and around well-made teapots), our better aspects are seductively invited to flourish.

This degree of aesthetic ambition would not have sounded in any way strange to the Zen Buddhist philosophers behind the Japanese tea ceremony. These theorists paid acute attention to the design of the teacups and teapots, because they felt that they could operate as powerful visual reminders of prized Zen tenets about modesty and forbearance. Minor blemishes were deliberately allowed to remain on cups so as to remind drinkers that imperfection is an inevitability to which we should graciously accommodate ourselves. The glaze was unevenly applied and the overall shape often a little wonky, so as to nudge us towards a serene acceptance of our own flaws. The cups were conceived of as small lessons of wisdom embodied in ceramic.

If a teacup can have the power to affect character, then so too must the most imposing of all the arts: architecture. In 1961, the government of what was then East Pakistan and is now Bangladesh started the construction of a new parliament building in the capital city, Dhaka. The country was deeply beset by economic problems and by intense ethnic rivalries; its administrative system tended to corruption; it was horrifically exposed to catastrophic cyclones and floods. But rather than try to reflect the actual country, it was decided to commission a building – by the great American architect Louis Kahn (1901–1974) – that could present a vision of the country as it might and could be in the future.

Kahn's complex of buildings in Dhaka are emphatically solid and enduring; they can bear the assaults of storms and floods; the logical, geometrical forms speak of a world in which civil servants and administrators make coolly rational judgements in the national interest, without reference

THE SIX-MARK TEA-POT.

Æsthetic Bridegroom. "It is quite consummate, is it not?"
Intense Bride. "It is, indeed! Oh, Algernon, let us live up to it!"

George Du Maurier, 'The Six-Mark Tea-Pot', *Punch*, 1880

to personal benefit; in the light-filled chambers and lobbies, there will be careful, serious discussion of long-term solutions; the parliamentarians and civil servants will become like the building and, via them, so too will the nation.

The building is intended as a kind of seduction. Generally we think of seduction only in its worst versions. But there is a good version in which we are gently but persuasively enticed to let go of our normal habits and develop in a hopeful direction. Seduction works not by sternly telling us to do something but by subtly conveying how nice it might be if we did so. It lures our senses and our imaginations; it foregrounds certain moods (un-panicked, sincere, quietly dignified) and gives us greater confidence in them; it implies that they are, or should be, normal. In the company of the right building (as in the company of the right friend) we find it easier to become the better versions of who we really are.

The Parliament building in Dhaka, like many a beautiful city, street, chair or teapot, matters because of its skill at encouraging the better sides of us. This is no idle or dispensable project. We are always on the verge of forgetting the lessons in goodness and fulfilment we know in theory – and lie at the mercy of messages whispered by our environment. We need to build lives in which we can arrange around us the kind of art that will daily bring the best sides of us to the fore.

TOP Tea bowl with a white slip decoration, Japan, Edo period, c. 1700–1724
Philosophy in a teacup

BOTTOM Louis Kahn, National Assembly Building, Dhaka, 1970

VIII
Appreciation

At the centre of our societies is a hugely inventive force dedicated to nudging us towards a heightened appreciation of certain aspects of the world. With enormous skill, it throws into relief the very best sides of particular places and objects. It uses wordsmiths and image makers of near genius, who create deeply inspiring and beguiling associations – and it positions works close to our eyelines at most moments of the day. Advertising is the most compelling agent of mass appreciation the world has ever known.

Because advertising is so ubiquitous, it can be easy to forget that – of course – only a very few sorts of things ever get advertised. Almost nothing is in a position to afford the budgets required by an average campaign, something overwhelmingly reserved for those wealthy potentates of modern life: nappies, cereal bars and hand sanitisers. This has a habit of skewing our priorities. One of our major flaws as animals, and a big contributor to our unhappiness, is that we are very bad at keeping in mind the real ingredients of fulfilment. We lose sight of the value of almost everything that is readily to hand, we're deeply ungrateful towards anything that is free or doesn't cost very much, we trust in the value of objects more than ideas or feelings, we are sluggish in remembering to love and to care, and are prone to racing through the years while forgetting the wonder, fragility and beauty of existence. It's fortunate, therefore, that we have art.

One way to conceive of what artists do is to think that they are, in their own way, running advertising campaigns, not for anything expensive or usually even available for purchase, but for the many things that are at once of huge human importance and yet constantly in danger of being forgotten.

TOP David Hockney, *Three Trees near Thixendale, Summer, 2007*, 2007

BOTTOM Albrecht Dürer, *Great Piece of Turf*, 1503

TOP LEFT Mary Cassatt, *Mother Playing with Child*, c. 1897

TOP RIGHT Pierre Bonnard, *Women with a Dog*, 1891

BOTTOM Vanessa Bell, *Interior with the Artist's Daughter*, c. 1935–1936

In the early part of the 21st century, for example, the English artist David Hockney (b. 1937) ran a major advertising campaign for trees.

At the start of the 16th century, the German painter Albrecht Dürer (1471–1528) launched a comparable campaign around the value of grass. In the psychological field, the French painter Pierre Bonnard (1867–1947) carried out an exceptionally successful campaign for tenderness, turning out dozens of images of his partner, Marthe, viewed through lenses of sympathy, concern and understanding. In an associated move, the American painter Mary Cassatt (1844–1926) made a good case for the world-beating importance of spending some time with a child.

These were all acts of justice, not condescension. They were much needed correctives to the way in which what we call 'glamour' is so often located in unhelpful places: in what is rare, remote, costly or youthful. If advertising images carry a lot of the blame for instilling a sickness in our souls, the images of artists reconcile us with our realities and reawaken us to the genuine, but too-easily forgotten, value of our lives.

Consider for instance Vanessa Bell's quiet picture of her daughter sitting in an arm chair, concentrating on the book she's reading. It's a seductive scene – but the charm Vanessa Bell (1879–1961) is interested in isn't expensive or remote. The room might have a few more books in it than our own, but the details, which are lovingly picked out, are modest: a simple rug, a plain vase, a few flowers. And the centre of the allure is the daughter's intent attitude, with her feet slightly tucked together. It's not fake glamour: it's a genuine highlighting of something lovely that we can directly pursue at little cost, if we want, in our own lives.

Art doesn't have to tantalise us with alluring visions of things we can never attain. It's capable of drawing our admiration to the easily forgotten, but very real, charms and dignity of everyday life. And it can – in this way – usefully reconcile us to the unavoidable imperfections of existence – a job that's not all it could be (but does have some genuinely nice moments); a relationship that's certainly not ideal – but does contain much that is, in less dramatic ways, quite pleasing; things which we could value more justly, perhaps, if more often, works of art shone their spotlight of loving admiration upon them.

Art can do the opposite of glamorising the unattainable; it can reawaken us to the genuine merit of life as we're forced to lead it. It is advertising for the things we really need.

IX
Perspective

Because of the way our minds work, it is very hard for us to be anything other than immensely preoccupied with what is immediately close to us in time and space. But in the process, we tend to exaggerate the importance of certain frustrations that do not, in the grander scheme, merit quite so much agitation and despair. We are inveterately poor at retaining perspective. Here, too, culture can help – by carrying us out of present circumstances and reframing events against a more imposing or vast backdrop.

Some extremely worrying-sounding things are, always, happening in the world. We are surrounded by a media industry that knows it must scare us to survive and that the one thing (despite its overt commitment to free speech) it must always censor is the idea that things might, on balance, be OK. One place we can turn to for relief is in a resource that powerfully reminds us that extreme difficulties are never new, that the worst sounding troubles can be survived and that it has (extraordinarily) often been a lot worse even than this. That antidote goes by the name of history.

When political events seem to have reached a new low, we might – for example – turn to the writings of the ancient Roman historian Suetonius. Born towards the end of the 1st century CE, Gaius Suetonius Tranquillus was an imperial administrator, chief secretary to the Emperor Hadrian and the first historian to attempt an accurate biographical portrayal of the rulers of the Roman Empire, from Julius Caesar down to Domitian. It's a shocking story. Suetonius's book, *The Lives of the Twelve Caesars* (121 CE), amounts to a catalogue of extraordinary follies and crimes of the first twelve men to rule the Western world. Amongst them, we find:

JULIUS CAESAR: A thief, a liar, an egomaniac and a murderer.

CALIGULA: A notorious psychopath who, to quote Suetonius, 'condemned [people] to the mines, to work at building roads, or to be thrown to the wild beasts; or else he shut them up in cages on all fours, like animals, or had them sawn asunder. Not all these punishments were for serious offences, but merely for criticising one of his shows, or for never having sworn by his Genius.' We also hear that the method of execution he preferred was to inflict numerous small wounds, but to avoid all major organs, and that he often gave the command: 'Strike so that he may feel that he is dying.'

NERO: Of him we hear that he: 'devised a kind of game, in which, covered with the skin of some wild animal, he was let loose from a cage and attacked the private parts of men and women, who were bound to stakes', and that he wandered through the streets at night randomly murdering strangers and throwing their bodies into the sewers.

VITELLUS: His ruling vices were gluttony and cruelty. He banqueted three or four times a day and he survived by taking frequent emetics. He used to give himself a treat by having prisoners executed before his eyes.

DOMITIAN: 'At the beginning of his reign he used to spend hours in seclusion every day, doing nothing but catching flies and stabbing them with a keenly-sharpened stylus'.

Though Suetonius writes about grotesque people – who were also at the time the most powerful people on the planet – he can leave us feeling remarkably serene. We might read him tucked up in bed, after news of the latest catastrophe. The experience is strangely reassuring, because at heart, it is a narrative of resilience.

Suetonius writes of earthquakes, plagues, wars, riots, rebellions, conspiracies, betrayals, coups, terrorism and mass slaughter. Considered on its own, it might seem to be the record of a society whose collapse must surely be imminent. But, in fact, Suetonius was writing before – and not after – one of the most impressive periods of Roman achievement, which would come fifty years later under the rule of the stoic philosopher and emperor Marcus Aurelius.

The disasters that Suetonius catalogues were compatible with a society heading overall towards peace and prosperity. Reading Suetonius suggests that it is not fatal for societies to be in trouble; it is, in fact, usual for things to go rather badly. In this respect, reading ancient history generates the opposite emotions to scanning today's news. Events have been much worse before and things were, in the end, OK. People behaving very badly is a normal state of affairs, and there have always been existential threats to the human race and civilisation. It makes no sense, and is a form of twisted narcissism, to imagine that our era has any kind of monopoly on idiocy and disaster. By reading Suetonius we enter unconsciously into his less agitated and more stoic reactions. He, and history more generally, encourage connection to what we need now more than ever: the less panicky, more resilient side of ourselves.

In a very different medium, a similar move is being made by the Japanese photographer Hiroshi Sugimoto (b. 1948) through his gigantic empty photographs of seas and oceans in a variety of moods. What is most notable in these sublime scenes is that humanity is nowhere in the frame. We are afforded a glimpse of what the planet looked like before the first creatures emerged from the seas. Viewed against such an immemorial backdrop, the precise discontents in our relationship, the frustrations in our work and the machinations of our enemies matter ever so slightly less. We regain composure not by being made to feel more important, but by being reminded of the minuscule and momentary nature of everyone and everything.

Hiroshi Sugimoto,
Atlantic Ocean, Martha's Vineyard,
1986

As our eyes wander over the vast grey swell of the sea, we are immersed in an attitude of gratifying indifference to ourselves and to everything about our laughably insignificant fate. The waters of time will close over us, and it will – thankfully – be as if we had never lived.

X
Conclusion

Works of culture can redeem us in a variety of ways, but we should never overlook the fact that they can do so only on one condition: that they are successful as works of art. It isn't enough that they should badly want to help us, that they should have powerful intentions to be companionable, serene or inspiring. They must also be these things in and of themselves. In other words, they cannot be mere manifestoes or declarations; they must, in addition, be good art.

That we need good art in the first place has to do with one of the deepest troubles of the human condition: we are generally committed to rejecting or ignoring all good advice unless we have first been extremely skilfully charmed or seduced into accepting it. The point was memorably elaborated on in the early 19th century by the German philosopher Hegel (1770–1831), who was deeply struck by the way in which good advice usually doesn't cut through into our lives. Extremely wise ideas have, since the beginning of time, been offered to humanity. The argument for kindness rather than cruelty or the long-term over the short-term have been won long ago in the pages of serious philosophical texts. But, as Hegel was painfully conscious, this has never in itself had much impact on how we actually behave. What counts, he realised, isn't simply the message, but also the medium.

And, he concluded, the very best medium for imparting ideas is good art. In his *Lectures on Aesthetics* (1835), Hegel suggested that the best art has the capacity to present important ideas in a seductive, captivating form. As he formulated it, art is the sensuous presentation of ideas. Sensuousness – beauty, lustre, charm, playfulness, wit – is no mere incidental add-on, it

Apollo Belvedere. Marble copy after a Greek bronze original by Leochares, 350–325 BCE, *Wisdom embodied in a sensuous form*

is what makes the difference between a message lodging in our minds and flitting straight in and out again.

Hegel had particular admiration for how the ancient Greeks hadn't restricted themselves to presenting their ideas as philosophy. They had managed to give them a more compelling form, as theatre, set to music, or sculpted out of stone. So for example, Apollo may have been the god of wisdom, but in order that his wisdom be remembered and adhered to, the Greeks had grasped that he needed a pleasing, and even at points physically enticing, outward form: that his hair had to be thick, his muscles akin to those of a great wrestler and his cloak teasingly drawn back. Only then would his wisdom emerge as properly believable.

A great artist isn't, therefore, just someone who sets out to help us live and die well. It is someone who knows how to seduce us into wisdom, so that we are at once instructed, entertained, charmed and gripped.

We need culture around us because we are so poor at retaining our equilibrium and maturity. The best lessons are constantly draining from us. We must have the right songs, films, history books, plays and images to hand to keep us from succumbing to rage and error. Culture is our emotional apothecary, a storehouse of humanity's finest bottled wisdom and compassion, with whose help we have the best chance of riding out our many inevitable moments of fragility and folly.

p. 287 TOP Caspar Netscher, *The Lace Maker*, 1662. Oil on canvas, 33 × 27 cm. Wallace Collection, London. Photo © Wallace Collection, London/Bridgeman Images

p. 287 BOTTOM Johannes Vermeer, *The Lacemaker*, 1669–1670. Oil on canvas, 24 × 21 cm. Louvre, Paris. Photo © Louvre, Paris/RMN-Grand Palais /Dist. Photo SCALA, Florence

p. 301 TOP Filippo Lippi, *Madonna and Child with Two Angels*, 1465. Tempera on wood panel, 92 × 63 cm. Galleria degli Uffizi, Florence. Photo Scala, Florence

p. 301 BOTTOM Titian, *Sacred and Profane Love*, 1514. Oil on canvas, 118 × 279 cm. Galleria Borghese, Rome, Italy. Photo Scala, Florence

p. 303 Sandro Botticelli, *Madonna del Magnificat (Madonna of the Magnificat)*, 1484–1485. Tempera and oil on wood panel, diam. 118 cm. Galleria degli Uffizi, Florence. Photo Scala, Florence – courtesy of the Ministero Beni e Att. Culturali e del Turismo

p. 308 From Jules Verne, *Vingt mille lieues sous les mers* (Paris: J. Hetzel, 1871). Houghton Library, Harvard University, Cambridge, Massachusetts

p. 310 TOP Captain Kirk with communicator, from the Star Trek Original TV series, 1967. Photo Mary Evans/Diomedia
p. 310 BOTTOM Communicator, from the Star Trek Original TV Series, 1967. Photo Chris Wilson/Alamy Stock Photo

p. 313 Xu Zhen, *ShanghArt Supermarket*, 2007/2014. Courtesy Xu Zhen and Madein Company

p. 316 Sainsbury Centre, University of East Anglia, Norwich, 1978. Designed by Norman Foster. Photo Sid Frisby/Alamy Stock Photo

p. 321 *The Extravaganza, or, The Mountain Head Dress of 1776*. Published by M. Darly, 1776. Print, 35 × 25 cm. Lewis Walpole Library, Yale University Library, New Haven, CT

p. 324 Claes Oldenburg and Coosje van Bruggen, *Dropped Cone*, 2001, Neumarkt Galerie, Cologne. Photo © Raimond Spekking/CC BY-SA 4.0 (via Wikimedia Commons) © The Claes Oldenburg and Coosje van Bruggen Estate

p. 326 James Craig, *To His Sacred Majesty George III… this Plan of the new streets and squares, intended for his ancient capital of North-Britain…* Map, 40.2 × 64.8 cm. Published in Edinburgh, 1768. Reproduced with the permission of the National Library of Scotland, Edinburgh, Scotland

p. 333 Patek Philippe advert, 2008. Image Courtesy of The Advertising Archives

p. 334 Calvin Klein 'Eternity' advert, 2010. Image Courtesy of The Advertising Archives

p. 345 Piet Mondrian, *Composition with Yellow, Blue and Red*, 1937–1942. Oil paint on canvas, 72.7 × 69.2 cm. Tate, London. Photo © Tate, London. © 2023 Mondrian/Holtzman Trust

p. 348 TOP François Girardon, *Apollo Attended by the Nymphs of Thetis*, c. 1666–1673. Apollo's Baths Grove, Chateau de Versailles, France. Photo Daniel Jolivet/CC BY 2.0

p. 348 BOTTOM Claude Monet, *The Cliffs at Étretat*, 1885. Oil on canvas, 65.1 × 81.3 cm. The Clark Art Institute, Williamstown, Massachusetts. Image courtesy Clark Art Institute (clarkart.edu)

p. 353 Thomas Jefferson, Monticello, Virginia, built 1772. Photo © Christopher Stark/ Dreamstime.com

p. 355 Agnus Dei, Lamb of God, stained glass window by William Warrington, 1856. Field Dalling, Norfolk, England. Photo Holmes Garden Photos/Alamy Stock Photo

p. 358 Northern rose window of Chartres cathedral, France, c. 1235. Photo Eusebius (Guillaume Piolle)

p. 374 TOP Gargoyle, Salisbury Cathedral, Wiltshire. Photo Coombs Images/Alamy Stock Photo

p. 374 BOTTOM Sussex armchair, c. 1860–1940. Manufactured by Morris & Co. Turned, ebonised wood with rush seat, 84.5 × 48.3 × 40.7 cm. William Morris Gallery, London Borough of Waltham Forest

p. 376 Aluminium Chair EA 103. Conceived and developed by Charles & Ray Eames in 1958. Photo Marc Eggimann © Vitra. © Eames Office LLC (eamesoffice.com). All rights reserved.

p. 408 Rogier van der Weyden, *Descent from the Cross*, c. 1435. Oil on panel, 220 × 262 cm. Prado, Madrid. Image © Museo Nacional del Prado © Photo MNP/Scala, Florence

p. 414 TOP Anselm Kiefer, *Alkahest*, 2011. Oil, emulsion, acrylic, shellac, chalk, lead and glass on canvas, 280 × 380 × 19 cm. Photo Ulrich Ghezzi. Courtesy Galerie Thaddaeus Ropac, London, Paris, Salzburg © Anselm Kiefer

p. 414 BOTTOM Jean-Baptiste-Camille Corot, *The Leaning Tree Trunk*, c. 1855–1860. Oil on canvas, 50.2 × 61 cm. National Gallery, London. Photo © The National Gallery, London/Scala, Florence

p. 419 Henri Matisse, *Reader*, 1918. Oil on canvas. © Succession H. Matisse / DACS 2023. Photo Bridgeman Images

p. 421 Christen Købke, *A View of Østerbro from Dosseringen*, 1838. Oil on canvas, 39.5 × 50.5 cm. Kunst Museum Winterthur, Stiftung Oskar Reinhart. Photo © SIK-ISEA, Zürich (Philipp Hitz)

p. 423 Andrea del Verrocchio, *Tobias and the Angel*, 1470–1480. Tempera on poplar, 83.6 × 66 cm. National Gallery, London. Photo © The National Gallery, London/Scala, Florence

p. 426 TOP Claude Monet, *Poppies, nearby Argenteuil*, 1873. Oil on canvas, 50 × 65 cm. Musée d'Orsay, Paris. Photo © Musée d'Orsay, Paris/ RMN-Grand Palais/Hervé Lewandowski/Dist. Photo SCALA, Florence

p. 426 BOTTOM Pierre-Auguste Renoir, *Picnic (Le Déjeuner sur l'herbe)*, c. 1893. Oil on canvas, 54 × 65.3 cm. Barnes Foundation, Philadelphia. Photo courtesy of the Barnes Foundation, Merion and Philadelphia, Pennsylvania

p. 429 Bernard van Orley (workshop of), *Virgin and Child*, c. 1520–1530. Oil on panel, 37 × 27.8 cm. Rijksmuseum, Amsterdam

p. 433 TOP Vincent van Gogh, *Still Life: Vase with Pink Roses*, 1890. Oil on canvas, 71 × 90 cm. National Gallery of Art, Washington, D.C., Gift of Pamela Harriman in memory of W. Averell Harriman, acc. 1991.67.1

p. 433 BOTTOM Vincent van Gogh, *Self-Portrait with Bandaged Ear*, 1889. Oil on canvas, 60.5 × 50 cm. The Courtauld, London. Photo © The Courtauld/Bridgeman Images

p. 437 Mel Gibson, *Braveheart*, 1995. Photo Moviestore collection Ltd/Alamy Stock Photo

p. 439 TOP The Life House, Wales, 2011–2016. Architect: John Pawson. Photo Gilbert McCarragher. Courtesy John Pawson Studio

p. 439 BOTTOM Francesco Borromini, San Carlo alle Quattro Fontane, Rome, 1638–1641. Photo Vladimir Khirman/Alamy Stock Photo

p. 440 TOP Jacques-Louis David, *The Oath of the Horatii*, 1784. Oil on canvas, 330 × 425 cm. Louvre, Paris. Photo © Louvre, Paris/RMN-Grand Palais/ Gérard Blot / Christian Jean/Dist. Photo SCALA, Florence

p. 440 BOTTOM Edmund Blair Leighton, *The End of the Song*, 1902. Oil on canvas, 128.5 × 147.3 cm. Private Collection. Photo © Christie's Images/Bridgeman Images

p. 455 George Du Maurier, 'The Six-Mark Tea-Pot', Punch (1880). Photo © Heidelberg University Library

p. 457 TOP Tea bowl with a white slip decoration, Japan, Edo period, c. 1700–1724. Glazed stoneware, height 7.9 cm × diameter (top) 14.3 cm. Rijksmuseum, Amsterdam

p. 457 BOTTOM Louis Kahn, National Assembly Building, Dhaka, 1970. Photo Muhammad Mostafigur Rahman/Alamy Stock Photo

p. 459 TOP David Hockney, *Three Trees near Thixendale, Summer, 2007*, 2007. Oil on 8 canvases (36 x 48 in. each) 72 1/4 × 192 3/4 in. overall. Kunsthalle Würth, Künzelsau, Germany. Photo credit: Richard Schmidt. © David Hockney

p. 459 BOTTOM Albrecht Dürer, *Great Piece of Turf*, 1503. Watercolour, pen and ink. 40.3 × 31.1 cm. Albertina, Vienna

p. 460 TOP LEFT Mary Cassatt, *Mother Playing with Child*, c. 1897. Pastel on wove paper, mounted on cardboard, 64.8 × 80 cm. Metropolitan Museum of Art, New York. From the Collection of James Stillman, Gift of Dr. Ernest G. Stillman, 1922. Inv.22.16.23. Image copyright The Metropolitan Museum of Art/Art Resource/Scala, Florence

p. 460 TOP RIGHT Pierre Bonnard, *Women with Dog*, 1891. Oil and ink on canvas, 41 × 32.5 cm. The Clark Art Institute, Williamstown, Massachusetts. Image courtesy Clark Art Institute (clarkart.edu)

p. 460 BOTTOM Vanessa Bell, *Interior with the Artist's Daughter*, c. 1935–1936. From the collection of the Charleston Trust. © Estate of Vanessa Bell. All rights reserved, DACS 2023

p. 466 Hiroshi Sugimoto, *Atlantic Ocean, Martha's Vineyard*, 1986. Gelatin silver print, 50.8 × 61 cm. © Hiroshi Sugimoto, courtesy Fraenkel Gallery, San Francisco

p 469 Apollo Belvedere. Marble copy after a Greek bronze original by Leochares, 350–325 BCE. Museo Pio-Clementino, Vatican, Vatican City, Rome. Photo © Kim Young Tae. All rights reserved 2023/Bridgeman Images

Text permissions

p. 74 T. S. Eliot, "Little Gidding", from *Four Quartets*, 1936. Copyright © 1936 by Houghton Mifflin Harcourt Publishing Company, renewed 1964 by T.S. Eliot. Copyright © 1940, 1941, 1942 by T.S. Eliot, renewed 1968, 1969, 1970 by Esme Valerie Eliot. Used by permission of HarperCollins Publishers. Used by permission of Faber and Faber Ltd

Also available from The School of Life:

The School of Life: On Self-Hatred

Learning to like oneself

A guide to emotional healing and living a more self-accepting life.

Behind many of our problems lies an often ignored factor: we don't like ourselves very much. It's because of self-hatred that we tend to neglect our potential at work and get entangled in unfulfilling relationships, that we lack confidence in our social lives and suffer from anxiety and despair.

This is a book that – with immense compassion – investigates the phenomenon of self-hatred. It asks where the feeling comes from, what it makes us do and how we might carefully overcome it. The tone is both hopeful and realistic.

We have probably spent far too much of our lives disliking ourselves and attacking everything we say, do or feel – while not even realising what we're up to. It's time to overcome our masochism and move towards the more self-forgiving and accepting relationship we should have had with ourselves from the start.

ISBN: 978-1-912891-87-0
£12.00 | $16.99

A More Loving World

How to increase compassion, kindness and joy

A book to encourage compassion and forgiveness, showing us how we can work towards a better and kinder world.

The modern world is richer, safer and more connected than ever before but it is – arguably – also a far less loving world than we need or want: impatience, self-righteousness, moralism and viciousness are rife, while forgiveness, tolerance and sympathetic good humour can be in short supply.

A More Loving World rallies us to remember how much we all long for, and depend on, love: how much we need people to forgive us for our errors, how much everyone deserves to be treated with consideration and imagination and how being truly civilised means extending patience and kindness to all, even, and especially, those who don't naturally appeal to us. With the right encouragement, all of us are capable of immense kindness. This book reminds us of our better natures and mobilises us to fight for the kinder, more loving world we long for.

Throughout, it frames love not as a romantic, idealistic fantasy, but as a serious and dignified force that can save us from meanness and strife, defend us against chaos and usher in hope.

ISBN: 978-1-912891-86-3
£12.00 | $16.99